FRONTIER BOOSTERS

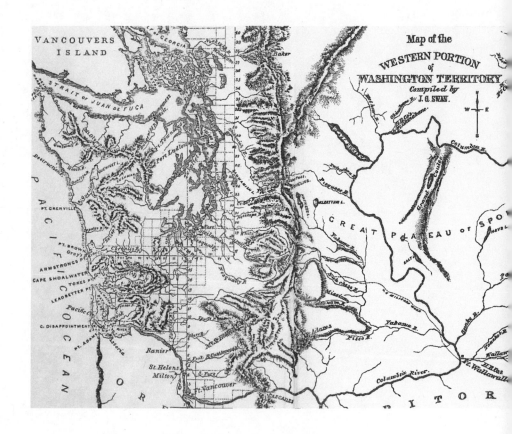

FRONTIER BOOSTERS

PORT TOWNSEND AND THE
CULTURE OF DEVELOPMENT IN
THE AMERICAN WEST,
1850–1895

ELAINE NAYLOR

McGill-Queen's University Press
Montreal & Kingston • London • Ithaca

ISBN 978-0-7735-4367-6 (cloth)
ISBN 978-0-7735-9188-2 (ePDF)
ISBN 978-0-7735-9189-9 (ePUB)

Legal deposit second quarter 2014
Bibliothèque nationale du Québec

Printed in Canada on acid-free paper that is 100% ancient forest free
(100% post-consumer recycled), processed chlorine free

This book has been published with the help of a grant from the Canadian Federation
for the Humanities and Social Sciences, through the Awards to Scholarly Publications
Program, using funds provided by the Social Sciences and Humanities Research
Council of Canada. Publication of this book has also been supported by the
President's Research and Creative Activities Fund at Mount Allison University.

McGill-Queen's University Press acknowledges the support of the Canada Council
for the Arts for our publishing program. We also acknowledge the financial support
of the Government of Canada through the Canada Book Fund for our publishing
activities.

Library and Archives Canada Cataloguing in Publication

Naylor, Elaine, 1943–, author Frontier boosters : Port Townsend and the culture
of development in the American West, 1850–1895 / Elaine Naylor.
Based on thesis (doctoral)–York University, 1999, under title: It's going to be a place
of commercial importance : frontier boosterism in Jefferson County, Washington,
1850–1890.

Includes bibliographical references and index.
Issued in print and electronic formats.
ISBN 978-0-7735-4367-6 (bound).–ISBN 978-0-7735-9188-2 (ePDF).–
ISBN 978-0-7735-9189-9 (ePUB)

1. City promotion–Washington (State)–Port Townsend–History–19th century. 2.
City promotion–Washington (State)–Puget Sound Region–History–19th century. 3.
Economic development–Washington (State)–Port Townsend–History–19th century.
4. Economic development–Washington (State)–Puget Sound Region–History–19th
century. 5. Urbanization–Washington (State)–Port Townsend–History–19th century.
6. Urbanization–Washington (State)–Puget Sound Region–History–19th century. 8.
Port Townsend (Wash.)–Economic conditions–19th century. 8. Port Townsend
(Wash.)–Social conditions–19th century. 9. Puget Sound Region (Wash.)–Economic
conditions–19th century. 10. Puget Sound Region (Wash.)–Social conditions–19th
century. I. Title.

HN80.P85N39 2014   979.7'9803   C2013-907992-0
                                              C2013-907993-9

CONTENTS

ILLUSTRATIONS AND MAPS

ACKNOWLEDGMENTS

In the course of researching and writing this book I have accumulated many debts, and I would like to take this opportunity to acknowledge my gratitude and appreciation.

I wish first to thank those historians of the North American West, past and present, who have guided and inspired me on my own journey into the past. I would also like to express my gratitude to the academic institutions that have sheltered and sustained me through the years: The Evergreen State College, York University, and Mount Allison University. I am also grateful to the publishers of the *Pacific Northwest Quarterly* and ABC-CLIO, Inc. for permitting me to reproduce material from previously published work: "Chet-ze-moka, J. Ross Browne, and the Great Port Townsend Controversy," *Pacific Northwest Quarterly*, 93, 2 (Spring 2002), 59–68; and "The Jacksonian Frontier," from *Jacksonian and Antebellum Age: People and Perspectives* (Santa Barbara, CA: ABC-CLIO, 2008).

This book has been published with the help of a grant from the Canadian Federation for the Humanities and Social Sciences, through the Awards to Scholarly Publications Program, using funds provided by the Social Sciences and Humanities Research Council of Canada; and a grant from the Mount Allison University President's Research and Creative Activity Awards Fund. Research for this book was aided by funding from York University, Mount Allison University, and the Social Science and Humanities Research Council of Canada through the Aid to Small Universities Program.

I would like to express my thanks to the staff at several libraries, archives, and historical societies who have generously assisted me in this research, including: the Jefferson County Historical Society, Port Townsend, Washington; Special Collections, University of Washington; the Resource Sharing Division, Scott Library, York University; the Washington State Historical Society, Tacoma, Washington; the Microfilm Research Room, National Archives at Seattle, Washington; and Mount Allison University Library, Sackville, New Brunswick.

I also wish to take this opportunity to express my appreciation to Kyla Madden of McGill-Queen's University Press for her advice and encouragement. Sandra Barry, Brittany Jones, Elaine Simpson, and Carolyn Smith have been invaluable in working with me to ready the manuscript for publication, and I am most grateful for their help through this process.

I owe special thanks to the scholars who have commented on drafts and/or been instrumental in the completion of this work, most notably: Penny Bryden, Marc Egnal, John Findlay, Alexandra Harmon, Molly Ladd-Taylor, Andrea McKenzie, Marge Samuelson, Adrian Shubert, David Torrance, Deborah Wills, and, of course, the manuscript's anonymous readers. In particular, I wish that Robert Cuff and John Saywell had been able to see the conclusion of this project. I am also very thankful to Dorothy McLarney and Clifford Bailey for their kindness in sharing their memories of early Jefferson County with me, and I am so sorry that they were not able to see how important their contributions have been to this book.

I am also very happy to be able to finally thank my good friends who have been supportive throughout my journey: Kelly Buehler, Linda Cupp, Marie Hammond Callaghan, Sally Payne, Frauke Rubin, and Sara Stratton. Last but never least, I wish to thank my family for their unfailing support: Peter Collins; Lawrence, David, and Eric Naylor; Shannon Naylor; Marianne Tomita-McDonald; and Brendon, Seth, and Nathaniel Naylor. To them, I dedicate this book.

Frontier Boosters is a community study. Its most basic premise is the assumption that, as a method of inquiry, such works have intrinsic value; that if writ small, they nevertheless better serve to illuminate the whole through focused, site-specific, but comprehensive investigation of significant historical issues and events. *Frontier Boosters* examines a particular locality on Puget Sound in frontier-era Washington: Jefferson County, Port Townsend – its principal town – and surrounding villages and rural areas. The study's goal is to further understanding of frontier settlement and economic development not only on that one frontier, but more broadly, and its findings argue for reassessment of certain aspects of these issues writ large. Historians, of course, have long been interested in frontier settlement, and the past several decades have seen a shift from an older, more rural focus in Western history to one that emphasizes economic development and town-building. More recently, historians have pointed to boosters as effective in instigating settlement and development, and boosters therefore have become increasingly important figures in the history of Western settlement. Nevertheless, reductionist notions about the identity of boosters – frequently described as land speculators, investors, or businessmen – continue to limit our understanding of who they were and what their role in development was. Such limitations create a disjuncture between the processes of development and the activities of ordinary settlers, one that minimizes the importance of individual settlers' expectations of, and support for development. This disjuncture also masks the influence of development upon the social dynamics of frontier communities. This study, then, calls for a more inclusive definition of boosters, demonstrating that, in at least one locality, development was embraced not just by land speculators and the like, but by many other residents. Further, as an issue of significance to many people, development thinking played an essential role within the community, especially with regard to social relations between ethnic and racial groups.

Another important feature of *Frontier Boosters* is its chronological reference. From a twenty-first century perspective it may seem that Seattle was destined to become the principal city of the Pacific Northwest. However, throughout much of Washington's long frontier period – from the 1840s to the 1890s – Seattle was but one of several towns in Western Washington (Port Townsend, Tacoma, Olympia, Seattle, Steilacoom, and Bellingham) whose residents expected that their town might very well become the Pacific Northwest's great city. This study, then, acts as an important corrective to a teleological approach in histories that begin and end with Seattle, and as such, obscure a portion of the history of Washington's early period.

Today, Jefferson County is sparsely populated, most notable for its beautiful scenery and the nostalgic appeal of Port Townsend's Victorian-era architecture. However, in the nineteenth century settlers believed the county possessed a brilliant future, and they tied their own hopes for economic opportunity and social mobility to the county's perceived potential. They dreamed that increasing numbers of people would immigrate and settle there, that industry and agriculture would flourish, that Port Townsend would become a leading West Coast city – even the metropolis of the Pacific Northwest – and that they and their children would live prosperous and happy lives. Were their dreams far-fetched? Not really. Jefferson County did indeed have attributes that suggested the possibility of significant economic development. Port Townsend was located at the entrance to Puget Sound, the waterway to the abundant timber resources that drove Washington's frontier economy. This strategic position made Port Townsend the obvious choice for the regional Customs Port of

Entry, and as headquarters for Customs, Port Townsend became an important seaport and shipping center. Further, the county was heavily forested. Its lumber mills and their attendant logging operations were integral to the developing Puget Sound "cargo" lumber industry, which during the latter half of the nineteenth century shipped millions of board feet of lumber by sea to California and other Pacific Rim points. County iron deposits were also thought to hold industrial promise, and it was assumed that county river bottoms, prairies, and logged-off lands would provide for agricultural development.

In their expectations of development, county residents were typical nineteenth-century Americans in that it was commonly believed that the frontier West would provide its settlers with economic opportunity not to be found in the more developed East. Much of this American optimism about the trans-Mississippi West derived from popular mid-nineteenth century theories that sought to predict where and how this frontier would develop, theories that privileged the founding of what were known as great cities. Where such future urban centers would be located was thought to be dependent on natural advantages such as potential transportation routes and abundant, nearby natural resources. The trick to seizing the advantages potential in frontier economic development was to predict or envision where a great city would most naturally develop and then to settle there and work with others to bring that vision into reality. Thus, development thinking was as much about the idea or concept of development as its reality. Such optimism about the West did not survive the frontier era. Yet, in the nineteenth century, American settlers often tied their individual hopes for prosperity to a specific place, and as elsewhere in the frontier West, Jefferson County residents expected, or at least hoped and dreamed, that successful county economic development would guarantee their own economic future. Jefferson County's history thus encapsulates the larger story of Americans' expectations of the frontier, a frontier thought to hold the key to individual economic opportunity and prosperity.

Development thinking was also formative in community affairs and social relations. At times residents' desires for county development, for instance, blurred class distinctions and ordered the allocation of urban space. This evolving culture of development was especially important in its influence on relations between Euro-Americans, resident Native Americans, and Chinese immigrants. An example of this is the trajectory of Port Townsend's participation in Puget Sound's widespread Chinese expulsion movement in the mid-1880s. The movement outside of Jefferson County was characterized by violent expulsions of resident Chinese from regional mining camps, towns, and cities. Yet, in Port Townsend, concerns that violence might rather drive away immigrants and investors had sufficient force to mitigate expulsion. Instead, some Euro-Americans instituted an economic boycott against Chinese labor and services, hoping that the boycott would produce similar results as violence had done elsewhere, but without discouraging development. The boycott was ineffective, yet anti-Chinese violence continued to be suppressed in the cause of development.

In addition to allowing for a deeper understanding of the issues described above, community studies also have the value of shifting attention away from the obvious: Today, Seattle is the great city of the Pacific Northwest, and Port Townsend is a small, charming, tourist destination. However, for neither town during Washington's frontier period was this future outcome clear. Like other Americans throughout the nineteenth-century West, the residents of both Seattle and Port Townsend dreamed of a future that reflected their own desires. How such very different outcomes for these two communities came to be is an important part of Washington's early history.

To further develop this point, initial economic development in the Puget Sound region was centered on the cargo lumber industry, which dispatched lumber from Puget Sound throughout the Pacific Rim in sailing ships. This industry was situated on the *western* side of Puget Sound, where Jefferson County forests provided much of the timber for milling, and county sawmills produced a significant portion of the lumber shipped. Port Townsend, as the Customs Port of Entry and an important shipping center, was at the hub of this industry. However, the primacy of the cargo industry did not survive the turn of the century, its demise in part deriving from the arrival of transcontinental railroads on the eastern shore of Puget Sound. This event, making possible the shipment of lumber by rail to the east, opened immense new possibilities for logging and lumber milling on the *eastern* side of Puget Sound, and the cargo lumber industry declined as the "rail" lumber industry expanded. Naturally, this had serious implications for development on the western shore and for Jefferson County. When nearly all approach to Puget Sound was from the Pacific Ocean, the Straits of Juan de Fuca, Port Townsend, and the forests and mill ports of the western side of the Sound appeared to many to be the beginning point for development. However, technology, as represented by the railroads, trumped the western shore's geographic location, shifting advantage to the eastern side of Puget Sound.

The decline of the cargo industry, however, was only one of several changes that brought an end to Port Townsend's bid for great city status: Jefferson County's failure to acquire a connection to any of the transcontinental railroads; changes in shipping technology that had a negative impact on Port Townsend's role in the region's sea trade; the crash of a real estate boom; and the economic devastation caused by the depression of the 1890s. By the end of the nineteenth century, Jefferson County residents' expectations of development had changed radically, becoming much less prescient and more focused on what could be done with circumstances as they were, rather than on an imagined future. This was in keeping with early twentieth-century trends throughout the Far West. By this time, significant development had occurred, and the visionary aspect of development thinking faded. Such frontier dreaming, dependent as it was upon a future yet unfolding, did not survive the reality of the post-frontier period.

FRONTIER BOOSTERS

The Culture of Development on the Frontier:

Boosterism, Class, and Race, 1850–1895

On the morning of March 4, 1891, broadsides appeared throughout Port Townsend, Washington, a seaport on Puget Sound and the largest town in Jefferson County.

> Let everybody who has the interest of Port Townsend at heart attend ... a public meeting [to] repudiate false reports ... now being circulated ... of the immorality of this place.

By 8:00 in the evening, the Red Men's Hall was crowded to overflowing with "all classes of society [indignant at the] stigma ... placed on the fair fame of [their] city" and eager to refute the "notorious libel" that gambling was a respectable activity in Port Townsend.[1] This meeting was Jefferson County's response to a political crisis, one which many residents believed was a threat to county development because it could damage the community's reputation with outsiders. In February 1891, Port Townsend attorney Morris B. Sachs, recently elected district court judge, was charged by the state legislature with "misbehavior, malfeasance and delinquency in office" for frequently gambling in public.[2] Judge Sachs did not deny his gambling; his defense was to claim that such a pursuit was a "fashionable and honorable passtime [sic] in Port Townsend [and that] some of the 'leading business men' ... of the city frequently gamble[d]."[3]

In the end, Sachs retained his office, acquitted by a narrow margin in the State Senate, because a majority of state senators thought removal was too high a price to pay for such "misbehavior."[4] However, it was not Sachs's gambling per se, but rather his assertion that gambling was an acceptable, popular recreation in Port Townsend that caused so much concern to townspeople. His claim was perceived to threaten the county's reputation, which in turn endangered its economic development, a project dear to the hearts of residents since such development promised individuals economic opportunity. According to the *Leader*, "unless some steps are at once taken ... a feeling of prejudice against Port Townsend in the minds of all respectable people throughout the United States" would arise. Already the town was "jestingly spoken of as a place where one of the requisites of admission to society is skill at playing faro." Port Townsendites needed to unite in "some expression of popular sentiment ... without delay" in order to protect the future of Jefferson County.[5]

Responding to the *Leader*'s call, residents of Port Townsend and the surrounding countryside assembled that evening and passed a series of resolutions condemning Judge Sachs. Declaring that the "community has been falsely stigmatized as a gambling community," they decried the "impression create[d] abroad" that the community's "citizens are devoid of moral character." Although it was unpleasant for individuals to be so characterized, what was even worse was that this should "degrade the name of our city in the eyes of the world." They asked "fellow citizens abroad to judge us not by the opinions of [those who would] further their own ends by casting a black cloud of universal immorality over ... our fair commonwealth."[6]

Why was this incident so important that it elicited a spirited public response? The answer lies in the concern many nineteenth-century residents had about Jefferson County's economic future. Because residents feared that Sachs's portrayal of the county would turn potential immigrants and investors to other, supposedly more respectable

0.1 (*Opposite*)
Bird's eye view of Port Townsend, Puget Sound, Washington Territory, no date. (Jefferson County Historical Society)

communities, an effective rebuttal was perceived to be imperative. Thus the "interest" the *Leader* hoped to find in the hearts of residents was the county's economic development, or boosterism.

NINETEENTH-CENTURY BOOSTERISM

Jefferson County boosterism, while unique in some local particulars, was not unusual. Boosterism – the thinking about, desire for, and/or the promotional efforts to accomplish development – was very much a phenomenon of the nineteenth century,[7] when the acquisition of immense reaches of continental land by the United States encouraged the movement of increasingly larger numbers of people westward,[8] and boosterist thinking was common currency. By the 1840s and continuing through the nineteenth century, booster literature was widely read,[9] and boosters' theories of economic growth "dominated nineteenth-century thinking about frontier development."[10]

By its very nature, nineteenth-century frontier boosterism was an interaction between reality and ideas, as much an exercise of the imagination as it was a practical program for development.[11] Boosters expressed "what many Americans believed – or wanted to believe – about ... the United States and its Great West": that expansion westward was inevitable and that the development of the frontier West's resources would naturally provide economic opportunity and social mobility unavailable in more settled regions, to those willing to participate in that development.[12] Such sanguinity was characteristic of frontier boosterism. Given American perceptions that the West was an undeveloped wilderness, Americans likened the frontier to a nearly empty canvas awaiting completion. If natural resources and transportation routes had been sketched in, presumably by the Creator, it was up to boosters and their supporters to finish the picture: to imagine and then to create the future. Once the canvas was largely filled, that is, once significant development had occurred, development thinking changed radically. Post-frontier boosterism was more pragmatic and focused on what could be done with circumstances as they were, rather than as imagined.[13]

Some of the earliest American thinking about westward expansion centered upon finding an American passage to India, a Northwest Passage, which would connect the United States and Europe to the wealth of Asia. The Lewis and Clark expedition ended any hopes for such a passage by water.[14] Thomas Hart Benton – a newspaper editor and long-time senator from Missouri, the gateway to the trans-Mississippi West – was an ardent supporter of American expansion into the West. His career in writing about expansion stretched from 1818 into the 1850s, and he argued that a combination of some far-west river system and portages, roads, and railroads might serve to connect the Pacific and Asia with mid-western and eastern waterways and markets.[15]

In time, such thinking was replaced by plans for a transcontinental railroad. Businessman Asa Whitney was the first to promote construction of a railroad from the Mid-west to the Pacific Coast, and he presented a memorial to Congress on January 28, 1845, proposing such a railroad. Congress took no action then, but by the early 1850s there was serious federal interest in a transcontinental railroad.[16]

Other expansionists placed a high priority on obtaining American ports on the Pacific Coast. For instance, a primary goal of the 1841 voyage of Charles Wilkes's United States Exploring Expedition was to establish the location of safe harbors on the Pacific Coast. Wilkes found only three consistently navigable bays or inland waterways along the West Coast: San Diego, San Francisco, and Puget Sound.[17] Thus, during the 1846 Oregon Country negotiations with Great Britain, President James Polk was determined to acquire "the Straits of Fuca, Admiralty Inlet, and Puget's Sound, with their fine harbors" for the United States.[18]

Beginning in the second quarter of the nineteenth century, ideas about western development placed increasing emphasis on the planning and creation of great cities or metropolises as transportation and commercial centers for the exploitation of natural resources within the West.[19] Such views initially focused on the interior United States, but ideas about great cities influenced development in the Far West as well. As thinking about frontier development was necessarily projected onto the future, the important task for boosters was to predict where a great city might develop and then convince other people to believe in that future city and invest capital or immigrate there or to the adjacent countryside. Boosters argued that the successful location of cities, especially great cities, was dependent upon "natural advantages," theorizing that cities would develop on sites favored by natural transportation routes: rivers and lakes, safe harbors – fresh and saltwater – potential canals, and later, railroads. Such sites would also be centrally situated near resources such as rich agricultural land, grasslands, and timber or mineral wealth.[20]

Such thinkers believed that cities were the ultimate expression of American progress.[21] However, understanding that cities developed in part from the resources of surrounding rural areas, boosters recognized the symbiotic relationship between city and country.[22] Thus, rural development – agriculture, ranching, mining, or lumbering – was perceived to be as necessary as urban development. In many areas the possibility of productive farming or stock-raising was the greatest lure for immigrants; in others, mining or logging and lumber mills drew settlers.

Of course, almost all boosters directly involved in promoting western frontier settlement and development, even those who only wrote about it, were interested in promoting a specific location, one in which they often had an economic interest. Regardless of the natural advantages of any given site, growth was dependent upon attracting immigrants and capital investment. There was little need to convince Americans that the West could provide economic opportunity and a better way of life – indeed, this idea was a given for most people throughout the nineteenth century.[23] Nevertheless, it was necessary to convince the public of the desirability of a specific townsite, area, or region.

Interest in the West and moving westward created an immense market for guidebooks, travel books, and magazine articles written by people who had visited or toured the West; and boosters sought to create a favorable public image of their town or region through such literature.[24] There were attempts to make the approaches to towns appear as prosperous as possible, and visiting writers were subjected to local lectures about a town's achievements and, more importantly, its great prospects.[25] However, visitors' reports were not always satisfactory, and frontier boosters of western towns, counties, states, and territories, multi-state regions, and railroads came to depend upon promotional material produced by themselves in the form of "maps, broadsides, books, posters, pamphlets, cartoons ... magazine and newspaper articles and editorials," and even letters written to folks back home, to attract the interest of immigrants and capitalists. Often produced in the Far West by individuals or informally organized, local groups of residents, such literature was widely read throughout much of the nineteenth century;[26] and boosters and booster literature and promotional materials were integral aspects of Western development.

BOOSTERISM AND THE HISTORIANS

Scholarly responses to boosterism have varied. Turner – his frontier thesis so long ubiquitous in Western history – relegated boosterism to the background by privileging rural individuals over town building and industrial development in the settlement of the West.[27] However, scholars who challenged Turner's idea that American democracy grew out of individual frontier experiences brought boosters forward, arguing as they did that democracy evolved from the necessary cooperative mechanics of frontier community development.[28] Urban historians continued the trend, addressing urban development through studies of frontier communities. Asserting the importance of urban development to the frontier, they found "urban promoters and urban visionaries ... most everywhere."[29] More recent work challenged the Turnerian rural focus even further by arguing that rural western development was dependent upon urban centers. William Cronon, for instance, writes that "the central story of the nineteenth-century West [is of] an expanding metropolitan economy [with] ever more elaborate and intimate linkages between city and country." Boosters played an important role in this story, devising theories about development, promoting it, and carrying it out.[30]

To a certain extent scholars who would bring boosters to the foreground have had to face a tendency in the academy to view boosterism from an ironic, dismissive perspective, one which may be traced to nineteenth-century writers such as Mark Twain, Charles Dickens, or J. Ross Browne. These writers were skeptical of boosters' often bombastic rhetoric, and their mockery may have helped formulate the idea that boosters were solely predatory – interested in personal gain, and willing to deceive not only others, but themselves, too, in a quest "to make lots of money."[31]

Why this interpretation has persisted is open to debate.[32] Howsoever, such thinking has prompted some scholars to focus their inquiries into boosterism on the contrast between booster rhetoric and the often harsh-lived experience of settlers. Such works have a propensity to be unforgiving of boosters,[33] and fail to acknowledge that "at times[,] western places indeed developed [in ways] that substantiated [boosterist] rhetoric."[34]

Writing partly in response to this literature, some historians have pinpointed the ways in which boosters were effective, concluding that boosters were indeed instrumental in western development: working to establish businesses and to attract capital investors and immigrants, railroad and steamship connections, and government support and institutions to their towns. In possessing greater or lesser degrees of perspicacity, they further influenced the success or failure of their community's development, especially as problem-solvers. Further, boosters contributed to the evolution of regional urban networks, argued by one historian to be requisite for economic development. Such works thus substantiate the credibility of boosters by drawing our attention to their influence and accomplishments in the development of the West.[35]

However essential, boosters' influence over development nevertheless must be seen to have been limited in many ways: by regional dynamics of economic growth and urban development;[36] by the type of natural resources available for exploitation;[37] and by the often overwhelming dependency of western development, both local and regional, upon large-scale, capital-intensive projects such as railroads or irrigation projects. As agents (witting or unwitting) of American expansion into the West, the accomplishments of boosters were often dependent upon economic parameters set by extraneous forces.[38]

Established as having at least important roles and influence in Western development – if with certain limitations – boosters have also been seriously implicated in the "destruction and exploitation of ... the land" wrought by development. In such environmental histories, boosters are again agents of American expansion and its cheerleaders, "romantic and ambitious visionaries, promoters whose resourceful and imaginative accounts about 'developing' the country knew few restraints." Articulating cultural assumptions about land use held by almost all Euro-American settlers, boosters believed that a rejuvenative nature would provide the wherewithal for individual and national prosperity.[39]

Necessary to the communication of ideas about development, boosters are seen further to have been instrumental in the creation of development thinking by variously formulating imagined regional concepts or "mental territories," or centering themselves in created regions, or – by lapsing into occasional regret at the changes brought about by the development they accomplished – adding nostalgia to late nineteenth-century development culture.[40]

By promoting and articulating a positive perspective on development, boosters imposed "a new layer of meaning upon the land in behalf of capitalism." Frontier booster literature, its voice so optimistic, futuristic, and triumphant, became a creative ingredient in the popular discourse or narrative of frontier settlement, providing justification for the conquest of the West even as it encouraged migration.[41] Indeed, as argued by David Wrobel, boosters are key to the creation of Western identity, being central "to the processes by which [thinking about] the West [was] constructed, elaborated, disseminated and sustained."[42] Thus, if Turner left boosters and boosterism out of Western history, post-Turnerian scholars have established their importance not only in the settlement and economic development of the frontier West but also in past and present thinking about the West. Further, they continue to shape our understanding of the West.

Boosters have been established therefore as undeniably important to the history of the American West. Nevertheless, our perception of their importance suffers from the need to better define who they were. Many works[43] have described boosters as discrete groups actively engaged in development, as land speculators, entrepreneurs, community elites, railroad officials, newspapermen and other writers, and so on.[44] Implicit in such a restricted or exclusive definition of boosters is the assumption that development was imposed upon the larger body of Euro-American settlers. Yet, there is much evidence in frontier Jefferson County to indicate that there was significant agreement with, and enthusiasm and support for, promoters' goals on the part of county residents.[45] Such evidence therefore suggests the usefulness of re-conceptualizing frontier boosterism, or development thinking, to include its function as an important articulation of ordinary residents' expectations of frontier settlement.

Further, as an issue of shared significance, development thinking permeated public discourse in Jefferson County, and was therefore a powerful force in community affairs not directly related to development. At times, it blurred class distinctions, influenced ethnic relations between Native Americans or Chinese and Euro-Americans,[46] and dictated the allocation of space within Port Townsend. If settlers found their desires for development clashing with other closely held notions such as racist or class-based assumptions, they often tried to reconcile the differences. Boosterism was therefore formative in the county's social dynamics and settler relations, setting in motion an evolving culture of development, a social role it may have played in other frontier regions as well.[47]

BOOSTERISM IN JEFFERSON COUNTY

Jefferson County is located on the Olympic Peninsula, the most northwesterly area of the United States excepting Alaska. Designated a county on December 12, 1852, and including the northern two-thirds of the Olympic Peninsula, it was divided in 1853, the northwestern portion becoming Clallam County. The subsequent remainder occupies an 1,805 square-mile strip of territory between the Pacific Ocean on the west and Puget Sound on the east, with the most northerly portion dividing Admiralty Inlet from the Straits of Juan de Fuca and Discovery Bay.[48] Between the western and eastern portions lies the Olympic Mountain Range. These mountains – the center of which is impassable by all but the most hardy of mountaineers – take up most of the county and effectively separate western and eastern Jefferson County. Nineteenth- and early twentieth-century Euro-American settlement in western Jefferson County was sparse and often of short duration, because the climate and terrain there are not friendly to farming, and any other significant economic development such as logging or tourism was impossible until the internal improvements of the 1930s, especially roads.[49] However, eastern Jefferson County was settled by Euro-Americans in the 1850s; it is this part of the county with which this work is concerned.

The shoreline of eastern Jefferson County includes several protected, deep-water harbors and borders on Puget Sound, which – as defined by marine historian Gordon Newell – stretches from Cape Flattery on the Pacific Ocean to the falls of Tumwater at Olympia,

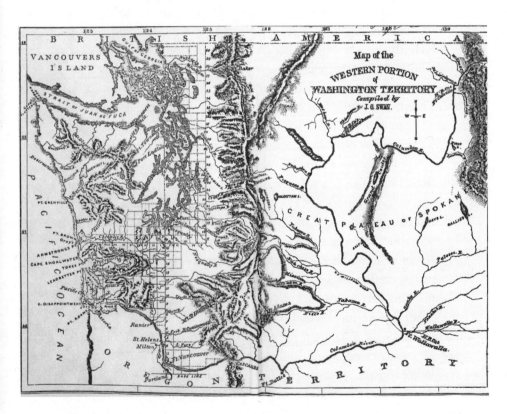

0.2

Map of Washington, drawn by James G. Swan, 1856.
(Harper and Brothers, Publishers)

and includes the Strait of Juan de Fuca, Admiralty Inlet, and Hood Canal as well as the Sound itself, the innermost body of water of the larger Puget Sound.[50] In the mid-nineteenth century the county's dense evergreen forests grew to the water's edge, the early economy was timber-focused, and Euro-American settlement was concentrated along the shoreline. Port Townsend, the largest town, was founded in 1851. Other centers of population were mill ports, the communities that developed around sawmills: Port Ludlow was established in 1853, Port Discovery in 1859, and Port Hadlock became a mill port in the mid-1880s.

Today, Jefferson County is a bit of a backwater.[51] However, during the latter half of the nineteenth century things were different. Then, Port Townsend was one of *several* small Puget Sound frontier towns – including Bellingham, Olympia, Seattle, Steilacoom, and Tacoma – which, during the Sound's decades-long frontier (from the 1840s into the 1880s), vied with one another for great city status. Thus, there were no instant cities on Puget Sound. If, by the end of the nineteenth century, Seattle had eclipsed all other contenders, during Puget Sound's frontier period, Port Townsend – touted by its boosters as the coming metropolis of the Northwest, even the "New York of the West"[52] – was a player in the regional great-city sweepstakes. Port Townsend was also central to Puget Sound shipping, and the forests and sawmills of Jefferson County were integral to the lumber industry that drove settlement and economic development in the region.[53]

At a time when urban development on Puget Sound was still largely imaginary, the first American settlers arrived in Jefferson County intending to develop and exploit its economic possibilities. Washington Territory's first governor, Isaac Stevens, had designated the county as an ideal site for a railroad terminus in his *Report of Explorations for a Route for the Pacific Railroad*;[54] and, building on Steven's prediction, county residents hoped that Port Townsend would become that terminus and a major Pacific Rim shipping center. They envisioned the future Port Townsend as an essential link in the passage to India, connecting the riches of Asia and the Pacific Rim with the rest of the United States and Europe. They dreamed of flourishing industries, prosperous farms, and a rapidly multiplying population, believing in the words of one early settler, that "no branch of business vigorously pushed along [in the county could] fail to pay."[55] Assuming that they had a stake in this future vigorous economy, many of the settlers strove to extend and maximize the county's economic potential; and many if not all residents espoused and supported this goal. Indeed, economic development was eagerly sought by ordinary settlers: boosters they were, whether more or less actively involved in promotion, and their "interest" made development a predominant county issue.

What follows is the history of boosters, development, and the culture of that development in frontier Jefferson County from its initial

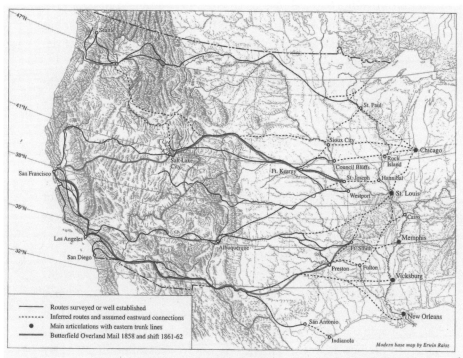

1. Pacific Railroad Surveys.
Based on "a hurried compilation of all the authentic surveys" to accompany the Report of the Hon. Jefferson Davis, Sec. of War, 1855.

0.3
Pacific railroad surveys. (Yale University Press)

Euro-American settlement in the early 1850s through the boom years of the late 1880s and very early 1890s. Throughout, Jefferson County is studied through the lens of boosterism broadly defined, affording the reader a better grasp of development culture as a phenomenon of consequence that was widespread among residents and fully integrated into community affairs and social dynamics.

The work draws on the idea that community studies provide essential building blocks for larger historical syntheses of history; that local histories where "one can see whole and read everything," provide opportunities "for research ... impractical in a [larger place]." Such studies are also more likely to "encompass [questions of] race, class [and gender]" than do broader studies[56] As a local study, therefore, *Frontier Boosters* allows us to analyze in situ and in detail the relevance of development thinking to frontier Jefferson County, but also suggesting that we extrapolate from this the importance of development culture on other frontiers.

Further, in examining this once pivotal, but now little known seaport of Port Townsend and its surrounding countryside, this study provides insight into the early settlement and development of nineteenth-century Puget Sound. This history is often overlooked, because from a twenty-first century perspective, the tendency is to privilege the history of Seattle – since the late nineteenth century, the premier city of the American Pacific Northwest.[57] Nevertheless, throughout much of Washington's long frontier period, Seattle's future status was not necessarily apparent. Then, the primacy of water-borne travel and trade that approached Puget Sound from the Pacific Ocean in sailing ships, the initial economic dominance of Puget Sound's western shore "cargo" lumber industry, and that industry's dependence upon Pacific Rim markets, all argued for the potential dominance of the west side over the eastern shore of Puget Sound. If their dreams failed to predict the future, this study nevertheless illuminates early Puget Sound history.

DEFINITIONS

It is impossible to discuss development thinking in Jefferson County without addressing the residents' concerns about the county's reputation. Naturally, boosters emphasized the county's potential for economic growth, and this was a constant theme in local booster literature. However, early in its history Port Townsend – through the published works of popular travel writer, J. Ross Browne[58] – became known as a very rough town, one which astute immigrants and investors might be wise to avoid. County residents took great pains to counter this reputation. At times the connection between development thinking and reputation is masked by what seems to be only a concern about whether or not the town was respectable. However, close examination reveals that residents' worries, at least in part, were founded in the belief that a good reputation was sine qua non to attracting immigrants and capital investment. What did boosters mean by a good reputation? In their promotional literature they emphasized – along with information about economic opportunities – certain aspects of county life that they believed would create a positive impression with outsiders.

Such emphases suggest an appropriate definition for reputation as perceived by residents of Jefferson County. For instance, in county newspapers and other booster literature, residents were favorably described as sober, industrious, and law-abiding. The presence of settled families in the community elicited enthusiastic comment. The establishment of social institutions such as churches, schools, fraternal orders, temperance groups, lyceums, and debating societies was also stressed. The orderly celebration of any public gathering was cause for self-congratulation, since this indicated that residents were law-abiding and sober, even when on holiday, and that public drinking and violence were under control. By way of contrast, shiftlessness, excessive drinking, especially in public, gambling, prostitution, and violent or lawless behavior were deplored.

Thus, boosters believed the county was more likely to be "well thought of" if it was known to be a community in which residents were hard-working, law-abiding, and preferably married, a community where respectable social institutions flourished and where public order was maintained. These characteristics were emphasized time and time again. Tensions surrounding this issue of respectability and reputation continued throughout the entire frontier period. Port Townsend's position as a shipping center was considered essential to county economic development. However, this same position almost guaranteed that the town would have a rough aspect. Shipping brought a large, transient male population to the town, one that supported "disreputable" institutions such as saloons, gambling halls, brothels, and cheap lodgings. The drive for economic development required that residents find some way to live with the disreputable aspects of life in Port Townsend and yet have a good reputation outside the county. Thus, a jealous concern for the county's reputation remained at the forefront of development thinking, as important a booster theme as was economic opportunity.[59]

In the late twentieth century, Port Townsend's waterfront – little changed since the building boom of the late 1880s – became and continues to be a tourist destination. Now promoters emphasize the rough aspects of Port Townsend's history, as well as the picturesque: majestic mountains, beautiful seascapes, and the Victorian-era homes and business blocks. Nevertheless, in the frontier period, image was focused on the county's reputation and commercial economic opportunity.

It is expedient to define several other terms as well. As discussed above, booster is broadly defined to include community residents who actively or directly promoted county development and those who espoused development thinking and/or supported boosterist goals but were less directly involved in promotional activities. As well, this work seeks to re-conceptualize our understanding of boosterism, and suggests that boosterism – defined as development thinking and the promotion of development – is as much about a culture of development as it is about the promotion of development. Thus, boosterism, boosterist thinking, development thinking, and development culture are used as complementary terms.

At another level, since frontier boosterism ("boost: to promote")[60] or promotion was focused on development – that is to say, converting the use of land so as to better exploit its resources and improve individual economic opportunities – boosterism and economic development are again complementary terms. In this sense development could be agricultural or industrial (logging, mining, canning fish, shipping, etc.). Although not necessarily, it often was centered on urban development. For Jefferson County residents, development meant increased Euro-American settlement; the establishment of businesses; local and outside investment in area industries; expansion of Port Townsend's capacities as a Pacific Rim shipping center and its potential status as the great city or metropolis of Puget Sound; promotion of agriculture; and acquisition of a rail connection to one of the transcontinental railroads.

Chapter 1 examines the growth of the shipping industry in Port Townsend and logging and the lumber and shipbuilding industries that shaped and sustained the smaller towns and the countryside. It demonstrates how the early timber and shipping economy, thought to offer abundant entrepreneurial opportunities, drew settlers especially interested in commercial economic development to Jefferson County. Chapter 2 examines "the Great Port Townsend Controversy" of 1858, which arose when humorist, travel writer, and Treasury official J. Ross Browne characterized Port Townsend as a disreputable "resort for 'beachcombers' and outlaws." This significant event established the importance of reputation to development thinking for Jefferson County, but also exemplifies the relevance of boosterism regionally in early relations between Indians and settlers, as well as the importance of local Native peoples to economic development. Chapter 3 looks at county promotional projects from 1859 into the 1890s, projects that were conceived by promoters – or those directly involved in development – but supported by other county residents: the booster press; a bitter campaign to retain the Puget Sound Customs headquarters in Port Townsend; efforts to establish a connection to a transcontinental railroad; and local and regional immigrant aid societies that plotted to entice immigrants and investment to the county. Chapter 4 considers issues surrounding the community's reputation as related to county development. As well, it sets out the ways in which some residents sought to resolve tensions between development and reputation: through redefining morality, but also allocating space so as to minimize contact between disreputable and reputable residents – all of which served to blur economic class lines. Chapter 5 discusses relations between Chinese and Euro-American settlers and demonstrates how development thinking effected such relations, especially during the 1885–86 Puget Sound Chinese expulsion movement. The chapter also demonstrates the important role Chinese played in economic development. The Conclusion describes the boom and bust of the late-nineteenth century in Puget Sound and Jefferson County. It brings to an end the story of frontier boosterism in Jefferson County.

Euro-American Settlement and Economic Development, 1850–1870

Significant Euro-American settlement in Washington's Puget Sound region originated in a lumber boom derived from the California Gold Rush. Legend has it that ships from San Francisco first entered Puget Sound in 1850 looking for ice to cool champagne for thirsty Gold Rush millionaires.

> [The ship's] masters were disappointed because they found a sunny inland sea at least as warm as San Francisco Bay and innocent of ice summer or winter … [Surrounded by soaring snow-capped mountain ranges] the northern waters were bordered with grand forests instead of frozen tundra. Then they saw that the forests might cover the failure of their mission. San Francisco … was as voracious for building materials as for iced drinks.

Although this story is surely apocryphal, Gold Rush Californians did have a tremendous need for lumber, and they did not have sufficient accessible timber close at hand. Early in 1850 California ship captains began sailing to Puget Sound, a region with seemingly endless supplies of easy-to-harvest timber.[1]

The resultant timber boom brought a sudden influx of settlers who, typical of settlers in other regions, were intent on building their own futures through economic development of Puget Sound. As lumbermen, merchants, sea captains, entrepreneurs, and town builders, they perceived frontier development to be the exploitation of natural resources, establishment of markets and trade, and creation of towns and cities. Early on, they established settlements such as Port Townsend, Steilacoom, Seattle, Port Ludlow, Port Gamble, and others. Some were aware of thinking about a "passage to India" and theories of great-city development, and since promotion was implicit in such ideas, the seeds of boosterism lay dormant in those first ships sailing north to harvest Puget Sound timber for California markets.[2]

"THE BEST GEOGRAPHICAL POSITION ON THE PACIFIC"[3]

During the late eighteenth century, four nations – Spain, Russia, Great Britain, and the United States – laid claim to the Pacific Northwest. The Spanish ceded their interest to the British in the Nootka Sound Agreements of 1790 and 1795; and by the Adams-Onis Treaty of 1819 they relinquished further claims north of the 42nd parallel – the northern boundary of California – to the United States. Russia abandoned its claims south of the southernmost tip of Alaska to the United States in 1824 and to Great Britain in 1825.

At odds over claims to what was then called the Oregon Country, the British and Americans had come to an uneasy joint occupancy in 1818. Primarily interested in exploiting the fur trade, the British – through the Hudson's Bay Company – exercised a virtual monopoly over the region into the 1840s. However, in the 1830s through the 1840s a small number of American missionaries bent upon Christianizing Native Americans settled in Oregon.

Starting around 1840, significant numbers of Americans wanting to establish farms migrated to the Oregon Country, primarily to the fertile Willamette Valley of present-day Oregon. Increasing pressure from American settlers and expansionists to resolve dual British and American claims to Oregon brought the two countries to the negotiating table. In June 1846 Great Britain and the United States agreed to a division of the Oregon County along the 49th parallel. The new American possession – which included the present-day states of

Oregon, Washington, Idaho, Montana, and much of Wyoming – became Oregon Territory in August 1848.[4]

When Oregon Territory was created, there were only a few American farmers living in the Puget Sound region, mostly near present-day Olympia. However, in 1850 migration to the region increased dramatically when the need for timber products in Gold Rush San Francisco prompted a timber boom on the Sound. By 1851 the settlers living in Oregon north of the Columbia River began to clamor for separate territorial status. In March 1853 Congress approved Oregon Territory's division into Oregon, in its present-day configuration, and Washington, which then included the rest of the territory. Present-day Washington is the result of further division in March 1863.[5]

The new territory's first governor was a former army officer and engineer named Isaac I. Stevens, his appointment political payback for supporting Franklin Pierce in 1852. He was an important booster for the Puget Sound region and shared with both Thomas Hart Benson and Asa Whitney[6] their belief in Puget Sound as an essential link in trade with Asia. According to his biographer, Kent Richards, Stevens wanted to promote the "development of the Northwest," but he also believed that his political career would be well served if he became "spokesman for [a frontier region] as ... Thomas Hart Benton had been representative of [an] earlier frontier." Stevens asked to be appointed Washington's first territorial governor, and he was so designated by Congress on March 17, 1853.[7]

Hoping to see rapid movement of settlers to Washington as well as development of the territory's lumber, mining, and agricultural potential, Stevens was committed to expediting treaties with the territory's Native Americans. Appointed territorial Superintendent of Indian Affairs at the same time he became governor, Stevens began efforts to extinguish Indian title to the land as soon as he arrived in Olympia, negotiating several treaties with groups of Washington tribes during the winter of 1854–55.

In keeping with his interest in Puget Sound, Stevens favored a northern route for the first transcontinental railroad and argued that it should terminate on Puget Sound, and he also requested that he lead the federal northern-route railroad survey team. He was

appointed its commander on March 25, 1853, and in early April
Stevens and the survey party started a slow progress to Washington.
The survey was completed in the spring of 1854, although Stevens had
left it earlier, arriving in Olympia, the territorial capital, in November 1853.[8]

In the railroad survey report, his "greatest propaganda effort" for
Puget Sound,[9] Stevens tapped into boosterist ideas about a passage
to India, arguing that the first transcontinental should follow the
northern route, one of its terminal points ending in Jefferson County.[10]
He wrote that such a railroad would "secur[e] control of the Asiatic
trade" for the United States, a trade which was "the great commercial
prize [from] ancient and modern times." It would, he argued, establish a commercial American world empire, placing the United States
"midway between the great centers of Asiatic and European population," as the route for all trade between Europe, the United States,
and Asia, lessening the distance for travellers between the eastern
United States and Asia, and between Europe and Asia. "From New
York to Shanghai by way of Cape Horn ... is 21,000 miles[;] by ...
the Cape of Good Hope ... about 15,000 miles. By ... the proposed
railroad and Puget Sound, the distance will be 7,800 to 8,000 miles."
Further, Stevens pointed out, sailing "from Liverpool to Shanghai is
14,400 miles. By [rail] and Puget Sound the distance will be 10,800
miles." Hence, once rail and steamship links were established, he believed trade and travel between Europe and Asia would cross the
United States using the northern railroad as the shortest route.[11]

Stevens's report was probably influential in persuading Congress
to charter a northern transcontinental line, which it did in 1864, two
years after the central-route railroad was approved. However, it was
not until 1884 that a northern-route transcontinental railroad was
completed. By the time the five railroad surveys were finished in the
late 1850s, Congress was too embroiled in the sectional turmoil that
led to the Civil War to act immediately upon any of the survey recommendations.[12]

Nevertheless, the connection between a passage to India and transcontinental railroads would continue to be important to Puget Sound
boosterism. Joined with theories about great cities, such thinking
would capture the imagination of Puget Sound settlers like Travers

Daniel, an early Port Townsend booster. Daniel was a territorial official and member of the Territorial Legislature; in 1859 he became founding editor of Port Townsend's first newspaper, the *Port Townsend Register*. He shared Stevens's vision about the international potential of Puget Sound, lauding its "position, commercially[, as] the best geographical position on the Pacific."[13] Puget Sound would connect "ships from the Indian Ocean, from Canton and Calcutta [which will] cross the Pacific and deposit their rich freight at the terminus of the great highway of the nations of the civilized world on Puget Sound."[14]

Daniel – who favored Port Townsend – joined with others to promote the idea of a great city on Puget Sound, one that would be the terminus for a transcontinental railroad, an important port of entry to the United States for the wealth of Asia, and the distribution point for the resources of the surrounding region to the rest of the world. In the meantime, however, the lumber boom provided Travers and other settlers with a more immediate, less visionary basis for economic growth and boosterism.

PUGET SOUND LUMBER BOOM: 1850–1854

In 1850 there were barely one hundred American citizens living in the Puget Sound region. Yet, by November 1853, when Stevens arrived in Olympia to take up his gubernatorial duties, he found bustling settlements dotting the shores of the Sound at Port Townsend, Port Ludlow, Port Gamble, Steilacoom, Seattle, and Olympia. By 1860 there were approximately 5,000 Euro-Americans living in the region, their economy focused on the lumber industry.[15]

Most of the Americans who migrated to the Oregon Country during the 1840s were farmers,[16] and farming would remain an important goal for many settlers who came to Puget Sound. Nonetheless, lumber was a greater factor in Puget Sound's development than agriculture.[17] The settlers eager to exploit the region's abundant stands of timber were accompanied by town builders, entrepreneurs, and others who believed the lumber boom would provide them with economic opportunities. By 1860 lumbering was firmly established, "a great industry [which] made possible the economic [growth] of the Sound, providing employment, markets for the produce of farmers, and trade for urban merchants."[18]

Commercial timber had been taken from the Northwest as early as 1787 by Briton John Meares, who led a venture to sell Northwest ship spars and furs in China.[19] Forced by weather to jettison his cargo in the middle of the Pacific, this first speculation ended in failure. Then, starting in 1827, the Hudson's Bay Company at Fort Vancouver developed a limited trade, exporting Northwest lumber to the Hawaiian Islands, California, South America, and perhaps China; and Hudson's Bay at Fort Nisqually sold the first cargoes from Puget Sound to the Islands and Victoria in 1848.

Gold Rush California, however, spurred the development of a lumber industry on Puget Sound.[20] Gold was discovered in California in the spring of 1848. By late 1849, San Francisco was the "greatest of all boom towns," but there was little accessible timber nearby to meet its building needs.[21] In 1849 ships from San Francisco began sailing to Oregon, seeking lumber from settlements on the Columbia River that provided the closest sources of timber for Californians. The 1850 Census enumerators counted thirty-seven Oregon sawmills with an annual production of 21,932,000 board feet, valued at over one million dollars – most of the lumber deriving from the area near present-day Portland, Oregon.[22]

The quest for timber soon shifted to Puget Sound, however. Entering the Columbia River was dangerous: the sand bars between the river and the ocean were so "hazardous that passengers and crews alike often fortified themselves with prayer or drink" before making the attempt. Vessels could be destroyed, and many either went aground and were disabled, or waited days or weeks to cross the bar. Once in the river, the trip upstream was slow and sometimes dangerous because of shifting shoals, and it was costly in terms of pilot and towing fees.[23] In contrast, rumors of the quiet water and deepwater harbors of Puget Sound beckoned; and sailing a little further north, ship captains found vast inland waterways with forests of easily harvested timber growing to the water's edge.

Puget Sound was the answer to California's lumber needs and raised expectations of another "gold mine" for those enterprising enough to go north for lumber. By the end of 1851 some dozen vessels were sailing regularly between the Sound and San Francisco, carrying cargoes of pilings and squared timbers – which cost eight cents a foot at ship side and sold for one dollar a foot in San Francisco – as well as ship's knees, "pieces of naturally crooked timber ... used in strengthening joints," shingles, and cordwood. Shipments of lumber awaited the construction of sawmills on the Sound.[24]

Lafayette Balch, master of the *George Emery*, was one of the first sea captains to carry such cargoes. An enthusiastic promoter for the Puget Sound region, he exemplifies the connection between the lumber boom, development, and boosterism, using the boom as a springboard for development and promotion. In 1850 he began to make regular trips between San Francisco and the Sound carrying timber products, some of which he contracted for from area settlers. In the same year he filed a claim under the Donation Land Claim Act of 1850, through which adult male citizens could claim up to 320 acres of land each if they were willing to cultivate it and live there for four years.[25] Balch established a townsite on his claim, building a trading post and hiring laborers to prepare his timber cargoes. By 1855 Steilacoom was an incorporated town of one hundred people with seventy homes, six stores, three hotels, some shops and a wharf, three sawmills, and a flour mill nearby.[26] Aware of the importance a local newspaper would have for promoting the growth of "his" town, Balch also persuaded San Francisco newspaperman Charles Prosch to immigrate to Steilacoom to edit the *Puget Sound Herald*, the second newspaper published in Washington Territory.[27]

It was Balch who brought the potential of Puget Sound timber to the notice of lumbermen Andrew Pope and William Talbot, who founded one of the largest and most successful of the region's lumber mills in 1853 in Port Gamble. He also encouraged two of the founders of Port Townsend, Alfred Plummer and Charles Batchelder, to settle there – pointing out to them how promising the site was as a center for the shipping that would develop along with the lumber industry.[28] Thus, lumber was the "green catalyst" for economic development and settlement on Puget Sound, drawing lumbermen and entrepreneurs ready to seize the opportunities created by the lumber boom.[29]

"NO BRANCH OF BUSINESS VIGOROUSLY PUSHED ALONG CAN FAIL TO PAY"[30]: SETTLEMENT OF JEFFERSON COUNTY, 1850–1853

James McCurdy, the native son of an early Port Townsend family, collected many of the stories of early settlers in his book, *By Juan de Fuca's Strait: Pioneering Along The Northwestern Edge Of The Continent*. He lends a sort of yeoman farmer glow to the stories of the early settlers.[31] For instance, according to McCurdy, Plummer, one of the founders of Port Townsend, came West because of "the soil hunger within him [rather than any] desire for sudden wealth." On the trip north with Balch, he reportedly carried a waterproof packet that "he guarded with jealous care," and when asked if the packet contained gold nuggets, he replied that it held "seeds." His companion replied: "By thunder, Plummer, you're right ... Gold won't fill your stomach when you're hungry, nor keep scurvy away when your system is crying out for fresh vegetables. I've a hunch that where we're going, them seeds will bring more than their weight in gold."[32]

Plummer did indeed plant his seeds. However, his activities were more those of an entrepreneur and town builder than yeoman farmer-like in nature, since besides his partnership with the other founders of Port Townsend, he was a saddle- and harness-maker.[33] Alert to the Puget Sound region's economic promise, Jefferson County's early settlers, including Plummer, were town builders, merchants, entrepreneurs, and lumbermen and therefore development-minded, their economic interests being tied to economic growth.

Between 1850 and 1852, thirteen settlers filed claims in Jefferson County under the 1850 Donation Land Act, receiving between 320 and 640 acres each. At least five of the claimants – H.C. Wilson, Alfred A. Plummer, Charles Batchelder, Francis W. Pettygrove, and Loren B. Hastings – believed that Port Townsend Bay, with its deepwater harbor and commanding location at the junction of Juan de Fuca Strait and Admiralty Inlet, was ideally situated for a shipping center. Wilson became a customs officer, working to have the Customs headquarters placed in Port Townsend, a move that was essential to developing the settlement's role as a shipping center. Plummer, Batchelder, Pettygrove, and Hastings platted the townsite of Port Townsend on their claims, sold building lots, and opened a trading post.

John L. Tukey chose land at Port Discovery suitable for logging, and John R. Thorndyke filed on a site at Port Ludlow ideally situated for the lumber mill he established with William T. Sayward in 1852. Thomas M. Hammond, J.G. Clinger, and Albert Briggs filed for claims near Port Townsend Bay.

Thomas M. Hammond was, among other things, a merchant and hotel keeper; J. G. Clinger, a "carpenter and joiner, contractor and builder, coffin maker and undertaker;"[34] Albert Briggs, a carpenter. Only four pursued farming as their primary occupation: Rueben Robinson of Chimacum and Ruel W. Ross, John Harris, and Benjamin Ross of Port Townsend.[35] Although almost all did some farming for their own needs,[36] most of the settlers were oriented towards commercial enterprises that were dependent upon economic growth. A closer look at these first settlers further underscores their commercial bent and commitment to development.

Many of the first settlers wanted to develop Port Townsend's potential as a shipping center, but H.C. Wilson was the first claimant to so envision Port Townsend. Wilson had clerked for Lafayette Balch in San Francisco before coming north in 1850 to work at Steilacoom. He initially saw Port Townsend Bay on the voyage into Puget Sound and recognizing its commercial potential determined to file a claim there. He became a customs inspector in 1851 and was instrumental in accomplishing the 1854 removal of the Puget Sound Customs Port of Entry from Nisqually to Port Townsend – an important step to establishing Port Townsend as a shipping center, since all shipping would thereafter make a stopover in the settlement. Although Wilson was an influential early booster, he soon disappeared from the record.[37]

In his late twenties, Alfred Plummer had come to California from Maine seeking his fortune. While operating a hotel in San Francisco, he met Balch, who hired him to work in Steilacoom. In December 1850 Plummer and his friend Charles Batchelder went north; sailing by Port Townsend Bay, Balch reportedly repeated Wilson's assessment of the bay. "That's one of the finest harbors on this Coast and is sure to become a prominent seaport ... I don't know of a better

1.1

Some of the first American settlers in Port Townsend.
(Jefferson County Historical Society)

place for you to locate." Inspired by the site's promise, Plummer and Batchelder decided to settle at Port Townsend, and they contracted to supply Balch with cut pilings and squared timbers as soon as they were established. After working in Steilacoom for the winter they relocated at Port Townsend Bay in April 1851.[38]

In October, the two men were joined by Francis Pettygrove and Loren Hastings. Both men were entrepreneurs, seeking a place with significant potential for economic development. Pettygrove was already a town builder, having founded Portland, Oregon, in 1844. Pettygrove had been a successful merchant in Oregon – the "principal commercial man in the [Oregon] country." Arriving in Oregon City in 1843, he quickly became the Hudson's Bay Company's principal competitor on the Columbia River, trading in furs, but also grain. He built a separate grain operation at Champoeg and opened another store in 1845 at what would become Portland. When salted salmon became a valued commodity, Pettygrove seized control of the market by refusing to sell his large supply of salt to competitors. Although Pettygrove first represented a New York mercantile firm, he eventually established his own, F.W. Pettygrove and Company, which ran two sailing vessels between Oregon and the Hawaiian Islands, trading grain and lumber. In 1849 he closed his Oregon businesses and went to California to reap the benefits of the Gold Rush close at hand.[39]

Loren Hastings was a dyer and wool carder by trade. He was born in Vermont, but in 1838 he migrated to Illinois, where he married and started a family. When he settled in Portland in 1847 he engaged in merchandising. It was there he became friends with Pettygrove. In 1851, after a six-month trading venture in Gold-Rush California provided him with a $10,000 nest egg, Hastings joined with Pettygrove to travel to Puget Sound, on the lookout to establish a new economic venture. Pettygrove was thirty-nine and Hastings, thirty-seven. Exploring the bays and inlets of Puget Sound, they found Port Townsend Bay a promising location, and meeting Plummer and Batchelder on the beach, they entered into a partnership with them to establish a townsite, sell building lots, establish a trading post, log timber, and make money.[40]

Other early claimants also looked to the economic opportunities offered by the region's timber. John L. Tukey, a native of Maine, had been a crewmember on one of the first California timber ships. While helping to cut a cargo of ship's knees and squared timbers at Port Discovery, he decided to go into the business for himself, and he filed a claim at Port Discovery, hiring all available men to ready timber for shipping to California. Later, Tukey sold or let that claim go, but staked another 500-acre claim nearby, which he continued to log. Tukey eventually sold part of this acreage and then ran a summer resort and model farm on the remainder.[41]

John Thorndyke filed a claim on sheltered Port Ludlow Bay and built a lumber mill there in 1852; he was joined in March 1853 by William T. Sayward.[42] Sayward was a forty-niner who had made and lost one fortune as a merchant at Placerville where a flood destroyed his property in 1851. Recouping his losses by practising law, he acquired enough capital to set up as a banker in 1852. With a nest egg of $15,000, he turned in 1853 to the timber business, buying three sailing vessels, the *Merchantman*, the *Sarah Parker,* and the *Williamantic*, which he put to work hauling timber from Puget Sound to San Francisco and selling lumber from Port Ludlow.[43]

He also established "Sayward's Line of Packets," which ran "regularly between Puget Sound and San Francisco." Beginning on July 30, 1853, Sayward advertised that he had "established himself at Port Ludlow where he ... will keep constantly on hand the largest assortment of Provisions, Groceries and Dry Goods in Washington Territory ... sell[ing] at wholesale or retail at the lowest price possible. And having a very large Launch, Clipper built, will forward them to any port on Puget Sound." In 1858 Sayward leased the Port Ludlow mill to Amos and Phinney for $500 a month, and built another lumber mill on Burrard Inlet, British Columbia, where he capitalized on the Fraser River Gold Rush. The 1860 census shows him, at least temporarily, back in Port Ludlow, but he then built a mill in Victoria, British Columbia, selling the Port Ludlow mill in 1874. He purchased the Port Madison sawmill in 1880 and operated it through the 1880s. He eventually retired to California, where he grew oranges until his death in 1905.[44]

Although survival in the early years of settlement required that residents be able to provide for themselves, especially in the matter of food production, it would be a mistake to allow that necessary self-sufficiency to obscure the settlers' intentions to build upon the economic potential of Jefferson County. As we have seen, most of the original settlers were entrepreneurs who settled in the county because they believed it offered economic opportunities in town-building and land speculation, merchandising, shipping, and lumbering.[45]

PORT TOWNSEND, 1850–1870: "ONE OF THE FINEST
HARBORS ON THIS COAST"[46]

In Port Townsend economic development was entered on shipping and commerce. The land adjacent to Port Townsend was unforested prairie. If it was unsuitable for logging, it was an excellent town site, and Port Townsend Bay's sheltered, deepwater harbor was ideal for the development of a shipping center. Port Ludlow and Port Discovery were mill ports, producing lumber, the region's primary export. They were established on deepwater harbors that had forests close at hand. Early shipments of logs were taken from forests that grew to the shoreline, although eventually loggers had to move further into the interior. Naval architects or ship builders established a small ship-building industry in Port Ludlow and Port Townsend. There were a few farms close to Port Townsend and in the Chimacum Valley on treeless prairie land, but the rural areas were primarily forested, furnishing necessary timber to the lumber industry and shipbuilders.

In 1854 Port Townsend was designated Port of Entry for the Puget Sound Customs District, acknowledgment that its deepwater harbor and proximity to the region's developing lumber industry made it central to Puget Sound shipping.[47] As Port of Entry, Port Townsend became a necessary stopover for the Sound's increasing commercial shipping, since international vessels passed through Customs on their way in and out of the Sound, and coastal shipping – ships that sailed only along the American Pacific Coast – stopped on its way out.[48] The United States Marine Hospital was located there in 1855.

1.2
Downtown Port Townsend, Water Street, circa 1860.
(Jefferson County Historical Society)

In 1858 there were approximately twenty Puget Sound sailing
vessels, each of which averaged six trips a year in and out of the
Sound. This meant a minimum of at least 120 vessel stopovers in
Port Townsend in that year. By 1868 some ninety sailing vessels
carried cargoes from Puget Sound, making 360 stopovers or more
in Port Townsend. Lumber was the usual cargo, although coal was
also shipped from Bellingham Bay. In 1857 the dollar value of Puget
Sound shipping was $543,574; by 1868 it was approximately
$2,000,000.[49]

This developing shipping industry provided entrepreneurial opportunities with relatively easy entry for residents of Port Townsend,
which became the "chief outfitting point for the shipping [in and
out] of Puget Sound."[50] By 1859 some 300 Euro-Americans and 200
Native Americans lived in Port Townsend,[51] in the midst of a growing

collection of warehouses, wharves, and mercantile establishments catering to shipping: ship's chandlers who carried merchandise of all sorts, butchers who sold salted meat to ships, bakeries which advertised ship's bread, and so on. There were three hotels; one, the Pioneer House, was "not surpassed by any public house in the Territory," and the American Chop House, which not only served meals, but was also a public bathhouse and barber shop. There were also businesses that serviced local residents: a stationary and book store, a pharmacy, and the chandlers who carried merchandise for local customers also. There were two physicians – one operated the Marine Hospital – two attorneys, a building contractor, and a land agent – all businesses benefiting from the growing sea trade, but also seeking further economic opportunity through county development.[52]

The United States Shipping Commissioner, pilots, tugboat captains and crew,[53] and shipping agents made their headquarters in Port Townsend. William Newton was the first of many such agents. Settled in Port Townsend by at least 1860, he advertised that he provided "crews and officers to any ships," arranged to unload vessels, and facilitated the movement of merchandise throughout the Sound region with his sloop, the *Sarah Newton*.[54] Newton was typical of many early settlers in that he made his profits from a variety of entrepreneurial activities, all connected to the shipping industry.

Because all Puget Sound shipping stopped in Port Townsend, it was a convenient place for ships to dismiss and rehire crews, and Newton turned a profit from the sailors, as well as the ships. In the early 1860s he operated a hotel, the Whalemen's Arms; in 1868 he advertised a boarding house for sailors with "boarding and lodging on the most reasonable terms." Newton also kept a saloon in Port Townsend for many years, and one in Port Discovery for a time.[55] He was joined in this profitable pursuit by others; six liquor licenses were issued to Port Townsend liquor dealers and three to mill port dealers in 1861.[56] By the 1870s, the saloons and other seedier establishments had proliferated, so that Port Townsend fairly "teemed with liquor ... gambling [and] prostitution."[57]

Because almost all of the early Puget Sound settlements perched between the dense forests and the Sound, water was the primary means for transporting mail, passengers, and consumer goods between towns and villages, or the outside world, and Port Townsend residents took advantage of this commercial opportunity.[58] At first, local travel was accomplished in Native American canoes,[59] small sloops such as Newton's, or lumber vessels such as Sayward's, but eventually steamers of ever increasing size replaced the canoes and sailing vessels. By 1864 three steamships also made regular runs between the Sound and San Francisco; a regular daily route linked Sound ports with Victoria beginning in 1869;[60] and Alaska was added to coastal steamship itineraries after 1867.[61]

The passenger vessels, some owned or managed by Port Townsendites, stopped regularly at Port Townsend, which enabled the town's merchants and shipping agents to draw advantage from local shipping on the Sound as well as coastal and oceanic shipping. Through local shipping they sold supplies to smaller Sound communities, and one Port Townsend firm, D.C.H. Rothschild, became "chief supply [house] for the extensive lumber and logging interests of the Sound." Agricultural goods grown in the Sound region – especially the lower Sound – were redistributed from Port Townsend throughout the Sound, as well.[62] Thus, the business of Port Townsend was commerce and shipping, and most entrepreneurial enterprises and employment in Port Townsend – excluding women who kept house for their own families – were dependent upon the shipping industry, successful commercial ventures, and economic growth.[63] (See Appendix.)

MILL PORTS AND LOGGING CAMPS: THE LUMBER INDUSTRY, 1850–1870

Saw milling was the economic mainstay of the mill ports, Port Ludlow and Port Discovery. Both were small villages, built on land owned by the respective mill companies, which included a wharf for loading the lumber onto sailing vessels, sawmill buildings, housing for employees, a general store – run by the mill company – a hotel, and a saloon. Shipbuilding – a smaller industry related to both the lumber and shipping industries – was also followed in the mill ports, especially Port Ludlow. There were also logging camps throughout the countryside, some of which became permanent settlements (see discussion of Quilcene below). It is also important to note that two of the three Kitsap County mill ports at Port Gamble and Seabeck (but excluding the Port Madison mill), because of their location across Hood Canal from Jefferson County, had strong economic ties to Port Townsend, and both mill companies, Pope and Talbot's Puget Mill Company and the Washington Mill Company – milled timber logged in Jefferson County, as well as Kitsap. Later, the Puget Mill purchased the Port Ludlow mill, and the Washington Mill Company relocated to Port Hadlock in Jefferson County following the destruction of the Seabeck mill by fire.

1.3
Moore and Smith Mill at Port Discovery, Washington.
(Jefferson County Historical Society)

In 1860 and 1870, Jefferson County was second only to Kitsap County in territorial production of lumber.[64] Port Ludlow's William Sayward had moved on by 1858. The mill continued to operate, however, under lease for $500 a month to Amos, Phinney & Co., with Arthur Phinney as manager of the mill and Zachariah Amos and W. Hooke handling marketing from San Francisco, where the firm also dealt in California redwood.[65] Phinney increased the mill's capacity considerably,[66] and in 1859 it produced and shipped 8,398,432 feet of lumber, flooring, and lath, 52,615 pickets, and 50,000 shingles to coastal and foreign ports during 1859, making fifty-six trips.[67] In 1866 poor management in San Francisco forced bankruptcy proceedings upon the company, but the business continued under the operation of Phinney, who bought the mill from Sayward in 1874.[68]

Logging continued at Port Discovery throughout the 1850s, and a sawmill was built there in spring of 1859 by S.L. Mastick & Co., of San Francisco. Between July 1859 and January 1860 the mill shipped 2,420,716 feet of lumber and 7,000 feet of piles.[69]

The Port Ludlow and Port Discovery mills were "cargo mills," built by San Francisco lumber merchants, with San Francisco capital, to mill lumber for California markets. (This was true for the mills in nearby Port Gamble and Seabeck, as well). Each firm had lumberyards in San Francisco and often other California locations as well, and general management was usually conducted from the head office in San Francisco, with one partner in residence at the mill.[70] There were also smaller mills, some of which – similar to the three King County mills – produced for the local market – for instance, L.R. Hoff's small sawmill at Chimacum Creek near Port Townsend and the Port Townsend Mill Company built by Port Townsend investors in 1881.[71]

With the exception of the owners of the smaller non-cargo mills, mill owners were largely absentee businessmen, their interest in Puget Sound devoted to resource extraction. The cargo mills dominated county and Puget Sound lumber for forty years or more, until transcontinental railroads changed the industry in the late 1880s and early 1890s, direct railroad transportation to the East making possible the eventual development of eastern markets (see Conclusion).[72]

Throughout the period of this study, the cargo lumber industry would remain essential to the economic agenda of boosters; however, local boosterism factored little in the mill owners' agenda.[73]

As we have seen, the industry began with the California Gold Rush. At the outset of San Francisco's building boom, merchants sold whatever lumber they could get their hands on, and, for a time, even cargoes of lumber brought around the Horn turned a profit. When enterprising sea captains such as Captain Balch found their way to Puget Sound, they returned with pilings, squared timbers, shingles, and cordwood, and their cargoes were snapped up.[74] Soon, San Francisco lumber merchants wanted a more reliable source of supply, and several decided to build sawmills on the Sound.

Sayward began construction at Port Ludlow in March 1853. J.J. Felt built a sawmill at Apple Tree Cove in Kitsap County about the same time. He moved the mill to a better site at Port Madison, and sold it to one George Meigs at the end of the year.[75] In June 1853 William Talbot of the newly formed Puget Mill Company[76] arrived to look for a suitable mill site. He preferred Sayward's Port Ludlow location but made do with nearby Port Gamble. That mill was in operation by September. Eventually, the Puget Mill Company would purchase the Ludlow mill following Arthur Phinney's death in 1878. At the same time they acquired a small mill at Port Utsalady on Whidby Island, and for some years they ran those two mills as well as two at Port Gamble. The Puget Mill Company was the most successful of the cargo mills, its Port Gamble mill continuing in operation until 1995.[77] During the summer of 1853, Captain William Renton constructed his first mill at Alki Point in Seattle, although eventually he would concentrate his prosperous lumbering activities at Port Blakely on Bainbridge Island in Kitsap County.[78]

By the end of the decade, several other San Francisco lumbermen moved to establish control of their lumber supplies. Adams, Blinn and Company built the Washington Mill Company at Seabeck on Hood Canal in 1857; Amos, Phinney & Co. leased the Port Ludlow mill; and S.B. Mastick and Company of San Francisco constructed the Port Discovery Mill Company in 1859.[79] The last important cargo mill, the Tacoma Mill Company, was built in the late 1840s by Charles

Hanson; it made its first shipment in December 1869.[80] All but the Tacoma Mill Company were located in Kitsap and Jefferson counties on the west side of Puget Sound.

When the first mills were built, it was expected that California would absorb their production. However, in late 1853 the nascent industry experienced a downturn, and falling prices and glutted markets settled into depression during 1854 and 1855. Unwilling to abandon their Puget Sound investments and believing that ultimately there was great potential for the industry, the lumbermen turned to foreign markets to take their unsold cut.[81] California remained the most important market for Puget Sound cargo mills, but by 1860 the Pacific Rim – the Hawaiian Islands, China, Australia, New Zealand, and the west coast of South America – provided a necessary cushion against the ups and downs of the California trade. This drew the Puget Sound economy into the international sphere and gave boosters cause for optimism about the region's economic future.[82]

Stabilized by foreign trade, the industry expanded. In 1858 Puget Sound cargo mills were able to produce 174,000 feet of lumber per day; by 1865 their daily capacity was 460,000 feet.[83] By 1870 $1.3 million of the $1.9 million invested in Washington manufacturing was invested in the lumber industry, and two-thirds of manufacturing wages were paid to sawmill workers.[84] Jefferson County's mill ports reflected these regional statistics in that most mill-port men were employed in saw milling, their wages sometimes supplementing family farms (see chapter 3). A few worked in shipbuilding.[85]

Saw milling and logging are inextricably linked one to the other. However, for much of the nineteenth century, logging on Puget Sound was done by independent *loggers*, a term that in the nineteenth century meant the owner of the logging operation (the men who worked for him were called variously lumbermen or laborers). Loggers contracted with the mills to supply them with logs. In Jefferson County, such logging outfits worked not only for the Port Ludlow and Port Discovery mills, but also for those nearby Kitsap County mills mentioned earlier – the Washington Mill Company at Seabeck and the Puget Mill Company at Port Gamble – which were located on the other side of Hood Canal from Jefferson County.[86]

1.4
Bull teams and logging crew on skidroad

   Logging was initially done by what were called hand loggers. Using axes and crosscut saws to fall trees onto the beach, they quickly shaped the trees into squared timbers and pilings or gathered logs into log booms. Timbers and pilings, as well as shakes and cordwood, were loaded directly onto ships, and shiploads of such timber products continued to be taken from the Sound into the late 1850s. Log booms were towed to a sawmill.[87] Logging became more complicated as the forest receded from the beach. In order to move logs out of the woods, a path had to be cut and trees cut down and laid across it. Delimbed, the trees would sink into the soft ground, making a road-bed or "skid road," along which logs were pulled by teams of oxen – twelve to twenty strong – to a point where they could be rolled into the water and put in booms.[88]

Such logging was done by small crews of five to sixteen men,[89] and it did not require a large investment of capital: cost and care of oxen or horses, some sort of rude housing for the laborers and a cookhouse, axes and saws, etc. If the logger did not have sufficient capital, the mills were willing to advance start-up funds – usually a few hundred dollars – to keep a camp going until the first boom was in the water. In return the logger agreed to sell his logs exclusively to the mill, and he often put up equipment, land, and logs as security.

Financial transactions, such as payments for logs[90] and wages (often paid to the "logger" as well as the logging workers) were paid through the mill's books. Once the contract was completed, outstanding debts were settled. The logger typically had a standing account with the mill for supplies of food and equipment, rental of boom chains, and towing fees – as did the laborers. Often very little cash changed hands, since both the logger and the men might spend most of their money at the mill store.[91]

It is arguable whether such loggers were "independent," or their operations profitable. Thomas Gedosch, who has studied the Seabeck Washington Mill, suggests that the loggers who contracted with the mill stayed in business only through remaining in debt to the mill. According to Gedosch, the mills kept an intermittent downward pressure upon log prices, which remained at $4 to $4.50 per thousand board feet between 1857 and 1870. It cost logging firms as much as $6.03 per thousand board feet for wages, food, equipment, repairs, and transportation. Throughout the 1870s and up to 1886 – the last year of Gedosch's study – log prices increased to as high as $6.50 in 1883, then dipped to $5.00 per thousand in 1885.

Such pressure meant that profits for logging companies were little or nothing. Further, wages for laborers working in the woods remained at a fairly steady level regardless of the price for logs, and those companies that contracted with the Washington Mill Company found that the mill often charged unusually high prices for the supplies – necessary equipment and food for the laborers – it furnished to the logger. One logger wrote the mill that he would have to deal with the Puget Mill Company unless things changed. He eventually went to work for the Port Blakely Mill. The mills carried large debts for their loggers; in 1890 the Puget Mill Company found that their loggers owed the mill $535,000. In 1887 Blackman Brothers, a logging outfit, owed so much to the Port Blakely Mill that Blackman agreed to settle up by turning over 1,800 acres of land with about 100 million feet of timber to the mill. However, not all loggers were able to settle up; in 1884 the owner of the Port Blakely Mill instructed its bank to make no more advances to loggers, since they had lost a great deal of money in past years through such practices.[92] Still, throughout the nineteenth century, loggers were kept going by the $75 monthly wage. Thus, loggers "had an income despite the fiscal condition of [the] company."[93]

Although running a logging company may ultimately have been an unstable investment, logging, nevertheless, drew settlers interested in economic opportunity and development to rural areas of the county. Certainly, logging could and was perceived to offer entrepreneurial opportunities to those who had little capital. Quilcene, for instance, was settled by men who logged – and sometimes farmed as well. In 1860, Hampton Cottle, the first settler in Quilcene – and his nephew, Samuel – cut ship's knees[94] for the Washington Mill Company, and Stephen Berry of Maine – another early settler – logged for the same mill.[95] In 1870 there were eight logging camps in the Quilcene area, and the population was a mixture of lumbermen, farmers, and their families.[96] For some settlers, working in the woods as laborers may have only provided an income to subsidize their farming, but for others it held out promise of "getting ahead."[97] Seven "loggers" running camps in the Quilcene area in 1870 owned real estate and personal property valued between $1,100 and $4,100, while the farmers listed their value between $520 and $2,600. Further, four of the men working as laborers in Quilcene logging camps in 1870 had become "loggers" working under contract for the Washington Mill Company during 1873–74.[98]

Shipbuilding was another industry closely connected to the sawmills, since shipbuilders depended upon the mills for lumber, and the mills sometimes commissioned lumber vessels and tugboats from independent shipyards. Some mills also established their own yards.[99] The county shipyards were never large. William Hammond employed perhaps ten men, both craftsmen and laborers, in 1860; Hall Bros. employed approximately thirty men when they operated in Port Ludlow during the 1870s and 1880s.[100]

County shipbuilding began in response to the need for small vessels – such as William Newton's *Sarah Newton* – for transporting mail, passengers, and consumer goods throughout the Sound. Franklin Sherman launched the first known county-built vessel in 1855 from Port Ludlow, a two-masted schooner of eleven tons that was followed by many such small sloops and schooners for use on Puget Sound.[101] Markets for larger vessels – up to 700 odd tons in size – developed in the 1870s. During the 1850s and 1840s, the cargo mills, which usually owned their vessels,[102] used ships that had come around the Horn.[103] However, as these eastern-made vessels began to wear out, lumbermen either contracted for vessels from Puget Sound shipbuilders[104] or established their own shipyards. The Washington Mill Company maintained a shipyard at Seabeck from 1876 to 1883, and the Puget Mill Company both purchased and commissioned Puget Sound-built vessels.[105]

Thus, commercial enterprises sustained the economy of early Jefferson County and made significant contributions to the overall Puget Sound economy: shipping and commerce in Port Townsend; lumber milling and shipbuilding in the mill ports, and logging in the rural areas of the county. In the minds of settlers, the county offered an array of economic opportunities for getting ahead, which, excepting the lumber mills – largely controlled by outside investors – were relatively less capital intensive: small beginnings from which settlers could imagine growing along with the county. Continuing economic development in Jefferson County was therefore seen as desirable, an issue of importance for many residents since their own prosperity was tied to county economic development.

"IT'S GOING TO BE A SITUATION OF COMMERCIAL IMPORTANCE"[106]

James G. Swan, one of Jefferson County's most important boosters, arrived in Port Townsend on February 14, 1859.[107] Swan had been a 32-year old Boston ship chandler when he decided to follow the

1.5
James Swan in Boston,
November 1870.
(Jefferson County
Historical Society)

forty-niners to San Francisco, arriving there in August 1850. Ostensibly an entrepreneur in search of his fortune, Swan worked in San Francisco for two years variously as a ship's purser, ship outfitter, and clerk. Perhaps more importantly, he also became a published writer, selling two articles about a November 1850 trip to the Sandwich (Hawaiian) Islands to the San Francisco *California Courier*.

After a time, Swan became dissatisfied with San Francisco. As a child he had been fascinated by stories his uncle told of an 1807 fur-trading expedition made to the Northwest coast on the Boston trader *Guatimozin*. Swan's uncle had been much interested in Northwest Coast Native American culture, and he passed his interest on to

1.6
James G. Swan sitting among his collections, reading.
(Jefferson County Historical Society)

Swan. In 1852, just as San Francisco was losing its allure, Swan was offered an opportunity to travel north with a friend – to Shoalwater Bay, now called Willapa – just north of the Columbia River in Oregon Territory. Here, Swan filed a Donation Land Claim for some 315 acres, harvested oysters for the San Francisco market, and sketched. He also travelled among and visited with area Native Americans, beginning a study of Northwest Native American cultures that would continue throughout his life. He compiled a dictionary of Northwest Indian dialects, and started writing *The Northwest Coast*, a memoir of his years at Shoalwater Bay replete with frontier burlesques, as well as serious reflections about Indians and their relations with Euro-Americans.

By 1855, Swan's rapport with resident Native Americans had earned him a reputation for expertise in matters relating to them, and he was invited by Governor Isaac Stevens to attend treaty negotiations between the southwestern Washington tribes and the federal government. Following this trip, Swan returned to Shoalwater Bay, and coming to terms with the fact that he was making too little money to stay there, he left his claim. He went first to San Francisco, but by the end of 1856 Swan was in Washington, D.C., gathering some background information for *The Northwest Coast* and working with J. Patton Anderson, Washington's territorial delegate to Congress. In December 1857 he was employed as secretary by the new delegate, former Governor Stevens.

Swan left Washington, D.C. in the fall of 1858 because Congress was in recess, and Stevens no longer needed a secretary. The sojourn was a momentous one for him, however, for he made the acquaintance of Spencer F. Baird, who was in charge of the new museum at the Smithsonian Institution. Baird had been impressed by Swan's acute observations of Southwest Washington Native Americans in *The Northwest Coast*, and he encouraged Swan to continue his study of coastal peoples.[108] Between 1857 and 1887 Swan wrote two books and several articles about Northwest Coast Native Americans, conducted two extensive expeditions to acquire items of Northwest Coast Indian manufacture for the Smithsonian, and accumulated his own large collection of artifacts. For the rest of his life – he lived until 1900 – Swan, although he retained a belief in the inherent superiority of Euro-American culture, attempted both to ameliorate the lives of the Native Americans he knew personally and mediate relations between the settlers and Indians. It is this for which Swan is typically most remembered.

Swan's time in Washington, D.C. was also important because of the influence Stevens appears to have had not only on Swan's immediate plans for the future, but also his ideas about frontier economic development. When the two men parted company, Stevens's advice to Swan was to go to Port Townsend. Stevens believed the town would be an excellent terminus for the projected northern-route transcontinental railroad, and he prophesied to Swan that "from its geographical position Port Townsend would become a place of commercial importance."[109] Swan acted upon Stevens's recommendation, arriving in Port Townsend in February 1859.

Before his employment and friendship with Stevens, Swan's ideas about frontier development were fairly simple. In *The Northwest Coast*, he promoted the potential of Shoalwater Bay as a harbor. He also mentioned the area's bountiful resources of seafood, fish, and game, which he thought would help settlers sustain themselves. Although he noted that some timber had been taken from the bay, he did not emphasize any potential for the lumber industry in Washington. He saw more promise in the development of a fishing station and trading post for the support of a fleet of whaling ships and halibut and cod fishermen.[110]

Swan's thinking about frontier expansion became more sophisticated, however, as he absorbed Stevens's ideas about American trade with Asia conducted through a northern-route transcontinental railroad, one terminus of which would be in Jefferson County. When Swan came to Port Townsend, he was armed with plans for a whaling station there, but also with up-to-date ideas about great cities and frontier development. He was eager to identify himself with the future of Jefferson County, and soon after his arrival he wrote a series of newspaper articles about Port Townsend and the county for the *San Francisco Evening Bulletin*, *San Francisco Daily Times*, and "various papers of the Territorial Press."[111]

Swan was encouraged by what he found in Port Townsend. The continuing development of commerce, shipping, and lumber augured well, he thought, for the county's economic future. Writing for the *Bulletin*, Swan described Port Townsend's "facilities for business accommodation [which are] equal to any ... in the Territory. It is a very desirable place for a permanent residence. The beauty of the location, its excellent harbor, its geographical position, and the fact of its being the port of entry for the whole Puget Sound district, combine to make it attractive to the merchant, ship-owner, and farmer," and echoing Governor Stevens, "It is safe to predict that it is destined to become a place of commercial importance."[112]

Although Swan's whaling station never materialized (his own commercial ventures were seldom successful), he stayed in Port Townsend – save for a few years spent at Neah Bay – for the remainder of his life. He died there in May 1900. Like other settlers whose survival required that they turn their hands to a variety of occupations and tasks, Swan was a sort of renaissance man. He worked in various capacities as a volunteer and paid employee of the Office of Indian Affairs; he collected both items of Native American manufacture and marine specimens for the Smithsonian. He became an attorney, was a notary public, probate judge, and county superintendent of schools. His specialty was admiralty law, and he served both as secretary to the Pilot Commission and as a commissioner.

He also was a persistent and seriously committed booster for Jefferson County. His most significant efforts for its development were through writing, dedicated lobbying for a county transcontinental railroad connection, and working to develop Puget Sound commercial fisheries. In 1859 he helped Travers Daniel prepare the first edition of Port Townsend's earliest newspaper, the *Port Townsend Register*, "a commercial sheet" dedicated "heart and soul to the ... interest of Washington Territory."[113] Swan continued to write articles about area development for the *Register* and other local and regional newspapers for his remaining forty-one years.

In 1868 he initiated correspondence with the general manager of Northern Pacific Railroad, arguing for Port Townsend's suitability as that railroad's Puget Sound terminus. Offering his services, he was hired in 1869 to assess and write a report about possible sites for the terminus. Of course, he recommended Port Townsend as the most promising, although his efforts failed. Tacoma was chosen, not Port Townsend, but Swan continued to attempt to establish a transcontinental railroad connection for Jefferson County into the 1890s. He also made extensive studies of Northwest fisheries for the United States Commission of Fish and Fisheries, hoping to see the establishment of viable commercial fishing on Puget Sound.

These were the most substantial of Swan's booster projects, but by no means all. Swan was able to envision and work for a transcontinental railroad connection or the development of a regional resource such as fishing. He was also interested in smaller aspects of development, as when he personally planted lobsters in Puget Sound, or advised area farmers though an article in the *Register* about how to cultivate cranberries.

If Swan stood out as a booster, nevertheless, he was one among many. Other residents shared his interest in county economic development which, it was assumed, would provide individuals with economic opportunity: merchants, shipping agents, and hotel barkeepers and bartenders in Port Townsend; ship carpenters and millworkers in Port Ludlow and Port Discovery; loggers in Quilcene and farmers in the Chimacum Valley; laborers throughout the county who worked for wages, but were also small producers or farmers – residents who expected the county's economic development to offer economic opportunities to them individually. Such thinking was at the heart of the county's settlement, and as such it had a relevance for many other residents beyond those such as Swan who were directly involved in promotional endeavors. Development was a countywide issue and "interest."

Port Townsend: "A Resort for 'Beachcombers' and Outlaws"[1]

Jefferson County's economic development received a blow in 1858 when J. Ross Browne, special agent of the United States Treasury Department and a much-published and popular travel writer, described Port Townsend as a "resort for ... outlaws." Browne's attack came in an official, but highly publicized, report to the Indian Commissioner on "Conditions of Indian Reservations in Oregon and Washington." Browne wrote: "with very few exceptions, it would be difficult to find a worse class of population in any [other] part of the world [than in Port Townsend]. It is known as a haven for 'beachcombers' and outlaws of every description."

Included in Browne's condemnation of Port Townsendites were members of the S'Klallam tribe who lived in and around Port Townsend; singled out for mention was the tribal leader Chet-ze-moka. "Once a powerful and intelligent chief," he now was, according to Browne, "much debased by the use of intoxicating liquors," and at the time of their meeting with Browne, his wives were "exceedingly drunk." The supposed drinking of Chet-ze-moka and other Indians formed the basis of Browne's denunciation of Port Townsend, since he blamed its settlers for Chet-ze-moka's degeneration. "The white population of Port Townsend" sold Chet-ze-moka his liquor: on each side of his "shanty" there was "a whisky shop from which he receive[d] continual supplies."[2]

THE DUKE OF YORK, QUEEN VICTORIA, AND JENNY LIND.

2.1

Chet-ze-moka and his wives, See-hem-itza and Chill'lil, 1864.
(Harper and Brothers, Publishers)

When the content of Browne's report was made public, it made a
sensation, raising an outcry from Puget Sound residents. West Coast
newspapers zinged as Browne and offended Port Townsendites and
others exchanged disagreeable comments in print.[3] Port Townsend
was again before the public eye in 1862, when Browne sardonically
mocked Port Townsend and Chet-ze moka – this time writing to a
large national audience in his "Coast Rangers" series, published in
Harper's New Monthly Magazine.[4]

That same year, a reporter for the Olympia *Washington Standard*
– inspired by Browne – decided "to spend a few days [in Port Town-
send] and take items ... the great notoriety" of the place making it
newsworthy. Perhaps inspired by Browne as well, Theodore Winthrop,
another travel writer, whose popular *Canoe and Saddle* was published in 1863, further added to Port Townsend's questionable fame.

2.2
Chet-ze-moka and See-hem-itza.
(Jefferson County Historical Society)

Winthrop wrote about visiting Port Townsend, where he hired Chet-ze-moka as a guide, and he characterized both town and man in much the same vein as Browne, derisively portraying Chet-ze-moka – or the Duke of York as he was known to Euro-Americans – as "ducally drunk." In 1862, a bid to remove the Customs office from Port Townsend to a supposedly less disreputable town was successful in part because the instigator emphasized Browne's characterization of the town[5] – all of which kept the controversy alive.

Browne revisited the incident himself in 1864, in "The Great Port Townsend Controversy," a chapter in *Crusoe's Island*, one of his many popular travel books. National attention ceased after the publication of *Crusoe's Island*, although there were anti-Browne references in Port Townsend newspapers for many years (see below). However, recognition of the controversy may have remained common for many years. Charles Nordhoff's 1875 travel book, *Northern California, Oregon and Hawaii* has pencil sketches of Chet-ze-moka and one of his wives, See-him-itza. These are the only Native Americans pictured in the book who are identified by name and title, which suggests that Nordhoff assumed that they would be familiar to some members of his audience.[6]

If the initial furor subsided, the controversy continued to rankle for years in the minds of Port Townsend residents, and given the great popularity of western travel literature – whether books, magazine articles, or guidebooks – it is not surprising that having acquired a national reputation, through several different publications, as a safe harbor for "beachcombers and outlaws" was considered injurious to county development. Nineteenth-century boosters were justly fearful of the impact negative images in widely read travel literature might have on development of a specific place, since such literature was of serious interest to potential settlers and investors. They believed making a favorable impression upon visitors was necessary, especially those such as Browne who commanded a national audience through their writings.[7]

In the case of Port Townsend, when Browne ridiculed the town as being disreputable, the question of the town's image with outsiders became focused upon its reputation, and thus integral to county thinking about development. Further, since the controversy linked the town's

THE DUKE OF YORK.
QUEEN VICTORIA.
Puget Sound Chiefs.

2.3
Puget Sound Chiefs: The Duke of York and Queen Victoria, 1874.
(Taylor and Francis Books UK)

reputation to that of Chet-ze-moka and the S'Klallam, some settlers
found it expedient to defend the reputation of the S'Klallam along
with the town's.

Development thinking also shaped relations between settlers and
the S'Klallam in other ways. Although prevailing federal policy argued for the removal of Indians from Euro-American society to reservations, in actuality, coexistence between Indians and settlers was an
established practice in the Puget Sound region during the frontier
period, and even beyond.[8] This coexistence was based in part upon
economic imperatives of development. in that many Native Americans were important and willing participants in the regional economy
(see below); and at least some boosters understood the advantages
of continued coexistence to Jefferson County's economy, and hence its

importance to development. While it is not clear how many S'Klallam were aware of the controversy, coexistence meant mobility for them. This mobility allowed them to seek wage labor and traditional foods such as salmon as they chose, affording them some economic control over their lives. Thus, many S'Klallam therefore also found some degree of coexistence acceptable.

The "Great Port Townsend Controversy," provides a window into the importance of boosterism, reputation, and coexistence between settlers and Native Americans. It also demonstrates the broader influence of development throughout the county in that development thinking was intertwined with relations between resident Native Americans and Euro-Americans, having an important influence on the course of such relations.

COEXISTENCE: "EMPLOYED AT ALMOST EVERYTHING THAT IS DONE ON THE SOUND"[9]

Common throughout the Puget Sound region, coexistence originated in economic circumstances, but also in certain characteristics of Puget Sound Indian culture.[10] The most numerous Native American group in Jefferson County was the S'Klallam, a Salish-speaking people, numbering at time of contact from 1,500 to 2,000 people living in thirteen villages – a population that had already been depleted by an earlier smallpox epidemic (see below). Their ancestors had migrated after 1300 CE from Vancouver Island to the southeast shores of the Strait of Juan de Fuca, their territory stretching along the Strait from Clallam Bay to Point Wilson.[11]

It is thought that they displaced Chemakuan-speaking peoples, of whom there were two remnants by the 1850s: one, the Pacific Coast Quileute; the other, the second Jefferson County Indian group, the Chimacum, a small tribe whose members lived on Port Townsend Bay.[12] The third group in the county was the Quilcene – Colceans or Kol-ceed-o-bish – a band of the Salish Twana, who lived along the northwest shore of Hood Canal. They were eventually incorporated into the peoples living on the Skokomish reservation, although during

the nineteenth century many returned to Quilcene Bay to fish, and some
worked for the Washington Mill Company at Seabeck.[13]

The Quilcene seldom appear in Jefferson County sources, and
except for their probable presence at the 1855 treaty negotiations,
they do not figure in the events discussed here. By the end of the nineteenth century, the Chimakum as a tribe were extinct, and even in
the early settlement period they were largely intermingled with the
S'Klallam and are rarely mentioned as a separate group.[14] Therefore,
for the purposes of this work, county Native Americans are defined
as S'Klallam. Further, neither coexistence in Jefferson County nor
S'Klallam lifestyle were unique, and many or even most of the tribe's
cultural characteristics were shared with other Puget Sound Indians.
Wherever possible, Native Americans discussed will be S'Klallam,
but characteristics and events generally shared with other Puget Sound
Native Americans are also used, as is general information relating to
Puget Sound coexistence.

There are two primary reasons that the culture of the S'Klallam
and other Puget Sound peoples gave rise to coexistence. First,
Native American lifestyle did not threaten the early, developing
Euro-American economy. Second, Puget Sound Indians were willing
to trade with, work for and with, and otherwise interact with Euro-
Americans because of the perceived benefits of such interactions to
their own individual status and worth. Indeed, their value and willing
participation in the Euro-American economy was the basis of coexistence, and such coexistence greatly facilitated early Puget Sound
development.

The S'Klallam were fishers, hunters, and gatherers who looked
seaward for much of their sustenance, being "almost exclusively maritime, depending mainly for support upon fish or the commodities
which they get in exchange."[15] Salmon, their most valued food, was
eaten fresh; when smoked and dried, it was a year-long staple sup-
plemented by other fish – rockfish, cod, halibut, dogfish – shellfish,
and seal. Roots, plants and berries, waterfowl, and game were also
eaten, and the S'Klallam travelled into the Olympic Peninsula interior
on gathering and hunting expeditions.[16] Important plants were "managed." Nettle patches were weeded, and the leftover stocks burned

in the fall; camas bulbs were divided and transplanted. It was also customary to fire prairie ground to encourage the proliferation of bracken fern, and to burn forest land so that fireweed and berries would spread.[17]

The winter months were spent in permanent settlements – occasionally fortified by stockades[18] – of large dwellings, or lodges, constructed of split cedar planks and shingles, which sheltered from four to six families. During the food-gathering months, however, tribespeople moved about to seasonal camps fishing, hunting, and gathering food. Extremely mobile by water, they travelled easily around the Sound, setting out in their cedar canoes to fish, gather foods, trade, or visit with kinsfolk and the settlers, but making less use of land away from the shoreline.[19] Settlers, whether lumbermen, merchants, or even farmers, perceived their economic interests to be less threatened by the maritime focus of S'Klallam lifestyle than was the case with Indians and settlers on other frontiers.

Robert Bunting has pointed out that ultimately the Puget Sound Indians' maritime culture depended upon the forest ecosystem, which would in time be radically changed by Euro-American settlement.[20] However, in the settlement period, this was not apparent, and the interests of Native Americans appeared to be little threatened by the settlers' lifestyles.

By the time the first settlers arrived in Jefferson County, the S'Klallam had had long experience with Euro-Americans. Initial meetings had followed in quick succession between 1788 and 1792. Crew members of the John Meares expedition to Vancouver Island visited Discovery Bay in 1788; two Spanish expeditions in 1790 and 1791 also landed in Discovery Bay; and in 1792 the Vancouver expedition spent two months exploring and charting the Strait of Juan de Fuca, Admiralty Inlet, Hood Canal, and Puget's Sound.[21] The Vancouver expedition found the S'Klallam eager traders, offering venison and fish for "Copper & Brass Trinkets for their Ears; they also took Iron with which Metal many of their arrows were barbed." Indeed, the S'Klallam had long been linked to other Native Americans in a vast Pacific-to-Plateau and Pacific coastal trade network that moved Native and Euro-American goods throughout the West.[22]

Interaction between Euro-Americans and the region's Native Americans continued, occasioned by the developing maritime fur trade, and later, the continental fur trade.[23] The S'Klallam traded with visiting British and American ships; may have made expeditions to Fort Vancouver; are known to have traded with the Hudson's Bay Company at Fort Nisqually – near present-day Olympia – beginning in 1833, and to have crossed the Straits to nearby Fort Victoria after it was built in 1843. They also worked for Euro-Americans, serving as guides and interpreters, and may have joined other Native Americans as farm laborers once the Hudson's Bay Company established an agricultural station at Fort Nisqually. In the resulting transactions, Indians and whites exchanged many goods: furs, marine oil, salmon, venison, baskets, and canoes for blankets, guns, tobacco, metal tools and implements, cloth, trinkets, and whiskey.[24] Thus, by 1850 significant economic interaction between the two groups was commonplace.

It is convenient to categorize the S'Klallam and other regional groups as tribes, but in doing so it is possible to lose sight of important cultural realities that facilitated economic relations between settlers and Indians. While members of a village or groups of villages often did identify themselves as belonging to the same unit, group members were also linked to other groups throughout the Sound by language, culture, and/or kinship since it was common, especially among the elite, to marry outside the village. Thus, S'Klallam, like other Puget Sound peoples, had kinsfolk living throughout the region, and they maintained "an extensive, well-ordered network of inter-community relations."[25]

On the other hand, not all Puget Sound Indians spoke the same language or shared exactly the same lifestyle, so that while many groups were linked to one another, they were disconnected from others. Further, at times groups with strong ties to one another were at odds, or even at war. Therefore, if Puget Sound Native Americans shared so many similarities that they have been classified as a "single culture" group by anthropologists, they were also extremely diverse.[26]

The prevalence of inter-group connections, but also the diversity of these groups created an inclusiveness that favored acceptance of Euro-Americans as trading partners and, later, as settlers. Further, according to historian Alexandra Harmon, trading had a multi-faceted importance to Puget Sound Native Americans. For one thing, because of their diversity, the S'Klallam and other tribes were adept at negotiating connections with people different from themselves, even in the face of opposition from such people. More importantly, success at negotiating such interactions was considered evidence of an individual's power, and such successes greatly heightened personal prestige. Trading also enhanced the individual's position or status in the community. Indeed, "although acquiring valued items was one object of trade, the items acquired were proof of and the means to personal relationships, and relationships were the true indications of a person's worth."

Thus, S'Klallam traders saw Euro-American fur traders and, later, settlers, as providing opportunities that were challenging and sometimes dangerous, but potentially advantageous.[27] Trading for merchandise, working for trade goods or money, establishing kinship through marriage or cohabitation between Native American women and Euro-American men, or just socializing with Euro-Americans had a significance for Native Americans that transcended the material value of tools, clothing, or trinkets, and was an essential aspect of the coexistence that grew between Native Americans and settlers .

This shared culture, but also the diversity of Puget Sound peoples, in combination with the status to be acquired by successful individual interaction with outsiders, furthered the economically symbiotic relationship between Native Americans and Euro-Americans. It was advantageous to fur traders. When settlers sought to trade or pay for the use of Native American skills or labor, the Indians' often willing association with them served the settlers well, which established an important economic connection between Indians and settlers. Indians perceived coexistence, at least some of the time, to be desirable as well.

TREATIES AND RESERVATIONS: "I COULD LOOK FOR FOOD WHERE I PLEASED, AND NOT IN ONE PLACE ONLY"[28]

Another factor that reinforced coexistence was the right-to-fish clause of the 1854–55 Puget Sound treaties. During the winter of 1854–55 most tribes signed treaties by which they transferred ownership of their lands to the United States in exchange for small reservations, specified government services, and annuities.[29] One intent of the treaties was to remove Native Americans to reservations, and if such removal had been achieved in Puget Sound, coexistence would have been impossible to maintain. However, certain factors combined to mitigate against removal. One was the right-to-fish clause in the 1854–55 treaties negotiated between territorial Governor Isaac Stevens and Puget Sound tribes. The other was the Native American perception of what the clause promised.

George Gibbs, one of Governor Stevens' advisors, recognized the necessity for Native Americans to continue their seasonal migrations for food until such time as they – he hoped – would successfully establish themselves as reservation-based farmers.[30] Another advisor to Stevens, Michael Simmons, believed continued Native American mobility would benefit the Euro-American economy.[31] Therefore, a clause was included in the treaties that promised:

"The right of taking fish at usual and accustomed grounds in common with all citizens of the United States, and of erecting temporary houses for the purpose of curing; together with the privilege of hunting and gathering roots and berries on unclaimed lands."[32] Native Americans interpreted this as a promise that their traditional mobile lifestyle would endure – indeed, they were assured of this by the negotiators.[33]

Until the beginning of the lumber boom in 1850, S'Klallam contact had been with those who sought to profit from their trade or hire their services. However, the first American settlers in Jefferson County – John Tukey, Alfred Plummer, Francis Pettygrove, or William Sayward, for instance – wanted to own and control the land and its resources.

Similarly, Washington's first governor, Isaac Stevens, who hoped to see the territory quickly fill up with settlers, placed a high priority on negotiating treaties that would extinguish Indian title to the land and remove them from the path of settlement. Meeting with Western Washington tribes at five different locations, Stevens effected four treaties – each almost identical to the other – that he believed would accomplish his goals.[34]

On January 25, 1855, he met with some 1,200 men and women of the S'Klallam, Chimakum, Skokomish, and Twana[35] at Point No Point on the northernmost tip of the Kitsap Peninsula. After a day and half of deliberation, the assembled tribespeople agreed to the treaty proposed by Stevens.

The negotiations were conducted in Chinook, the trade jargon.[36] Chinook was more ideally suited to simple transactions, and there may have been misunderstandings on the part of the Native Americans. Nevertheless, many Native Americans present had had years of experience in communicating with Euro-Americans, and two of the advisors who accompanied Stevens at the Point No Point negotiations were also experienced in talking with Puget Sound Native Americans. Further, some of the Indians at Point No Point made clear their reluctance to sign the treaty, voicing a variety of concerns, all of which suggests that they did understand the treaty negotiations, or, at least, a great deal.[37]

Che-lan-the-tat, a Twana, said he did not want either to sell his land or go to live where the "Great Father" wished. Deprived of his traditional mobile lifestyle, he was afraid that he would "become destitute and perish for want of food." Another man, Shau-at-seha-uk, spoke of his emotional attachment to his traditional lands. "I do not want to leave my old home, and my burying ground. I am afraid I shall die if I do." Nah-whil-uk shrewdly said that he did not want to sell his land: "It is valuable. The Whites pay a great deal for a small piece and they get money by selling the sticks [timber]." Hool-hol-tan stated that he did not "like to go on a reserve with the Klallam ... in case of trouble there are more of them than of us ... Let us keep half [you] take the rest."[38]

When Chet-ze-moka spoke he emphasized the treaty's promise of continued mobility, which may have swayed the assembly: "My heart is good ... since I have heard the paper read, and since I have understood Gov. Stevens, particularly since I have been told that I could look for food where I please, and not in one place only ... We are willing to go up the Canal [where the reservation was to be] since we know we can fish elsewhere."[39]

Chet-ze-moka was cheered, and, although there was still sufficient opposition to the treaty for the meeting to be adjourned without resolution, by the next morning the Indians had decided to accept the treaty. Chet-ze-moka presented a white flag to Stevens; and Chimakum leader Hul-kah-had told him, "We give our hearts to you ...

in return for what you do for us." Then, the treaty was signed, gifts were distributed and everyone dispersed.⁴⁰

Stevens expected the treaties to facilitate further settlement in the Puget Sound region by concentrating Native Americans as much as possible on reservations. Thus contained, they were to be taught farming and encouraged in the acquisition of "civilized" habits by Euro-American personnel.⁴¹

The "right-to-fish" clause in the treaties, however, expressed the intention that the Indians would provide for themselves through fishing, gathering foods, hunting, and taking part in the Sound economy until the process of reform was complete. Stevens and his advisors may have meant the right-to-fish clause to be applied only temporarily, but in the immediate post-treaty years funding to develop the reservations was lacking. There was no money to make them attractive to Native Americans or to provide sufficient staff to manage them. Native Americans lived on or off reservations as they pleased and continued working for or trading with settlers, living among them, and moving about the region fishing, hunting, and gathering food. This was the situation when Browne visited Port Townsend, and it continued to be true throughout the Puget Sound region for many years.

In the late nineteenth century several trends united to produce a more vigorous application of federal Indian policies on Puget Sound. On the one hand, immigration to Washington Territory increased – the Euro-American population went from 5,000 in 1860 to 25,000 in 1880 – and expectations of an economic boom upon completion of the transcontinental railroad in the mid-1880s created a more competitive environment with regard to land and other resources. There was then less tolerance of off-reservation Native American activities and residence, especially on the part of new settlers. At the same time, the federal government, influenced by religious reformers and reiterating reformist ideas of the past, determined to accomplish the isolation of Native Americans upon reservations where they would be protected from "corrupt" influences and taught by agents, missionaries, and teachers to be Christian, sober, sedentary farmers.⁴²

It proved impossible to force Puget Sound Indians to live on the reservations, however. Some chose to do so, either because the reservation was on their traditional lands, or because they wanted protection from Euro-American harassment. But many refused to remove to reservations, or, as Alexandra Harmon explains, they "devised ways to take advantage of opportunities afforded by the reservation system without conforming wholly to administrators' expectations of them."[43]

Even when individuals did move to a reservation, there was nothing to prevent them from leaving if they so desired. As Chet-ze-moka said at Point No Point: "I have been told that I could look for food where I pleased, and not in one place only." Assured by "American treaty negotiators ... that they would be allowed to work or gather goods off reservation, Indians did so.[44] As for the S'Klallam, their assigned reservation was seventy-five to one hundred eighty miles away from their villages and "usual and accustomed places"; few were willing to relocate to the Skokomish Reservation. Instead, bands worked to maintain themselves in their traditional region, very often living and working in coexistence with Euro-Americans (see further discussion below).

During the post-treaty years, the S'Klallam and other tribes continued to fish, hunt, and gather foodstuffs. They also participated in the settler economy, where they were accepted as supplying needed labor, services and even markets, especially for whiskey.

They sold potatoes they raised, venison, and berries to settlers. They continued to harvest salmon and other fish and shellfish. They hunted seals off the coast and caught dogfish, rendering the oil to be used by the logging industry to grease the skids logs were hauled along (see chapter 1). They carried freight and passengers in their canoes, and worked as agricultural laborers, domestic servants, loggers, lumber mill-hands – the S'Klallam worked in the mills at Port Ludlow, Port Discovery, Port Gamble, and Seabeck – and cannery packers.

Indian women sold craft work such as mats and baskets, and during the harvest season whole families travelled to the hop fields near Seattle to work.[45] Some women married or lived with white men, or sold sexual services to them. For instance, the 1870 Jefferson County census listed fifty-one Indian women as "keeping house," a term which designated a conjugal relationship with the male head of household, rather than one as a servant. There were three Native American housemaids living in Euro-American homes, and twenty-eight women from British Columbia living in beach settlements at Port Townsend and Port Ludlow whose occupation was listed as "housework." Twenty male "laborers" lived in the beach settlements as well. There were eighty-one children with Native American mothers and Euro-American fathers.[46]

Thus, in Jefferson County, and elsewhere on Puget Sound and other areas of the Northwest Coast, Native Americans maintained themselves, often living in proximity to settlers. They continued, at least in part, to follow their traditional mobility, refusing to be finally "removed" to reservations. Further, many settlers acquiesced in this coexistence, which had an important economic connection to development.[47]

Recorded memories of the settlement period in Jefferson County reflect this coexistence. According to James McCurdy's pioneer informants, when the Hastings-Pettygrove party landed, they were greeted by a large number of S'Klallam, who gave friendly assistance in the landing. A consultation between groups followed, which "ended amicably, and it is a gratifying fact that the truce thus established ... on the beach at Port Townsend in '52 was never broken, but has endured unto this day.[48] Lach-ka-nim, the elder son of Chet-ze-moka, shared a similar memory in 1936 with a Washington Pioneer Project interviewer. Then in his seventies, Lach-ka-nim looked back and lamented that "the boasted benefits of civilization brought no welfare or happiness to my people, and perhaps we would have been more in number today if we could have lived as our ancestors lived before us." Nevertheless, he also made reference to peaceful relations between the S'Klallam and the settlers, remembering that his father was "a warm friend of the white people; he liked them and they liked and trusted him ... I have always tried to do as he would have done, and I have many friends among the white people who have known me all my life. We have never quarrelled and never will."[49]

COEXISTENCE AND TENSION

All this evidence of coexistence does not negate the fact that coexistence was fraught with ambiguity and tension. For one thing, despite the importance of Indians to the economy and the connections between development, reputation, and the S'Klallam, not all boosters agreed on the necessity for defending coexistence. Nor did they all see the S'Klallam as necessary to economic development. In Jefferson County, as elsewhere, some settlers made intermittent demands that restraints be placed on Native American mobility and other behaviors, or that the Indians be confined to their reservation. Often such demands were voiced as concern that the S'Klallam threatened development. There were also periodic official attempts to enforce removal. Further, although Euro-American settlement provided Puget Sound Indians with opportunities for trade and status enhancement, nevertheless it irrevocably changed Native American life, and there were episodes of intimidation and violence and resentment between settlers and Indians.

Even before contact, Puget Sound Indians had suffered depopulation from European diseases; it is estimated that the first smallpox epidemic killed a majority of Puget Sound peoples[50] – timing of the epidemic is debated but falls somewhere between 1774 and 1782.[51] Its effects upon the S'Klallam – and others – were observed by members of the 1792 Vancouver expedition, who noted the presence of pockmarked individuals and deserted villages.[52] Smallpox epidemics continued during the post-contact period, the last occurring in 1862, although the S'Klallam and other Puget Sound Indians were especially hard hit by the smallpox epidemic in 1853, which had been preceded by the measles epidemic of 1847–48.[53] All of the epidemics caused, to a greater or lesser extent, social and cultural breakdown. Tuberculosis, influenza, dysentery, and syphilis plagued Puget Sound peoples as well.[54]

Over time, traditional eating habits and crafts were altered. As early as 1841 S'Klallam were reported to have been growing potatoes at Port Discovery,[55] their cultivation to eventually replace the gathering of native bulbs and roots, and it became more common to preserve salmon by salting it rather by drying it. Traditional cloaks and skirts made from shredded cedar bark or cloth – woven of mountain goat hair, duck down, fireweed-plant cotton, and shearings from small white dogs specially raised for their wool – were gradually replaced by European clothing. Euro-American tools and weapons replaced some traditional ones – although traditional fishing gear continued to be used.[56] As well, kinship relations and conflict resolution were seriously affected by Euro-American society.[57]

There were episodes of resentment, anger, intimidation, and violence between Native Americans and Euro-Americans. For example, although Chet-ze-moka was friendly with the settlers, his brother Klows-ton, also called King George, reportedly disliked the settlers a great deal. He believed that he had been cheated by Plummer, one of Port Townsend's founders, who had promised that the federal government would pay the S'Klallam for the land taken by settlers. Although some small annuities were eventually paid after 1859, when the treaties were ratified, nothing was forthcoming throughout the 1850s. Klows-ton is said to have often gone into the founders' trading post, making to purchase an item from the store but then insisting that the purchase price be considered as an advance on his land payment. He came to so resent the settlers that he eventually left Port Townsend and did not return.[58]

In 1852, violence threatened when the Port Townsend S'Klallam told settlers that they must not plant any crops; they were so frightened that they called for the USS *Active* to come from San Francisco and make a display of force. According to McCurdy, the *Active* anchored in the Bay and fired a few shots.[59]

Violence broke out in 1854, when United States soldiers and Port Townsend town officials searched for the murderers of two men. In the resulting skirmish several S'Klallam were arrested, but four men, two S'Klallam and two soldiers, were killed, and twenty-eight canoes were destroyed. Later, after three men were convicted of the murder and held at Fort Steilacoom, they – along with some other prisoners – escaped to a S'Klallam camp on Hood Canal. Soldiers followed and demanded the escapees' surrender. When their demands were refused, the soldiers destroyed the camp and a winter's supply of salmon, reportedly killing five S'Klallam. Then, taking Chet-ze-moka hostage, they held him until the escapees were returned to the army to be hanged.[60]

In 1861 the S'Klallam wife of John Allen, a Dungeness settler, was murdered, and Allen blamed the S'Klallam for her death. When in retaliation he shot and killed a S'Klallam man, violence threatened to break out as S'Klallam and settlers confronted one another across the Dungeness River. Further bloodshed was prevented, however, when Allen paid "the relative of the dead Indian a sum of money."[61]

There were settlers who believed that development would best be served by either establishing more control of the S'Klallam or removing them from Port Townsend. In 1860 a letter-writer who identified herself or himself as M.V.B. complained to the *Register* that Port Townsend was "obnoxious" because its buildings were "interspersed with rude constructed Indian huts from which a vast amount of filth does emanate," and the Indians themselves had "the most meretricious characters extant." Their presence in town "will deter emigration, and expel that part of the community which is inclined towards morality."[62]

The same *Register* reported that the question of the removal of the resident Native Americans from Port Townsend was soon to be addressed by the city trustees, a necessary move since the homes of the Indians took up "much valuable property that is needed for building purposes." Also, "the unsightly appearance of the smoky, filthy huts of the savages, [and] the appearance of the ... occupants, who wander about our streets, exhibiting themselves in a manner offensive in the eyes of decency [in other words, scantily clothed by Euro-American standards] is a matter that the city government will do well to attend to."[63]

In June 1860 a city ordinance made any permanent Indian residence illegal within the city limits and forbade temporary "mat lodges or tents" or the building of fires except on the beach at the edges of the town.[64] What immediate effect this ordinance had is not known. There was still a permanent village on Port Townsend Bay in 1871, and S'Klallam and other Native Americans continued to live on the beach into the twentieth century.[65]

Ideas about control or removal continued to resurface over the years. In 1862 the smallpox epidemic was the impetus for another plea – this time from *The North-West* – for the removal of Indians from Port Townsend, both because of perceived health hazards and their negative effect on the town's future. (The editor had no apparent sympathy for the plight of the Indians.) "Aside from the important consideration of present safety from the ravages of a loathsome disease, the growth and prosperity of the towns on the Sound, morally and socially, depends upon the exclusion of the Indians ... from their municipal bounds." He argued that "a hundred Indians" living within a town would "not so much enhance the value of real estate as the advent of one family of civilized, honest and industrious whites." Further, he said that if the Indians were removed to their reservation, "the unenviable reputation our community has gained would be less deserved, our natural resources would rapidly develop, society would improve and strengthen."[66]

In 1879, Port Townsend residents petitioned the city council to remove Native American encampments from within the city "as we deem that the presence of Squaw Brothels has hitherto been a nuisance." And, in the same year the *Democratic Press* called for the removal of those Native Americans living "on the beach north of this city [who] lead a life of debauchery that is a disgrace to any community ... They should be kept on their reservations and only allowed to leave for a few days at a time."[67] In 1890, the *Leader* campaigned for the removal of "Siwash Brothels," or dance houses – bars with music where customers were expected to buy their dance partner a drink when the music stopped, which was often. Such establishments – where the female partners might be prostitutes – were "a menace to the future good name of [Port Townsend]," the Indians working in them "a class that do much injury to a city like Port Townsend."[68]

The S'Klallam people successfully resisted control and removal, however, seeking to establish a secure base for themselves in their traditional homeland. As early as the fall of 1860, Chet-ze-moka enlisted the aid of Swan in requesting of the Superintendent of Indian Affairs that a S'Klallam reservation be set aside near Port Townsend on Marrowstone Island, apparently a response to the fear of removal, pursuant to ratification of the Point No Point treaty in 1859.[69]

In June 1870, Che-ze-moka met in Swan's rooms with Congressional Representative Garfielde to discuss a similar request.[70] However, nothing came of Chet-ze-moka's efforts. Indeed, quite the reverse. In 1867 an official of Indian Affairs had visited Port Townsend and tried to persuade Chet-ze-moka to "return to the Reservation on Hood's Canal" – which suggests that he had been there for a time. He refused.[71]

Then, in 1871, Edwin Eells, the agent for the Skokomish Reservation, directed Port Townsend city officials to burn the S'Klallam's Port Townsend shoreline village, and he made the S'Klallam pack their belongings into some twenty canoes, which were towed to the Skokomish Reservation by a steamer.

In an account derived from S'Klallam oral tradition, S'Klallam historian Mary Ann Lambert relates that as the canoes were pulled away from the beach the Indians, "looking back at their ancestral homes, could see their village in flames, burning rapidly to the ground." When they arrived at the Skokomish Reservation "the canoes were cut loose ... Sadly the Clallams [sic] paddled to shore and sat dejectedly in their canoes, staring unhappily at the shore." In a very few days, however, the S'Klallam returned "by cover of night ... to the heap of ashes which was their Port Townsend village."

Following their return, Chet-ze-moka tried unsuccessfully to arrange compensation for the loss of S'Klallam homes; perhaps discouraged by his failure to help his tribe's people, Chet-ze-moka relocated on land across the bay from Port Townsend, where he lived until his death in 1888.[72]

During the 1870s and 1880s, growing immigration to and investment in the Puget Sound region created increasing pressure on land and other resources, and the appeal of coexistence lessened for many Euro-Americans. Nevertheless, S'Klallam continued to fend for themselves, through participation in the Puget Sound economy, and fishing and other traditional food-gathering activities.[73] Ultimately they successfully resisted removal to the Skokomish Reservation.[74]

An outstanding example of S'Klallam determination was Jamestown. In 1874 a group of 200 Dungeness S'Klallam under leadership of Jim Balch secured 210 acres for $500 and founded the village of Jamestown near Sequim in Clallam County. They were joined by S'Klallam from the Elwah, Port Discovery, and Port Townsend bands.

Other S'Klallam purchased land at Port Discovery, Elwah, Clallam Bay, and Port Angeles. As well, a sizable settlement developed on Port

Gamble Bay near the Puget Mill Company, where many S'Klallam men worked. According to Myron Eells, "only a little of [the land acquired was] first class land [but] they ... used it for gardens and as a place for a permanent home so that they should not be driven from one place to another, more than for farming."[75]

Jamestown was – in part – a response to Dungeness settlers' petitions calling for removal of the band to the Skokomish reservation. However, the efforts of the S'Klallam to build villages or individual homes of their own met with approval from other Euro-Americans,[76] as when, for instance, the Port Angeles correspondent to the *Argus* wrote that "the Clallam [*sic*] Indians in this vicinity are building good houses and are clearing and fencing in considerable ground for farming purposes without government aid or the benign influences of those martyrs known as Indian agents."[77] Thus, coexistence continued with the support of some Euro-Americans who recognized that the S'Klallam had a purpose within the settler economy, an economy important to county development.

Today there are three federally recognized S'Klallam tribes, their reservations located within traditional S'Klallam territory, all attributable to S'Klallam persistence and determination to continue as a people.[78]

"THE GREAT PORT TOWNSEND CONTROVERSY"

J. Ross Browne, however, viewed S'Klallam independence in a very negative way as reflected throughout "the great Port Townsend controversy."[79] Browne was an inveterate traveller best known for his humorous and irreverent writings about "adventures in exotic lands." Beginning in the early 1840s through the late 1860s he wrote numerous books and many travel articles and commentary for *Harper's New Monthly Magazine*, and he "created for himself an enviable reputation as a satirist and author of works on travel." During the same period he was employed by the United States government in various capacities, the last as Minister to China, 1868–69, and he wrote several detailed reports for investigations he conducted for the

federal government. From 1853 to 1860 he was a special agent for
the Treasury Department headquartered in California, and he "was
a ubiquitous figure from Port Townsend, Washington Territory, to
Galveston, Texas."[80]

Browne visited Washington and Oregon in the late summer of
1857, on assignment to investigate the "conditions of Indian[s]" in
the two territories and inquire into the origins of the Indian War of
1855–56. He travelled over 2,000 miles and visited six reservations
and four agencies, where he examined the accounts of Indian agents,
met with Native American leaders – one of whom was Chet-ze-moka
– and listened to testimony from Euro-American settlers about the
recent war.[81]

Browne brought to his investigation a decided critique of the effects of American expansion on Native Americans. He had sympathy
for the situation of Native Americans and thought that they had been
dispossessed in the worst possible way. However, he considered this
dispossession an unavoidable aspect of what he called progress.[82]
With regard to Northern California, he noted that settlers had taken
the land from the Indians "without recompense ... kill[ing] them in
every cowardly and barbarous manner that could be devised."

Even when the government intervened, it served Native Americans
little better. California's experimentation with the emerging reservation system during the 1850s only served to enrich its administrators
– men of "intemperate and disreputable habits ... who spent their
days in idleness and their nights in brawling grog-shops." While "immense numbers of Indians were fed and clothed [and educated] – on
paper," in reality, they barely managed to survive by seeking subsistence on non-reservation lands.[83]

Nevertheless, while he argued for humane treatment, he believed
that federal policies, especially the idea that Indians should be removed to remote reservations, best served Native American interests.
He believed that on reservations Indians would be protected from
the venality and cruelty of Euro-Americans and taught "civilization."
Browne harbored a romanticized belief that the California Spanish
mission system could provide a blueprint for instructing "this [Native
American] race in the acquisition of civilized habits ... by this humane
system of teaching many hostile tribes ha[ve] been subdued, and en-

abled not only to support themselves, but to render the Missions highly profitable establishments."

He also believed that the younger generation of Native Americans would be the most apt pupils, and he proposed that Indian children be sent to school from the age of five. When they turned fourteen, he suggested that they be separated from their parents, boys to be apprenticed to farmers and girls to learn to do domestic work.[84] Over time, however, the failures of the reservation system in California convinced Browne that the only effective reservation was a military fortress that would prevent any contact between Indians and non-Indians. Without complete separation, he feared, Indians would "suffer speedy extinction."[85]

Thus, any form of Native American independence was anathema to Browne. As many before and after him, Browne believed that Native Americans should be Americanized, and, in the process, be sequestered on reservations. He found much therefore of which to disapprove in the "conditions" of Indians on Puget Sound.

For Browne, the coexistence between Puget Sound Native Americans and Euro-Americans was "a condition worse than pure barbarism [in which] large bands of Indians [are] permitted to roam at large, committing petty depredations wherever they can, lounging idly about the farms, consuming the substance of the settlers, affording a profitable trade [in whiskey] to the worst possible class of whites that can infest any country."[86]

He believed Port Townsend and Chet-ze-moka to be outstanding examples of such degeneracy. In describing his visit to Port Townsend on August 25, 1857, he maintained that Chet-ze-moka and his wives were degraded by their association with Euro-Americans. He also emphasized the perceived moral depravity of Port Townsend's settlers. Chet-ze-moka was "once a powerful and intelligent chief,[87] but [was] of late much debased by the use of intoxicating liquors." He lived "in a large shanty built of slabs and boards, within the limits of the town." There was a whiskey shop placed on each side of his home, "from which he derives continual supplies. Within the past year he has scarcely ever been sober."

Browne also noted that at the time of their meeting, Chet-ze-moka was accompanied by his two wives, who were "exceedingly drunk."

Further, according to Browne, Chet-ze-moka had "knocked a few teeth out of [See-hem-itza's] mouth [and] a few days before he had given [Chill'lil] a black eye." Browne wrote:

> We took our departure, very much impressed with the scene. It was a sad commentary upon the morals of the white population of Port Townsend ... During my stay there, I formed the opinion that the Duke of York [sic] and his amiable family were not below the average of the white citizens residing at that benighted place. With very few exceptions, it would be difficult to find a worse class of population in any part of the world ... It is notorious as a resort for 'beachcombers' and outlaws of every description.[88]

Browne submitted his report to Indian Affairs in January 1858 where it was read by James Swan in his capacity as secretary to Isaac Stevens. Swan reported the contents to Stevens who, once the report was made public, sent copies to Washington Territory,[89] where the report met with great disapproval. The Steilacoom *Puget Sound Herald*, for instance, defended coexistence saying that Indians "worked and are employed at almost everything that is done on the Sound." Further, said the *Herald*, lumber mills, logging camps, farming, and shipping could not get along without the labor of Indians, a far cry from Browne's description of "bands of Indians ... permitted to roam at large ... lounging idly ... affording a profitable trade to the worst possible class of whites [whiskey-merchants]."[90]

Understandably, however, it was in Port Townsend that opposition to the report was strongest. A letter to the *San Francisco Bulletin* demanded that Browne "be kind enough to inform us when or where you saw any of us pursuing any other than an honorable calling for a livelihood." Browne had "wholly and most wrongfully misrepresent[ed] a community of as peaceable, industrious and law-abiding citizens as can be found anywhere ... We, in self defense, say you have done us great injustice."[91] A letter to the *San Francisco Globe* "indignantly den[ied] that the Duke had ever knocked a tooth out of [See-hem-itza's] mouth ... [and Chill'lil] enjoyed entire exemption from a black eye."[92]

Browne replied with characteristic sarcasm, wondering that respectable citizens would confuse themselves with beachcombers, since he had not. Writing in the *Globe*, he insisted that although he would "submit to your report and take the [See-hem-itza's] teeth back," he would not take back "[Chill'lil's] eye." He wrote that her eye "was certainly black; darkly, beautifully black. It was not only black, but the vicinity was blue, green and yellow, with a touch of neutral tint in the background. I hold on to the eye, gentlemen, and will never give it up."

He continued, saying that he had never seen "any of you drunk" and he certified that the inhabitants of Port Townsend did not "habitually use whiskey as a beverage." Or, with irony, at least, not whiskey made in Port Townsend, "which is said to be made of alcohol, tobacco, cayenne pepper, mustard, vinegar, strychnine and salt water. I blame no man for refraining from the use of that sort of whiskey."[93]

Writing in 1864, Browne went so far as to claim that the "controversy" was the making of Port Townsend. He said that Port Townsend had such a familiar name that during the Fraser River gold rush "thousands who had no particular business there went to take a look at this wonderful town, which had given rise to so much controversy ... There was a brisk trade in city lots on speculation, and Port Townsend began to look like a city."

Indeed, when "the Fraser River bubble burst, nobody was killed at Port Townsend," for which, Browne contended, he was responsible. Thanks to himself, Browne wrote, "[Port Townsend] had a strong reputation, and could still persuade people that it was bound to be a great city at some future period ... I was the means of building up the fortunes of Port Townsend ... it has been clearly demonstrated ... that 'whisky built a great city.'"[94]

Needless to say, the settlers – recognizing the corrosive nature of Browne's humor – disagreed. They wanted their community to have a good reputation, not a strong one, and the town's development was the result of their hard work, not whiskey!

References in letters to regional newspapers debunking the controversy continued for some time, and for many more years the local editors made teeth-gnashing comments in the local papers about

Browne and his "abusive" descriptions of Port Townsend and its residents, both Euro-American and Native American. For example, in February 1860, a Port Townsend correspondent to the *San Francisco Bulletin* exclaimed that, "A community that can support a paper like the *Register* must be composed of different people than are represented to be here by the Ross Brownes ... of the press."[95] *The North-West* deplored in August 1860 that, "In times past ... our community has been ... outraged by a sort of literary trash purporting to be a detailed account of everything Indian, in which the material and embellishment alike found source in unhealthy and vain imaginings."[96] And, using a touch of irony themselves, some Port Townsendites referred to bad whiskey as the "Ross Brown" [*sic*] compound.[97]

A November 1867 *Weekly Message* wrote about the audience at a Sunday school concert: "We would have been glad had Ross Browne and other traducers of this town been present and seen how many among the audience were composed of old beachcombers, as the sarcastic Browne called them." Their presence at a Sunday School function was "evidence" that these "men from the logging camps and farms have souls capable of appreciating the harmonies of the children's choir, and hearts big enough to contribute to the support of the Sabbath School."[98]

In 1868 Browne's writings were compared "for truth [to] the famous tales of Sinbad the Sailor," and in 1869, the "Report of J. Ross Browne, on the Mineral resources of the State and Territories west of the Rocky Mountains," was described as "consisting of a good deal of error. [It is] about as reliable as the reports [to] the Commissioners of Indians Affairs."[99]

As late as 1878, Swan commented on the controversy when writing to historian H.H. Bancroft about the early settlement period. Dismissing Browne as a "writer more witty than reliable,"[100] he also opined that Chet-ze-moka and his wives "had become historical characters by [Browne's] fertile pen."

Swan was perhaps the most effective defender of both Port Townsend and Chet-ze-moka. He was acknowledged as having some authority on Indian matters, and his status as outside observer and published writer challenged that of Browne (see above). Swan arrived in Port Townsend in 1859.[101]

Writing for the *San Francisco Evening Bulletin*, Swan asserted that "those persons who have formed an opinion of Port Townsend ... from the report of J. Ross Browne" would find that far from being a "God-forsaken place where a traveller might think himself fortunate if he escaped with his life," Port Townsend was an up-and-coming place, destined for great things. "The facilities for business accommodation are equal to any ... in the Territory [and the] 'beachcombers' and 'outlaws' ... have left the place." Of late there had been "no rioting nor drunkenness among either the whites or Indians ... The whole conduct of citizens and strangers was such as reflected well on their characters as law-abiding and order-loving persons."[102]

When Swan discussed Chet-ze-moka, he spoke with the knowledge of prior acquaintance. Wanting to impress Chet-ze-moka and, through him, his tribespeople with the power they represented as Americans, Port Townsend settlers had sent Chet-ze-moka in 1852 on a visit to San Francisco. Swan, a friend of the ship captain who transported Chet-ze-moka, played host.[103]

According to Swan, however badly Chet-ze-moka may have behaved when he met Browne, the S'Klallam leader was "a very intelligent and very reliable Indian." Further, he was now "very sober," and the rest of the S'Klallams resident in Port Townsend were sober as well. "In fact, during a residence at Port Townsend of nearly six weeks, I have not seen a single drunken Indian." Swan gave credit for this last to the local Indian Agent, Captain R.C. Fay, for "rooting out and driving off the few low scoundrels who made an infamous living by selling liquor to the Indians."[104]

All in all, in his *Bulletin* pieces, Swan depicted a town of economic promise with an established and growing business community and sober residents, Euro-American and Native American. Further, as to coexistence, instead of corrupting the S'Klallam, and thereby sinking to a level even more depraved than the supposed depths of S'Klallam existence, the settlers, in the person of the local Indian Agent, had helped the Native Americans become sober, too.

There is a ludicrous aspect to the "Great Port Townsend Controversy," and at least one historian, Murray Morgan, has presented the controversy in a jocular way.[105] However, it is worthy of serious analysis, given the importance attached to it by the participants.

As a well-published travel writer, Browne's writings had influence. As pointed out by David Hamer, throughout the West those settlers who sought local development believed that such development depended, in part, upon positive public images, especially those conveyed through travel literature. A good impression with the federal government was important as well. That development-minded Port Townsendites sought to counter the negative images of Port Townsend broadcast by Browne in popular publications, newspapers, and a government report is not surprising.[106]

Certainly, Swan believed the episode was important enough to mention to Bancroft twenty years later. Local newspapers made humorous but derogatory comments about Browne for ten years or longer, and given that such media depended upon maintaining a cogent dialogue with their local readers, such comments argue for the continued popular relevance of the controversy. That the controversy was so tied to the question of reputation suggests the popular relevance of concerns about reputation, as well. Reputation may have been an important issue for boosters without the controversy, but coinciding, as it did, with the nascent phase of development culture, Browne's attack gave an early and continuing development focus to the question of Port Townsend's disreputableness.

The settlers had variously invested their time, energy, money, and dreams in the town's future. Being made a national laughing stock by such a popular writer was thought to put that future in jeopardy, and they were eager to counter Browne's depiction of them as disreputable, to establish that the town consisted of "peaceable, industrious and law-abiding citizens" who did not drink too much; that, by implication, Port Townsend was a promising town for investors and immigrants.[107] Such reassurances to outsiders would remain a vital development strategy throughout the nineteenth century (see chapter 4).

It is easy to understand why the settlers defended their own reputation, but it may be less clear why they defended that of Chet-ze-moka and the other S'Klallams – why they made haste to deny See-hem-itza's missing teeth and Chill'lil's black eye, or why Swan characterized the whole town – Euro-American and Native American – as orderly and sober.

There are two reasons. One is that Browne blamed the degeneration of the S'Klallam upon Port Townsend settlers. They, he claimed, provided the whiskey responsible for Chet-ze-moka's degradation. By denying that Chet-ze-moka was violent towards his wives, the settlers denied his drunken behavior, and through establishing Chet-ze-moka's respectability, they emphasized their own. When Swan assured his readers that the S'Klallam were no longer drunks because Fay – Indian Agent and a local resident – had swept away the "few low scoundrels"[108] who sold whiskey to the Indians, he not only established the sobriety of the S'Klallam, but promoted the reputableness of Port Townsend's settlers.

Second, coexistence between the settlers and Indians produced sufficient economic rewards for coexistence to be generally acceptable to many members of both groups (see above). Removal of the S'Klallam to their reservation seventy-five miles away would have destroyed that coexistence, a coexistence that most importantly for the settlers provided a labor force important to economic growth and development. Thus, development and the S'Klallam were inextricably linked, both through their economic role and the perceived need by some boosters to support coexistence.

The great Port Townsend controversy established Port Townsend's reputation as an important development concern, with rehabilitation an imperative. Further, because Browne identified coexistence – which already had an economic imperative – as the crux of Port Townsend's disreputableness, some residents also defended that relationship between settlers and S'Klallam, characterizing both groups as law-abiding and orderly.

"A WRITER MORE WITTY THAN RELIABLE:"[109] BROWNE, NATIVE AMERICANS, PORT TOWNSEND, AND REPUTATION

To Browne, his vignette of town and tribal leader proved that the close contact with settlers common on Puget Sound was dangerous for Indians. However, the great Port Townsend controversy illustrates the degree to which J. Ross Browne's understanding of Indian/settler

relations on Puget Sound was misguided. Browne saw "large bands
of Indians permitted to roam at large ... in a condition worse than
barbarism, [prey to] the worst possible class of whites than can infest
any county."[110]

In reality, however, Indians were at work surviving Euro-American
settlement with better wisdom than demonstrated by Browne or
other federal officials. Coexistence was far more complicated than
the symbiotic association between whiskey peddlers and whiskey
consumers perceived by Browne.

Browne believed that Native Americans should be isolated and
protected. However, if Browne's mockery of Chet-ze-moka and Port
Townsend was a satirical argument for reservations, Port Townsend
boosters – even those who favored removal – saw his writings as an
assault on economic development.

It is little wonder they thought his writings fighting words. His description of Port Townsend suggested that it might be the last place
on earth where anyone would want to settle. Said Browne, "surrounded by a jungle of pine [*sic*] and matted brush, through which
neither man nor beast can penetrate [, it is] indeed, a remarkable
place." Its houses were few in number and crudely built from "pine
[*sic*] boards, thatched with shingles, canvas, and wooden slabs," the
streets "curiously ornamented with dead horses and the bones of
many dead cows ... by reason of the peculiar odor ... no person can
fail to recognize Port Townsend [even] in the darkest night."[111]

From describing the location, Browne went on to decry the businesses of the town claiming that: "the principal articles of commerce
... [are] whisky, cotton handkerchiefs, tobacco, and cigars, and the
principal shops [are] devoted to billiards and the sale of grog." Mis-
chievously describing the drinking habits of the settlers, he attacked
their character: "I do not believe you habitually drink whisky as a
beverage – certainly not Port Townsend whisky, [anyway] for that
would kill the strongest man that ever lived in less than six months,
if he drank nothing else. Many of you, no doubt, use tea or coffee at
breakfast, and it is quite possible that some of you occasionally venture upon water."[112]

Browne's description of Chet-ze-moka created the image of a foolish drunkard, one who, moreover, routinely beat his wives. The Duke

looked "very amiable and jolly [but] stupefied by ... whisky." When it transpired that his visitor had brought no whiskey, he said "'Oh, dam!'... turning over on his bed and contemptuously waving his hand in termination of the interview – 'dis Tyee no'count!'"

This description of Chet-ze-moka – "once an intelligent and powerful chief" – laid siege to the integrity of the settlers since "the degraded condition of [Chet-ze-moka] and his tribe [was due] to the illegal practice on the part of the citizens in selling whiskey to the Indians."[113] Given the national forum Browne commanded, his attack required counterattack.

If Browne's scurrilous description of the town and its residents – both Indian and non-Indian – was assumed to define Port Townsend, then Jefferson County's future was at risk. The settlers' letters and the partisanship of James Swan were only the beginning of an extended defense of the town's reputation that became integral to development schemes. The good reputation of Port Townsend and its friendly relations with the S'Klallam were prominently touted throughout the frontier period as if J. Ross Browne still skulked in the background, waiting to malign "that remarkable place," Port Townsend.

Booster Activism: Jefferson County, 1860–1880

In 1853, H.C. Wilson wrote to a family member that in Port Townsend "no branch of business vigorously pushed along [would] fail to
pay whether it be Agriculture, Fishing, Lumbering, or Mining."[1] In
1859, James Swan echoed Wilson's optimism that Port Townsend
was "destined to become a place of commercial importance."[2] Nevertheless, such hopefulness seemed unwarranted in the intervening
years. While Port Townsend had captured the Puget Sound District
Port of Entry, so important to the town's development as a shipping
center, a depression in the lumber industry during the mid-to-late
1850s had a negative effect on Puget Sound shipping, and hence Port
Townsend's economy. The 1855–56 Puget Sound Indian War and
raids by Native peoples from British Columbia and Alaska – such as
the incident on August 11, 1857, when Isaac Ebey, a resident of
Whidby Island was beheaded by raiders – discouraged new immigrants and frightened many resident settlers into blockhouses or
flight. J. Ross Browne, for instance, noted deserted farmsteads and
fleeing settlers during his 1857 visit, although arguably, the Indian
War of 1855–56 placed far greater stress on the non-hostile S'Klallam
than on county settlers. Confined to a small area, the S'Klallam were
unable to fish or gather foods in quantity; unable to work for wages
and prevented from buying the ammunition to hunt game for sale to
settlers, they suffered from lack of income and food.[3]

When Browne's attack on the settlement came in 1858, it must have seemed to mark a nadir in the boosters' ambitions. Nevertheless, as the 1850s drew to a close, the lumber industry recovered momentum, and fears of warfare with Indians receded; hopefulness about the county's prospects for the future experienced a resurgence. Further stimulated by the necessity to defend Port Townsend's reputation from Browne's acid-dipped pen, boosters embarked upon efforts to promote county development.

Throughout the 1860s and 1870s, however, county development was hampered by a stagnating Puget Sound economy. In 1860 lumber was all on Puget Sound, firmly established as Washington's leading industry.[4] By 1870, $1.3 million of the $1.9 million invested in Washington manufacturing was invested in the lumber industry; two-thirds of manufacturing wages were paid to sawmill workers, and thirty-one of the thirty-eight steam engines operating in the territory powered sawmills. Almost all lumber production derived from the Puget Sound region, especially its west side, with Kitsap County the largest producer[5] and Jefferson County the second largest.[6]

Contrary to the expectations of early Puget Sound and Jefferson County promoters such as Lafayette Balch or H.C. Wilson, though, the lumber boom of the early 1850s did not have a gold-rush effect upon Puget Sound. Initially established to supply lumber to gold-rush San Francisco, the industry had also developed other Pacific Rim markets during the 1850s. Access to markets beyond California was limited by transportation costs, however, and the industry tended to stagnate. Overall mill production grew little during the 1870s, increasing only slightly by 1880. In that year, despite the commercial potential of its myriad stands of timber, Washington ranked only thirty-first in national lumber production.[7]

The larger Pacific Northwest economy was more diverse: agriculture, mining, and fishing, as well as lumber, were important facets of that economy. During the 1860s, most economic growth was derived from mining, which had less effect on Puget Sound.[8] Canned salmon, wheat, and livestock joined Pacific Northwest lumber and metals in the world market during the 1870s, but they would not be either produced or shipped from Puget Sound until the late 1870s. The first canned salmon was from Columbia River stocks. Puget Sound canneries began operation in 1877, and Puget Sound and Alaska canneries soon were outproducing those on the Columbia River. Wheat was first shipped from Puget Sound in 1876, but it was not until the Northern Pacific Railroad's Cascade line was finished in 1887 that wheat grown in eastern Washington became a major export from Puget Sound.[9] Regional diversity could not alter the fact that lumber, its growth limited, remained the mainstay of the Sound economy. This in turn limited shipping and ensured that population growth – from approximately 5,000 in 1860 to 25,000 in 1880 – would be slow.[10] Ultimately, large-scale development on Puget Sound awaited a transcontinental railroad connection, the completion of which was dependent upon a timetable set by American and even global expansion.[11]

Jefferson County boosters – those actively engaged in promotion and their supporters – were aware of the importance of a transcontinental railroad to the region's development. Governor Stevens's northern route railroad report had recommended that such a railroad end point should be Puget Sound with a Jefferson County port as one of the terminuses, and county residents were hopeful that this important connection would promote development not only of the Sound, but also of the county. Boosters also understood the necessity of outside capital investment to such development, and much of their energy would be devoted to drawing such investment.[12]

Nevertheless, if many of their hopes for the future were pinned upon a transcontinental railroad and other large-scale investment, completion of which was largely beyond their control, county residents – much like boosters in other areas[13] – nevertheless pursued locally based, non-institutionalized promotional projects that they hoped would stimulate some county development, from individual projects such as letter writing, to more formal efforts such as booster journalism, development of local resources, and, in the 1880s, membership in a multi-county immigration society, the purpose of which was to promote settlement in the county.[14]

Conversant with current theories of development about the passage to India and great cities, they considered Port Townsend's situation as a shipping center essential to county development. They agreed that growth required the development of transportation routes – not only railroads, but county roads and shipping – and they sought to exploit natural resources beyond timber. Understanding that the countryside was as necessary for economic growth as Port Townsend, boosters worked to bring investment and immigrants to the whole county. One point of disagreement was whether or not immigration should precede or follow investment, but whether one or the other, immigrants were as important a target for promotion as was capital investment. This chapter examines some of the locally determined development efforts beginning with the booster press.

LOCAL NEWSPAPERS: JOURNALISTIC BOOSTERS

As on other frontiers, newspapers[15] played an important role in promoting Jefferson County and facilitating a lively local and ongoing discussion of development issues. Beginning with articles published by James Swan from 1859 to 1861 in the San Francisco and Olympia papers and continuing with local newspapers, such journals were enthusiastic boosters. The county's first publication, the *Port Townsend Register*, described itself as "a commercial ... not a political sheet,"[16] and dedicated "heart and soul to ... the Agricultural and Commercial interest of Washington Territory."[17] It was published intermittently between December 23, 1859 and September 13, 1861, with three editors: Travers Daniel, William Whitacre, and Henry Sutton. James Swan was its commercial reporter throughout most of this period, writing a column, "Commercial and Marine Matters." *The North-West* promised to be "a family and commercial newspaper" and to promote "the Commercial and Agricultural Interests of Washington Territory."[18] It also had a short life – from July 1860 to late 1862. John Damon, and for a short time, Victor Smith, were its editors.

Al Pettygrove, son of Port Townsend founder Francis Pettygrove, started *The Weekly Message* in May 1867. He sold it to a prominent Port Townsend businessman, Enoch Fowler, and it folded in 1871. In 1870 Pettygrove established the *Puget Sound Argus*; its focus was "General Intelligence and Home Interests." Pettygrove sold the *Argus*, but it continued publication under various owners and editors until its plant burned to the ground in 1890. Throughout, it was a vehicle for boosterism, and Allen Weir, its editor from 1877 to 1889, was an especially active booster. In his salutatory editorial, he announced that he wanted to develop a "commercial newspaper" and promised that "whatever of the great natural and artificial resources of the Puget Sound country still remained undeveloped or unknown to the world, it will be the object of our earnest labor to unveil to an extent limited only by our ability."[19] *The Democratic Press*, first published on August 31, 1877, determined to "promote the external and internal prosperity of [the] Territory," as well as represent the interests of working men.[20] Its editors, H.L. Blanchard and Frank Meyers, conducted weekly battles with Allen Weir of the *Argus*, often over conflicting theories of economic development, although they wrangled over politics more often.[21]

While claiming devotion to territorial interests, these papers were in actuality fiercely parochial. The *Port of Entry Times* was more honest about this than some, admitting that it was "devoted to general news and the best interests of Port Townsend" and its future as a "business center and railway terminus."[22] The *Port Townsend Call*, published between 1885 and 1910, and the *Port Townsend Leader*, published from 1889 to the present, also promised to promote the commercial interests of the county rather than those of the Puget Sound region.[23]

These newspapers make for colorful reading. As one Port Townsend historian has noted, although "small in size, [they] made up for the deficiency by the force and eloquence of their utterances [which were] personal ... abusive and ... contemptuous of libel statutes.[24] However, they were more than amusing copy for their nineteenth-century readers. These frontier newspapers not only reported local, but also regional and national news; they provided space for advertisements, as well. Because editors exchanged newspapers with one another and reprinted articles from regional and other local newspapers, they also disseminated regional and territorial news, issues, and attitudes throughout the Puget Sound area. Newspapers often had political agendas as well, and declared themselves either Republican or Democratic. For instance, *The North-West* was owned by J.P. Keller, a wealthy Republican and mill owner.[25]

Local newspapers were perhaps most important as vehicles for development and as a forum for discussion of development-related issues, and it was not unusual for a frontier newspaper to begin publication at the behest of a local property holder wanting "to boom his town." Given the less formal nature of frontier promotion, editors and their newspapers were an essential aspect of development: everyone read them, and, in a frontier community, newspapers were a forum for community discussion through the many letters to the editor, a frontier blog of sorts.[26] Historian David Hamer argues that "one of the main functions of [the booster] press ... was to suppress information about, or divert attention from, the darker, grimmer, less hopeful aspects of urban life."[27] However, Jefferson County newspapers often initiated or published discussion and debate about development issues – through letters to the editor and editorials – which did not pull punches with regard to negative aspects of life in Jefferson County. Nevertheless, part of the agenda of local newspaper editors and owners certainly was to inform the outside world of the advantages and potential of their particular locale.

Indeed, *The North-West* promised to be "a medium through which our hardy and adventurous pioneers [can] transmit to their friends at a distance ... accounts of the resources [of the area] and that by means of a wide dissemination of facts ... immigration might be induced."[28] Thus, when newspapers published long, descriptive articles extolling county virtues and prospects for development, the editors expected that copies of such articles would find their way to potential settlers. They were often sent to far-away friends and relatives by local residents who were eager for development – or just lonely for neighbors – and editors sent their newspapers to San Francisco, Victoria, and other regional towns, as well as to the East Coast to be marketed by news dealers there.[29]

According to one frontier editor, Charles Prosch, such copies were read by individuals but were also "devoured ... by assemblages, with the utmost avidity." Because interest in immigration to the West was high in more settled areas, whole neighborhoods would "collect ...

in one place and have somebody read aloud to them all that the paper contained, including sometimes even the advertisements." It would be "then borrowed and passed from hand to hand, perused and re-perused until it was literally worn to shreds, and still the people continued reading as long as a shred remained." Perhaps an exaggerated comment, but frontier newspaper editors expected to reach beyond their local audience, and they depended upon county residents to help spread the word to outsiders who might be prospective immigrants or investors.[30]

Early newspaper editors also sent breaking news to the outside world, as in March 1858 when the *Puget Sound Herald* dispatched the first information of the Fraser River gold strike to San Francisco, shipping "column slips" to a news dealer who sold them "like hot-cakes."[31] And, once there was telegraph service, editors availed themselves of this method for publicizing the region, wiring news releases to newspapers in other regions.[32]

In keeping with their promotional agenda, editorials and commentary often functioned as "testimonials" to county growth – as when an 1860 *Register* reported with pride that there were "no less than seven buildings in the process of erection, some of them of large size[, a] bakery ... hotel ... livery stable ... small store and office ... dwelling houses ... a blacksmith shop and forge," and further building activity was expected in the coming summer. Minor growth, perhaps, but to the *Register* it was "constant and permanent." Although "every one has the chronic cry of 'hard times' in this region, yet ... we see no reason why the business prospects for this city are not fully equal to any place in the Territory."[33]

Such local newspapers were a forum for discussions of county development, and editors, reporters, and resident letter writers advised, criticized, and prodded each other over development issues, often suggesting appropriate investment opportunities that would appeal to local residents. *The Weekly Message* proposed that investment by local residents in a dry dock or marine railway – for hauling large ships out of the water for repairs – would be advantageous to the county. "We do not need [much] outlay ... [Thirty thousand dollars would fund the necessary railway for pulling steamers and large ships from the water] ... suitable buildings for carpenter and blacksmith shops, sail and rigging lofts and a well-stocked chandlery store ... Let us have a marine railway or dry dock at once." Similarly, *The Message* lauded a local fisher and wholesaler for his initiative and urged a tugboat company to add another tug to its fleet.[34]

The North-West scolded county residents, maintaining in one article that true progress was slow because "we are too 'fast'" and ready to give up "if we cannot make a fortune in a week." Solid growth required time and effort. At the same time the writer, John Damon, offered an analysis of the local economy. He argued that "the man of capital" could and did profit by "importing certain marketable commodities for consumption in the settlement," but such business practices only provided quick profits for the entrepreneur and expensive commodities to customers. However, such a "man of capital ... could more than double the profits which the first operation would secure," if he invested in the manufacture of goods locally or in agriculture or animal husbandry. "Port Townsend alone, consumes on an average three beeves in two days, or five hundred and thirty-five head per year, beside mutton and pork. For this beef alone, the neat little sum of $16,650 is sent to Oregon, every cent of which could be saved to our farmers." Investment in locally produced agricultural goods would provide profits for individuals, offer less expensive goods to consumers, and keep capital in the Territory. In the same way local dairy farming and poultry raising were deemed to create slow but sure growth. "Let us have the farms and stock raisers. Let us keep our money at home.[35]

Newspapers were also actively involved in specific development issues. When turmoil over removal of the Customs House from Port Townsend erupted in 1861, two editors of *The North-West* played leading roles in the event.

THE BATTLE FOR THE CUSTOMS HOUSE

J. Ross Browne's attack on Port Townsend's reputation in 1858 was an implicit threat to its economic future. In 1862 Victor Smith, a Special Agent and Customs Collector for the Puget Sound Customs District, explicitly endangered that future when he instigated pro-

ceedings to move the Port of Entry from Port Townsend to Port
Angeles – an almost uninhabited harbor forty-five miles west of
Port Townsend.

The Puget Sound Customs District was established in 1851 with
Olympia its headquarters or Port of Entry.[36] However, in 1854, Customs operations were moved to Port Townsend because of the town's
deepwater harbor and the centrality of its location to the important
developing westside lumber industry (see chapter 1). Customs was a
valuable asset for Port Townsend, the basis for its status as a shipping
center and integral to its economy; without it, the town would have
had little likelihood of maintaining itself as a thriving shipping center.
While the ensuing battle for the Customs House brought less national
attention than the Browne controversy, it was a more serious concern
with widespread county interest in the affair, as landowners, Grand
Jurymen, Marine Hospital patients, and others protested Smith's
agenda. The incident also reinforced the importance of reputation.
Smith argued that Port Angeles would be superior to Port Townsend as the headquarters of Customs by reason of its geography, but
he also emphasized Port Townsend's notoriety, referencing J. Ross
Browne's writings and stating that so disreputable a town was inap-
propriate as the Port of Entry to the region.

Victor Smith was a Port Angeles landowner, a partner in a real estate venture to develop the site, and perhaps its most important
booster.[37] He was also known as particularly corrupt, exhibiting a
"disproportionate preponderance of his organ of acquisitiveness,"
throughout his time in Washington Territory.[38] He had been an Ohio
newspaperman and real estate speculator, and he was appointed
Treasury Department Special Agent for the Pacific Coast and Customs Collector for Puget Sound in return for his work in the 1860
Republican presidential campaign. Arriving in Port Townsend on July
30, 1861,[39] Smith characterized himself as a reformist, bent upon
streamlining the Customs operations and reducing its maintenance
costs. He claimed in his first semi-annual report of April 4, 1862, to
have significantly reduced the annual costs of collecting customs revenue, maintaining lighthouses, and running the U.S. Marine Hospital
for the Puget Sound District.[40]

His reforms were unpopular with Port Townsendites, however.[41] The Marine Hospital patients complained that the savings made in food for the hospital were at their expense; it was not "fit for the sick." The meat was fatty salt pork and beef, hard bread rather than soft, and little of that. "This is not the diet laid down in the Government Regulations!"[42] Smith was also criticized for employing his father as a lighthouse keeper and his younger brother as a customs inspector.[43]

Then Smith announced his plan to relocate the Port of Entry. Addressing the issue in the local and territorial press, Smith said he had been directed by the Treasury Department to follow the advice of "former special agents and other parties to investigate the 'unfortunate temporary location [in Port Townsend] of the Port of Entry for Puget Sound,' and the natural fitness of Port Angelos [*sic*] for a permanent location." After due consideration, he had come to the conclusion that removal of Customs to Port Angeles would be in the best interests of the public.[44]

Smith argued several points: that the Port of Entry should be a safe harbor closest to the ocean – Port Angeles was forty-five miles nearer the ocean than Port Townsend – (interestingly, when the Customs House was moved from Port Townsend to Seattle in 1913, it was to bring it to what, by this time, had become the *center* of shipping activity); that Port Townsend was inconvenient for ships travelling to ports west and north of Port Townsend; and that if Customs was located in Port Angeles – which is directly across the Strait of Juan de Fuca from Victoria – it would draw trade to the American side of the Strait from British Columbia, trade which at the time was going to Victoria. Thus, claimed Smith, Port Angeles was geographically superior to Port Townsend, its location more convenient for shipping and likely to increase American commerce.[45]

Smith's most important points, however, were based on the perceived disreputable characteristics of Port Townsend as depicted by Ross Browne. As editor of *The North-West* for six weeks and a frequent correspondent to other territorial newspapers, Smith was an eager exponent of his own views about removal. He wrote the *Overland Press* that "a most respectable" number of Port Townsendites would be willing to "sacrifice all their investments [in Port Townsend] for the sake of a residence where ... there was a good harbor, fresh water and provision for a school, a church and other improvements desirable in a place of residence."[46] Expanding his argument in *The North-West*, Smith argued that Port Townsend could prosper without "a pitiful little Customs House that don't [*sic*] collect so much in a year as a well-driven shoe shop should in six months." But first, residents would have to make drastic changes in the town before "the over-true pictures drawn of this village by Ross Browne," would cease to prejudice investors and settlers against Port Townsend. It would be necessary first to refashion the town into "a more desirable, not to say possible, place of residence for families." If the "town proprietors" wanted to attract families and men of substance they should "invest in schools, local newspapers and churches [rather] than in lending [their money] at three per cent per month ... to induce young men to open ... 'rum mills.' [Thus we] barb ... the arrows of our up-Sound enemies, [Seattle and Olympia] by destroying our reputation."

Smith – with irony – wrote that he was not opposed to all drinking establishments. "The 'mills' aforesaid, are all well enough in their way and their keepers among the best men in the village." But some balance was necessary. "If there were fewer saloons, or if some other kind of business was sandwiched thicker in between them," and if the town also had "a policeman or wharf-watchman [to] prevent those most disgraceful scenes [displays of drunkenness or soliciting by prostitutes] that too frequently occur here when a passenger steamer ventures to the dock. Other desirable improvements might be named – a water company, Blacksmith shop, liberal newspaper support, etc, etc, – tho' enough has been said to indicate the direction of village enterprise."[47] According to Smith, not only was the harbor at Port Angeles a more suitable geographic location for the Port of Entry, but Port Townsend was also too disreputable.

Port Townsendites, of course, disagreed with Smith. As to geographic location, it was pointed out that the U.S. Coast Survey of 1858 had concluded that without a lighthouse the spit at Port Angeles was a danger to navigation, that the harbor had a "sticky bottom," and that while there was fresh water close to shore, "extensive [mud] flats render it hard to obtain." In contrast, Port Townsend's harbor was "favorably situated" for Puget Sound shipping with shelter from the weather, a "hard, sandy bottom," and with a wharf and mercantile establishments close at hand.[48] Further, after Smith was accused of being one of five partners in the township of Port Angeles – where he built a home and farm – it was argued that he only wanted to move Customs to Port Angeles for his own "pecuniary gain."[49]

John Damon, editor of *The North-West*, led the protests against removal, although initially Damon and Smith were friendly with one another. Soon after Smith arrived in Port Townsend, he arranged for Damon to become a Customs Inspector, and he took over as editor of *The North-West*. However, the two men fell out – why is not clear – and six weeks later Damon returned to his editorship entirely at odds with Smith. He devoted whole issues of *The North-West* to the controversy, presenting a detailed defense of the suitability of Port Townsend's location for the Port of Entry, raising the issue of Smith's proprietorial interests at Port Angeles, and in general attacking Smith's integrity as a government official.[50]

Concern over the removal was also more general. In the late winter of 1861, Joint Resolution No. 3, "Relative to the Collector at Port Townsend," was introduced in the Territorial Legislature. The resolution accused Smith of "using his official as well as personal influence to procure the removal of the Port of Entry" from Port Townsend to Port Angeles, "in the property of which latter site the said official has a pecuniary and landed interest." Further, such a removal was not desired by "the people of any section of the Territory." It was contrary to the best "interests of that commerce which is so important to the well-being of all our communities, and can advantage none save such as would mar the general prosperity for their own personal aggrandizement." It requested that the resolution be forwarded to the Territorial Delegate in Congress "with the earnest request that he use his best endeavors to prevent the removal contemplated."

While a select committee recommended the resolution's passage, the larger Assembly requested more evidence about Smith's "pecuniary and landed interest" – an interest that Smith vehemently denied. Accordingly, three affidavits were sent to the Legislature, in which

Port Townsend founders, Albert Briggs and F.W. Pettygrove, and John Damon each swore that Victor Smith had talked in their presence about his partnership in the township of Port Angeles and about his plans to turn the town into a rival for Victoria, British Columbia. The affidavits failed to sway the Legislative Assembly, however, and the resolution failed.[51]

Protest continued, however. One January morning, "a haggard looking effigy was seen suspended from the truck [*sic*] of the pole at the Custom House ... it was labelled to represent Victor Smith, Esq., Collector." Damon was eager to maintain a certain distance between the majority of Port Townsendites and the "rowdies" who hanged Smith in effigy, although the incident implies a popular element to the protests against the removal of the Customs Port of Entry from Port Townsend.[52] Smith himself capitalized on the disreputableness of the event, telling his patron, Treasury Secretary Salmon Chase, that "the ruined grog shops of Port Townsend, heretofore sustained by the drunken sailors ... admitted to board in the Hospital, hung me in effigy."[53]

During a regular meeting of the U.S. District Court in February 1861, the grand jury tried to make a formal complaint to the court about Smith. "Outraged and insulted by ... certain remarks and assertions made by one Victor Smith ... that the Grand Jury was subject to the influence of E.S. Fowler [local wharf owner, merchant, and ship chandler]," the jury asked the court to either exonerate them or to silence Smith "from further insulting the character and integrity of this body." The presiding judge believed their complaint was out of order, and he refused to consider it. His decision aroused great resentment; and one juryman was so exercised in his response to the situation as to merit a $20 fine and release from his duties as a juryman.[54]

In May 1862 Smith left Port Townsend for Washington, D.C., to be present for Congressional consideration of the removal; machinations against him locally continued. The Olympia *Washington Standard* recorded one such local incident in which Justice E.P. Dyer – knowing full well that Smith was absent – issued a summons for Smith to appear in court "to answer to a complaint of one Billy Armstrong, to recover the value of certain 'ictas' (Chinook for small things) sold and delivered, amounting to some $40." Rather than serving notice on Smith's resident wife, Sheriff J. G. Clinger served a copy on the Deputy Collector of Customs. The scheduled day in court arrived with no member of the Smith family present, and Dyer "rendered judgment by default [and] advertise[d] a horse [belonging to the Smiths] for sale under execution issued on said judgment." Mrs Smith, in accordance with territorial law, "claimed the horse on behalf of herself and husband as exempt from execution, it being [their] only domestic animal."

Dyer summoned three townsmen to "determine the question of exemption," and after hearing the evidence, two of the men declared the horse exempt. The third disagreed, however, and another panel was also unable to agree on the question. Dyer declared that "the horse will be sold."[55] The final outcome of this particular situation is not known. That harassment continued is indicated by Mrs Smith's letter to her husband saying that she had "been made to suffer in many ways and severely by the miserable rabble of Port Townsend."[56]

Smith's opponents carried their protests to Washington, D.C. Before leaving for the capitol, Smith appointed Lt J.H. Merryman, an officer of the revenue cutter *Joseph Lane* to serve as Acting Collector.[57] During Smith's absence, Merryman claimed to have become convinced that Smith had never posted bonds for his position as Collector, and further, that Smith had embezzled funds from the Treasury Department. Merryman both wired and wrote the Treasury Department about his findings.[58] Meanwhile, Congress had approved the removal of Customs to Port Angeles; and Smith, learning of Merryman's complaints against him, convinced Secretary Chase that what appeared to be withdrawals of funds from government accounts were merely monies shifted from one account to another, thereby retaining Chase's support.[59]

Smith returned to Port Townsend August 1, 1862, onboard the U.S. Revenue cutter *Shubrick*. Disembarking, he approached the Customs House, only to be refused entry by Merryman, who requested that he show "his authority or commission." Smith answered, it "was in the safe." Merryman replied that Smith knew that his bonds had never been filed, and that he had never had authority to act as Collector. In light of these facts, Merryman said he refused to surrender his acting authority to Smith.

The two men wrangled for a time. Smith then returned to the *Shubrick* where he "caused her guns to be double shotted as it is said with shell." He had them aimed at "the property and persons of [Port Townsend]. He then caused a body of armed men to be marched on shore, and by force took possession of the Customs House," removing all official documents.[60] The *Shubrick*, with Smith aboard, steamed away to Port Angeles, which was now the Port of Entry. Smith probably thought that this was end of the incident.[61]

Smith, however, had run afoul of territorial officials as well as Port Townsendites. According to his biographer, territorial politics were particularly "vituperative" in this period. Washington, a Democratic Party stronghold throughout its short history, was in shock as "the new Republican party's presidential coup of 1860 provid[ed] lucrative patronage appointments to strangers." There was turmoil between resident Republicans and "the Tribe of Lincoln," those outsiders appointed by the President. In addition, divisions within the Democratic Party and cross-partisan coalitions were customary as politicians jostled with one another for power. Smith, a supporter of Salmon Chase, was seen to represent different interests than several of the leading territorial Republicans, especially Territorial Governor William Pickering and Surveyor General Henry Anson, who were both personal friends of President Lincoln. Acting Collector Merryman, who had personal ties to Pickering, Anson, and Lincoln, was also a member of a different faction from Smith. The animosity between Smith and his fellow Republicans boiled over with the issue of the Customs removal.[62]

In the wake of the *Shubrick* incident, Governor Pickering, ex-Governor Henry McGill, and other territorial notables visited Port Townsend to investigate complaints about Smith; following was a warrant for the arrest of Smith and the commanding officer of the *Shubrick*, "on a charge of assault with intent to kill." Attempts were made to serve the warrant, but Smith evaded arrest.[63]

Charges were brought then against Smith during the fall session of the Third District Court. He requested a change of venue, and the session was moved to Olympia, where the grand jury brought indictments against him for, among other things: embezzling upwards of

$20,000 in government funds (this was based on Merryman's find-
ings); for receiving kickbacks from Dr Allyn whom he had placed in
charge of the Marine Hospital; for "converting to his own use and
embezzling a portion of the provision and apparel and furniture of
the [federal government] vessel called the Jefferson Davis" when the
vessel was sold; for "unlawfully engaging in the purchase of public
lands." He was also charged with "unlawfully and in high misde-
meanor be[ing] concerned or interested in carrying on the business
of trade or commerce" in Port Angeles, where he was a landholder
and hoped to become a town builder. The U.S. Prosecuting Attorney
added a charge for assault with intent to kill – referring to the August
1, 1862, *Shubrick* incident.[64]

In November 1862, Treasury Department Special Agent Thomas
Brown investigated and absolved Smith from the charges brought
against him; and the indictments were nullified in February 1863 by
Solicitor of the Treasury Edward Jordan at the order of Secretary
Chase.[65] Territorial political antagonism for Smith continued though,
and in May 1863 Anson Henry convinced Lincoln that he should
have Smith removed from his position as Customs Collector. However, Smith was reappointed Treasury Department Special Agent for
the Pacific Coast, a position from which he had resigned in 1862. In
1865, Smith drowned in a shipwreck en route to Puget Sound from
San Francisco.[66]

With the death of Smith, the fortunes of Port Angeles declined.
L.C. Gunn, who had followed Smith as Collector, was succeeded by
Fred A. Wilson in March of 1865. Wilson was a Port Townsend man,
and he moved to return the Port of Entry to Port Townsend. Free of
opposition from Smith, Wilson was successful, and on July 25, 1866,
the Port of Entry for Puget Sound returned to Port Townsend after
an absence of almost four years: "There was great rejoicing upon the
re-establishment of the headquarters. The old cannon on Union Dock
– owned by Captain Tibbals – was fired and Wilson was tendered
the thanks of the community at a public ovation held in his honor."[67]

Jefferson County had had a close call. The Customs House was
crucial to Port Townsend's development potential, but its more immediate economic situation also must have suffered with the removal

of Customs. Indeed, when Port Angeles lost the Port of Entry in 1866, development and immigration there dwindled to little or nothing. Writing many years after the battle for the Customs House, newspaper editor Allen Weir described Port Angeles as "a small town [established] about twenty years ago when it was the port of entry … when the [Port of Entry] returned to Port Townsend a little later, a general decline in the growth of the place commenced. All that there is of it at present is a few houses, not all of which are occupied."[68]

Smith's biographer, Marian Parks, emphasizes the importance of politics in her analysis of this event. Certainly, politics was an important component, but the economic aspect was at least as important for Smith and Port Townsend residents. Political patronage gave Smith the power to set in motion the removal of Customs to Port Angeles; and partisan divisions contributed to his removal as the Collector.[69] Be that as it may, development was at the core of the battle for the Customs House. Victor Smith came to Washington Territory with a background in frontier land speculation. By his own admission, he believed that if the Port of Entry was moved to Port Angeles, that town would become a commercial rival to Victoria. Further, not only was Smith a Port Angeles landowner, at least two of the people who had previously recommended the removal of Customs to Port Angeles owned land there – Lt John W. White of the *Jefferson Davis* and former Customs Collector M.H. Frost. Smith used their recommendations in building his case for removal.[70]

Although Smith denied throughout the controversy that moving the Customs House would make any difference to Port Townsend's future, he, as well as Port Angeles landowners White and Frost, certainly understood the importance of Customs to Port Angeles's commercial development and community promotion. Shortly after Congress approved removal of the Port of Entry to Port Angeles, Smith sent a news release to several regional and national newspapers which announced that Customs had relocated in Port Angeles, which was "convenient to commerce, has the lands of the Elwha Valley on the west, and the equally rich farming district of Dungeness on the east." There were nearby coalmines and "four mountain streams of the purest water come into the bay within the town site, and with fall enough for any desirable [industrial] purpose."

In connection with the "classic" location of the now *late* [Smith's italics] Custom House on Puget Sound, it may be asked whether our California traveler – ex-Special Agent Ross Browne – will be able, with the aid of Harper's wood cut, to "do justice" to the realization of his official dream – the removal of the port of entry for Puget Sound and the Straits of Fuca? West Coast readers will remember his humorously scathing *Sketches of Port Townsend* [*sic*] – "that brackish-watered beach on a storm-swept roadstead, whose people have respect unto Clootchmen [Chinook jargon for Native American women] but do profitably devour the male Indian with strychnine whisky and each other with slander-sharpened teeth.[71]

This wily piece of promotional prose attributes to Port Angeles necessary conditions for development then current in boosterist thinking. It exemplifies not only Smith's own boosterism and the importance of reputation – as established·by J. Ross Browne – in the competition between these rival towns, but why the struggle over the Customs House was so hard-fought.

COURTING THE RAILROAD

With the return of the Port of Entry to Port Townsend, county boosters shifted their attention to railroads. The importance of railroads to Western economic development has been a frequent subject of discussion; certainly, the advent of transcontinental railroads drastically altered the Puget Sound region, allowing the development of new markets for the lumber industry, spurring other industries, and bringing thousands of immigrants to the area. Long before the event, Puget Sound boosters longed for the Midas touch of the railroad, and residents were stricken with what one Portland newspaperman called "terminus disease." Newspaper editors sang the praises of their respective communities and denigrated those of rivals. Real estate speculators wooed potential investors, and one company advertised lots in several towns and sites – one of which was Port Townsend. Ads suggested that buyers purchase something in each of Clark's

Additions, since "the probabilities are that the Northern Pacific Railroad will touch at two or more of the places named, which will insure the purchaser a large profit upon his investment." There were even two breweries named for the railroad: Seattle's North Pacific Steam Brewery and Steilacom's North Pacific Railroad Brewery.[72]

Jefferson County may have flirted with railroads longer and less successfully than any other Puget Sound community, as several lines were built which connected some Jefferson County towns and other Olympic Peninsula towns to one another, but none of these tracks left the Peninsula. Thus, while at one time or another from the late 1860s into the 1890s, residents sought to establish a railroad connection to the outside world, their efforts ultimately came to naught. However, at end of the Civil War, Jefferson County residents were hopeful that the railroad was on its way: "The time [would] soon come when the whistle of the locomotive and rattle of the cars [would] wake the echoes of the Northern wilderness, which is destined soon to 'blossom as the rose.'"[73]

Railroads were still in their infancy when New York merchant and railroad enthusiast Asa Whitney made the first serious proposal for an east-to-west transcontinental railroad in 1844. At the time, Congress was unwilling to take the project, but by the early 1850s there was serious interest in the undertaking, and on March 3, 1853, Congress authorized the Secretary of War to arrange for five surveys of possible routes for a transcontinental railroad.[74] However, when the railroad surveys were made available to Congress, the question of a transcontinental railroad had been displaced by sectional politics.

After the Confederate states had seceded, Congress was able to come to agreement upon the issue of transcontinental railroads. The Pacific Railway Bill of 1862 granted charters to the Union Pacific Railroad and Central Pacific Railroad to connect California and the East by rail: this line was completed on May 10, 1869. The Northern Pacific Railroad, chartered in 1864 to build a railroad between the Great Lakes and Puget Sound, began construction in 1871.

During the intervening period of 1864 to 1871, Puget Sounders had suffered pangs of anxiety and despair. Portland was the leading city of the Pacific Northwest, but Puget Sound residents believed that the Northern Pacific Railroad would shift regional dominance to the

Sound.[75] Echoing Isaac Stevens's assumption that Puget Sound would be the end point of a northern-route railroad, Washington Governor Marshall Moore told the 1869 Territorial Legislative Assembly that a railroad connection would put Puget Sound in the center of "the great highway of trade and travel, extending from Liverpool and Havre to Hong Kong and Yokohama." Railroads are "the true alchemy of the age, which transmutes the otherwise worthless resources of a county into gold ... Wherever the iron track [is] laid, and the whistle heard, 'the wilderness has been made to bud and blossom as the rose.'"[76]

In 1870, the federal government allowed the Northern Pacific to change the suggested western terminus from Puget Sound to the Columbia River. Puget Sound residents were outraged: "The Almighty ... decreed that any great north continental railroad should terminate on Puget Sound."[77] Portland property values increased, while they languished in Puget Sound. Nevertheless, there was still hope. According to the *Weekly Message* a railroad connection between the Columbia River and Puget Sound would be built, and although "Puget Sound at present is but a *cul-de-sac* ... let a means of communication with the interior and with Oregon be opened, and it will be like tapping a pent up lake. The tide of commerce will flow through and make for itself a channel which will force all northern roads to come to Puget Sound as the best means of communication with the ocean."[78]

The *Weekly Message* was correct; construction soon began on a track from Kalama, Washington – on the Columbia River, near Portland – to Puget Sound. Puget Sound residents again looked forward to the enlivened economy and growing population that would follow in the wake of the railroad. Communities resumed efforts to capture the Puget Sound terminus, and in Jefferson County, James Swan took up the task of promoting Port Townsend.[79] Writing on December 3, 1868, he argued the benefits of Port Townsend to Thomas H. Canfield, general agent for the Northern Pacific Railroad. Referring to his long acquaintance with the late Governor Stevens, who, he said, had always been of the opinion that Port Townsend would be an ideal terminus, Swan enumerated this and several other points in Port Townsend's favor. One was, "ease of approach [to Port Townsend] from the ocean." Prevailing winds that made it difficult for sailing vessels to manoeuver once they sailed past Admiralty Inlet made it easy for vessels to sail up the Strait of Juan de Fuca as far as Port Townsend: "There are no good harbors [past Admiralty Inlet] that can be approached by sailing vessels without having to resort to towing very frequently during the year, but sail vessels as well as steamers can at all times reach Port Townsend ... easier and with less loss of time than any other point on Puget Sound."

Swan continued, saying that the water at "Commencement City" (Tacoma) and Seattle was too deep for consistently safe anchorages, while at Port Townsend the water was a perfect six to seventeen fathoms. In order for the railroad to reach Port Townsend, it would come from the Columbia River to Olympia. Track would be laid from Olympia along the Hood Canal, a task facilitated by the stands of timber along the shores of the canal, which would provide necessary wood for bridges.[80] Further, "a ship could sail direct from New York with a cargo of Railroad iron, which could be landed at any desired point on Hoods [sic] Canal."

Assuring Canfield that Port Townsend was surrounded by the hinterland necessary to support a potential metropolis, he said, "the whole of the rich valley of the Chahalis [sic] ... and the valley of the Willopah, [sic] the garden of the Territory ... would be tributary to a city at Port Townsend, and could furnish supplies for a population larger than the dreams of the most sanguine enthusiast could ever hope to place on this peninsula."[81]

In early May 1869, Swan and an engineer made a reconnaissance of Hood Canal by canoe. All the more convinced of the practicality of a route along Hood Canal, he wrote again to Canfield, assuring him of the suitability of Port Townsend.[82] Eventually, Canfield hired Swan to write reports detailing the advantages and disadvantages of several Puget Sound ports, and to act as host for various parties of visiting railroad officials and other dignitaries. In November 1870, Swan suggested that an important commercial link could be made between the Amur River in southern Siberia – then the boundary between Russia and China and a rendezvous point for whaling ships – and Puget Sound, an idea Stevens had propounded in 1859, and Swan had written about in 1860.[83]

In January 1871, Swan met with eight of the county's landowners to gather signatures on agreements that would deed land to the railroad if it decided to locate its terminus in Port Townsend within a year. In March he made another trip down Hood Canal, this time accompanied by a Northern Pacific Railroad engineer, H.C. Hale. As reported by the *Weekly Message*, the trip "proved the fact of the practicability and facility with which a railroad can reach ... Port Townsend ... It now remains to be seen what action the committee of the directors will take."[84]

Swan's work came to naught and all hopes were dashed in 1872, when Tacoma was chosen terminus. There was a certain logic to Swan's argument about the suitability of Port Townsend for a terminus, as well as to Seattle's assumption that it would win the terminus. However, the Northern Pacific preferred the sparsely settled village on Commencement Bay. Tacoma was closest to Kalama, an important point because the Northern Pacific was running out of money. Further, the railroad and its affiliates, the Oregon Steam Navigation Company and the St Paul and Tacoma Land Company, would able to make a return on waterfront and other lands they had purchased for speculative purposes. Bringing the track to the water's edge, they built wharves and engaged in the sea trade; no rail service was provided to other Puget Sound communities at this time.[85]

In September 1873, financial difficulties brought construction of the westbound track between Kalama and Bismarck, North Dakota, to a standstill. Jay Cooke's bank, which had financed the Northern Pacific, failed, ushering in the depression of the 1870s. The region would have to wait a decade for further railroad construction. It was not until 1883, thirty years after Stevens's survey, that the entire line was finished, and Puget Sound finally received its transcontinental link – via the line built earlier between Tacoma and Kalama, Washington, on the Columbia River. The Cascade line, which connected Seattle and Tacoma to the Northern Pacific more directly, did not begin operation until 1887.

Although disappointed by the failure of efforts to snare the terminus, at least one Jefferson County booster expressed confidence that the county would not fail to grow – with or without the Northern Pacific railroad. Even before the loss of the terminus, frontier optimist

Al Pettygrove wrote with true frontier optimism that there was still the possibility that the Union Pacific would establish a connection between Port Townsend or Port Discovery and Salt Lake City.[86] And regardless of where the railroad terminated, "the different places along the Sound will have advanced in importance, and it will matter little where the investment is made in real estate, an increased value is sure to accrue."[87]

Further, according to Pettygrove, there were other opportunities for growth in the county. Recent developments in the fishing industry and commercial links with Alaska held promise. These were "causes of prosperity ... which have come to us quietly, without flourish of trumpets, or influence of rail-roads or saw-mills. They will be the means of insuring a permanency to Port Townsend, and create a healthy business far better for us than the feverish rush of speculators in corner lots and water rights."

Returning to what was perceived to be Port Townsend's strongest point, Pettygrove – whose faith in the future was seemingly boundless – reiterated that "Port Townsend is and will be the Port of entry [sic] for the Puget Sound district and always from its geographical position must be a point of commercial importance." It did not matter where the railroad terminated since all shipping "bound for that terminus from the coast must pass by and stop at Port Townsend first, and thereby, be a direct benefit to our people." Resorting to a theme favored by frontier boosters who wanted to be encouraging despite disappointments, Pettygrove wrote, "our growth has been slow, but it has been sure, and we think the prospects for this place never were in so cheering condition as at the present day."[88]

THE IMMIGRATION AID SOCIETY: IMMIGRATION, CAPITAL INVESTMENT, AND AGRICULTURE   ·

Immigration was as important to the economic vision held by county residents as the Port of Entry or transportation routes. Boosters understood that people were essential to frontier development, and many believed that, by itself, an increase in population would stimulate economic development: "The benefits which will accrue to ... those who come among us ... as well as to the Territory by their settlement can be neither few nor uncertain. The larger our populations, and the more our resources are worked, the greater will their extent appear and demand for labor augment."[89]

Appeals to immigrants often took the form of agricultural promotion, although boosters hoped to see the area opened up to farming for many reasons. As early as 1860, John Damon of the *North-West* promoted agricultural development in the belief that until the Territory could produce as much of its own food as possible, it would be sending its capital needlessly out of the Territory (see above).[90] Later, H.L. Blanchard, county entrepreneur, developer, and editor of the *Democratic Press* argued that farming, in particular butter and cheesemaking, would contribute to the area's prosperity: "For in the successful working of ... several industries, alone, hinges our posterity. The time has come when it is not safe to look to the [lumber] mills alone for our advancement."[91]

Those boosters who believed that Port Townsend was a potential metropolis, drawing on current booster theories, believed that such "a city [would need a] garden [to] be tributary ... and ... furnish supplies."[92] For instance, Al Pettygrove of *The Weekly Message* noted that the Northern Pacific terminus would have to be surrounded by "good farming land," and in keeping with this idea, he urged the construction of a road from Port Townsend to Olympia, which would allow the establishment of a hundred farms in a country "destined to make the very garden of the Sound ... the soil being of the very richest description."[93]

Understanding that a metropolis would require a "garden," Pettygrove argued that a well-populated hinterland would not only grow food for the city's inhabitants, but agricultural products to export as well. Further, rural inhabitants would provide a market for goods manufactured in the city. And, he added the fanciful rejoinder that a beautiful countryside was also necessary because "humanity was not created to inhabit the desert. Withdraw from it the verdure which clothes the valley and hill, and you deprive it of half its existence, of its pleasures ... Neither brain, capital, or labor have any inclination to coasts covered with sand."[94] Thus, boosters considered agricultural development essential to urban expansion and encouraged farmers to immigrate to the county.

They also encouraged laborers – woodworkers, miners, seamen, masons, female domestic servants, and so on, broadcasting that, "the field for laborers is increasing with the opening up of new industries every year. No country in the world, of equal extent, holds ... a brighter prospect for steady and remunerative employment than does Western Washington ... Its prosperity [is] almost wholly within itself ... it is so diversified in its resources that nothing necessary to the attainment of the highest condition of prosperity and civilization seems lacking." However, the pamphlet's author cautioned that "no smart young man ... should fancy that, because this ... Territory [is] so far away, it is just the place for him, and post off here with a sort of dime novel hallucination that he will somehow get suddenly rich ... For the benefit of all such we would say that we have already on hand a large number of disappointed adventurers that sudden wealth has not yet overtaken and probably never will."[95]

Boosters wooed entrepreneurs of all sorts, from institutional administrators to craftsmen. A promotional booklet suggested that "Port Townsend, by reason of its enchanting scenery, clean surrounds, and eminently healthful location, presents one of the finest sites in the world upon which to establish some high institution of learning." Also, "there is a bed of potter's clay within one mile of the city, that is about 20 feet thick, easy of access and of good quality, and there can be no question but this industry could be established here and made to pay because there is nothing of the kind on the Sound.[96]

Not all boosters, though, courted large-scale immigration, arguing that until sufficient industrial development took place there would not be enough markets for immigrant farmers' produce or jobs for immigrant laborers. Said one, "Capital will not follow the people but people will follow capital."[97] However, by and large, county boosters saw immigrants as essential to commercial development.

In 1879 Allen Weir, editor of the *Puget Sound Argus*, joined with twenty or more Port Townsend and county residents to form the Immigration Aid Society. The idea for such a group did not originate with Weir. Seattle had formed its own society earlier in the year, and both Seattle and Jefferson County's efforts were in keeping with an increase in more formalized ventures of local boosters through immigrations clubs or societies. Port Townsend's society, however, had its particular beginnings in Weir's concern that boosterism – which had previously been organized informally – was flagging in the county.

> Every breeze that comes from the East and South brings to our ears the sound of immigrant foot-falls ... yet the business men of our city and vicinity raise not a voice to invite them here ... [We] mention these matters in no spirit of jealousy toward any other locality, but to inspire some of the good citizens of Jefferson, Island, Clallam, San Juan and Whatcom with a spirit of laudable emulation. We have virgin soil and undeveloped resources, enough to spare for thousands of husbandmen, mechanics and capitalists. Let persistent and systematic effort commence at once.[98]

Members of the community took his idea to heart. By the end of June, the *Argus* reported the call by "a number of the citizens of Port Townsend" for a "mass meeting ... to take preliminary steps toward disseminating useful and reliable information concerning the lower counties on Puget Sound."[99] The meeting was held, "several pointed and stirring speeches were made," and the participants resolved to form an organization to disseminate "reliable information relative to the climate, resources and productions of the lower counties on Puget Sound." There were various tasks for members: to communicate with residents of nearby counties about joining forces; to arrange with the territorial Surveyor General for a survey of the "Quillyhute" valley – in the west end of the county to which boosters hoped to entice farmers; and to organize and publish a pamphlet for distribution to interested immigrants.[100]

On July 17, Weir reported that "the society is in a flourishing condition," the constitution and by-laws had been printed, and the program for the next meeting was already set. James Swan was invited to read a paper about Port Townsend's "prominence as a probable railroad terminus," and one Captain Stratton of Port Angeles to talk about Puget Sound fisheries.

In 1880, the Jefferson County society joined with other societies to form the Immigration Aid Society of North-western Washington, and in the same year *Northwestern Washington: Its Soil, Climate, Productions and General Resources with Detail Description of the Counties of Jefferson, Clallam, Island, San Juan and Whatcom* – a fifty-page booklet written by members of the society – was edited and published by Allen Weir to be distributed for twenty-five cents a copy.

The society was controversial in that it was championed by one newspaper – Weir's *Argus* – and criticized by the other – *The Democratic Press*. Initially, the *Press* was favorably disposed towards territorial societies, suggesting that they quickly amass "a full and accurate statement of the agricultural, lumbering and mineral resources of our Territory, together with the cost of getting here." Thus, "we might receive a large percentage of the immigration which would help materially to develop this Territory."[101] However, the *Press* – self-proclaimed voice of the local Democrats and the working class – and the *Argus* – the local Republican sheet – seemed determined throughout the *Press's* brief history to disagree, and it was not long before the *Press* did an about-face, opposing the society.

In April 1880 the *Press* made a two-pronged attack on the society, arguing that industrial development should precede immigration. In "San Francisco Capital and Puget Sound," editor Myers looked back on the history of the Puget Sound region, a region once "hardly known" but now developed with outside capital from San Francisco lumbermen and others. It was thanks to the efforts of such non-residents that there was any population in the Puget Sound region. Myers chastised those who complained about the profits that enriched outsiders. Such critics, he wrote, forgot the wages earned by local people that stayed in the country, and they failed to realize that most local capitalists had too little money to fund either railroads or industries that would really change the area's economic circumstances. The true interests of the area "demand a cheerful submission" to outside capital in order to develop the territory.[102]

In "An Immigration Boom," Myers reiterated the importance of the lumber industry to the region, suggesting that since lumber, the principal employer, was currently in an economic slump, encouraging immigration to the area was lunacy. "Every town is crowded with mechanics and laboring men who barely earn enough to buy the necessaries of life; the cause of which is the depression in the lumbering business." Society members were only trying to draw attention to themselves "for the purpose of making political capital," or for their "own selfish interests." No "substantial business men" had taken any heed of the society. Further, he argued that the laboring men of the area wondered why more men should be encouraged to come to the region when there was insufficient work for those already residing in the area and farmers pleaded that they could not find markets for their goods. "Until there is more capital invested here [to encourage immigration is pointless] as capital will not follow the people but people will follow capital."[103]

The complaints of the *Democratic Press* about the Immigration Aid Society struck a chord with some of its readers, which suggests that there was broad community and cross-class interest in development and the society.[104] "Citizen" agreed with Myers that members of the society were "pot-house politicians." He did not believe that respectable citizens and business people supported the effort. "Cumtux" thought that businessmen should precede ordinary immigrants, so that there would be employment for all. "Workingman" complained that there was little enough work for residents, and "Phelix" said farmers could not sell what they grew as it was. "Puget Sounder" suggested that the only people to get any good out of the Immigration Aid Society would be "men who own steamboats and hotels and stores ... What we need is money to develop our lumber and mineral wealth which will create a demand for farm produce and labor."[105]

The *Argus* responded that the *Press* "has brought upon itself the merited contempt of all our right-minded, public spirited citizens," since the society was bringing an influx of capital to the region. On their way were immigrants with varying sums in capital: $7,000, $1,500, and one group from "the Baltic provinces, a party of 600 men and women, with 300 children and $75,000 in money." Said Weir, Meyer's behavior is "a deliberate and traitorous attempt against the welfare of the community from whence he obtains his daily bread [and] he has already lost patronage.[106] The *Press* retorted that it was a" free and outspoken journal" that would "not change its course through fear of losing a few subscribers or of incurring the ill-will of a few unscrupulous politicians.[107]

Myers was correct that large-scale economic growth and immigration in the territory was dependent upon significant outside capital investment.[108] However, criticism of the Immigration Aid Society by Myers and the letter-writers did not imply a rejection of development, but rather a disagreement of just how to promote development.[109] Not only was Myers firmly in the development camp, former *Press* editor H.L. Blanchard, for whom Myers had worked, and Dr H.C. Willison, the owner[110] of the *Democratic Press*, were also deeply involved in county development.[111] Blanchard was one of the original trustees of the Puget Sound Iron Company of Washington Territory, incorporated July 28, 1879, with offices in Port Townsend and the mill located in nearby Irondale.[112] When iron ore was discovered in Chimacum Valley farmland, the landowners, William Bishop, William Eldridge, Olaff Peterson, and John Lindley, suddenly become active boosters, were willing to lease the right to mine the ore for a royalty of twenty-five cents a ton *as long as it was reduced to finished pig iron within the county* (author's italics). Blanchard, accompanied by D. W. Moor, who became an operating officer of the mill, traveled to San Francisco to find capital to develop the mill. They were successful, although by 1882 controlling interest in the mill had fallen to San Francisco residents when it was reincorporated as the Puget Sound Mill Company of California. Many of the original stockholders retained stock in the new company, and Blanchard and Moor both were mill superintendents for a time, although the mill closed in 1889.[113]

Willison owned property in Irondale, and – looking ahead – in 1883 he, Samuel Hadlock (one of Blanchard's partners), and Robert K. Latimer incorporated the Irondale Real Estate and Manufacturing Company for the purpose of developing the Irondale area. Willison also built and operated a hospital in Port Townsend, although he lost it during the depression of the 1890s.[114] Hadlock was a partner – with San Francisco capitalists – in the Western Mill and Lumber Company, which built a mill in Port Hadlock and then sold it to the burned-out Washington Mill Co. in 1886.[115] When Myers claimed

that outside capital was necessary for large-scale economic development, he wrote from a position of involvement with developers such
as Blanchard and Hadlock, who had had to seek outside capital in
order to develop Jefferson County industry in iron and steelmaking
and lumbering.

However much county boosters disagreed about how to promote
development – in keeping with other Western Washington residents
– they concurred with one another about the supposed viability of
agriculture in Jefferson County.[116] In western Washington, unlike
some portions of the mid-west where farmlands may stretch as far
as the eye can see, good agricultural land was found in pockets surrounded by forests and mountains. For instance, alluvial land east of
Puget Sound proved to be fertile and became known for its dairy and
truck farms[117] The Olympic Peninsula also had fertile areas, especially the prairies that dotted the landscape, and in east Jefferson
County there was land which was successfully farmed: prairies and
some reclaimed marshland near Port Townsend; the Chimacum Valley, not especially suitable for croplands but able to support dairy
farms; Marrowstone Island with its poultry farms and berry fields;
as well as Leland Valley and the Tarboo Creek Valley.[118]

The best farming land, however – the prairies which were clear of
timber – was taken by the earliest settlers,[119] and farmers who came
later had to buy from the earlier landholders or rent to obtain tim-
ber-free land. Otherwise, they bought forested land, marshland, or
tidal flats. Clearing forested land was very labor-intensive. The huge
stumps of fir and cedar trees could take a lifetime to rot, and "even
with dynamite, [it took] a man and a horse 400 hours of labor per
acre" to clear forested land for farming. As mentioned above, there
were farms in Jefferson County, but valuable farmland was less common than the boosters claimed, especially since forested land, once
cleared, tended to be unsuitable for agriculture.[120] Although the number of Jefferson County farms increased over time, a sizable number
were not full-time market, or even subsistence, farms. Rather they
were "stump farms" where the men worked regular or part-time jobs
in logging camps, sawmills, or construction and farmed in their spare
time. Indeed, *North-Western Washington* mentions this fact, that
farmers could work in the sawmills and logging camps and touted

such available work as an incentive for families wishing to establish farms. On such farms, of course, wives and children probably did much more of the farm work than the "farmer."[121]

Nevertheless, boosters argued for the development of county agriculture as well as the desirability of opening up prairie lands in west Jefferson County or of sparsely wooded fertile river bottom lands that could be easily cleared[122] D.W. Smith of the Immigration Aid Society rhapsodized about freshwater marshland in the Chimacum valley, which would be easy to drain, and about land with soil composed of "nothing but fine gravel and sand of a reddish tint, and apparently, as hard and impenetrable as a rock" but which produced "the finest, most forward and luxuriant garden of potatoes, peas, onions, strawberries, &c. &c." Weir assured readers that "the good land" was not all taken, and as long as prospective farmers were "the kind of m[e]n … [who do] not expect to make a good home here without making an effort in earnest," then the county would develop.[123]

Much of the county, however, was good for little else than growing trees. Misled by the wealth of timber that the land produced, as well as the general "green-ness" of the countryside, boosters and others believed that all soil in the region was equally fertile, and praised the lumber companies for clearing timber land, thereby making it available for agriculture. "It is strange indeed if land that produces such a dense growth of timber will not produce grain, vegetables and fruit."[124] Such enthusiasm is understandable. The technology for scientific testing of soil fertility did not exist at the time, and even "as late as 1931, the State Director of Agriculture for Washington advised prospective settlers to choose land with plenty of big stumps because such land was certain to be fertile."[125] The information and technology necessary to correctly assess agricultural potential was not available, but because a surrounding "garden" was an essential part of "great city" thinking, and because immigration – either before or after capital investment – was perceived to be necessary for growth, encouraging development of county agriculture was seen to be an essential aspect of county promotion.

By 1880 the Puget Sound region – and the Pacific Northwest as a whole – was poised at the beginning of a period of exponential growth spurred by the expected completion of the transcontinental railroad.

Between 1860 and 1880, the Puget Sound population had only increased from 5,000 to 25,000. By 1890 there were as many as 100,000 people. Although most of the immigrants settled on the east side of the Sound – Seattle went from a population of 1,107 to 42,837 during the 1880s – Jefferson County experienced growth as well, as its population of 1,712 in 1880 grew to 8,368 in 1890, sufficient numbers to foster the continuation of optimistic expectations for economic opportunity and growth.[126] However, as development continued to be a county concern, residents grappled with the issue of county reputation, especially that of Port Townsend.

"The Great Notoriety of That Place"[1]: Reputation and Development in Jefferson County, 1858–1890

Travellers making their way to Port Townsend or Jefferson County's mill ports in the mid- to late nineteenth century encountered a landscape of uncommon beauty. The approach from the Pacific Ocean via the Strait of Juan de Fuca – the way most travellers would have arrived before the completion of the northern-route transcontinental railroads – passes by "a dark sea-wall of mountains with misty ravines and silver peaks"; in its forests, which then often grew to the water's edge, "trees a hundred feet high [were] by comparison with the lofty peaks above them, made to appear as if … but grass." Upon arrival, travellers found Port Townsend situated on a "lovely bay" behind which were the " great mountains" of the Olympic Range, "standing guard."[2] Looking from Port Townsend, a viewer saw close at hand a "sun-reflecting bay" with sailing ships riding at anchor; in the distance tree-covered peninsulas and islands floated against the "majestic panorama of [the Cascade] mountains in almost every direction." Dominating the Cascades' "lofty irregular peaks" was Mt Baker, "towering, like Saul among the prophets, 'head and shoulders taller than his brethren.'"[3] The county's other ports were set among equally magnificent scenery.

Such impressive vistas, however, were juxtaposed with the seedy appearance so typical of frontier towns and villages. Frontier Port Townsend stood on a sand spit one and a half miles long and one-third of a mile wide. On its western edge, a swampy lagoon – eventually to be filled in – cut into the town. Described with irony by one visitor, it was a "beautiful pond of stagnant water, [giving] the place a healthful appearance all the year round."⁴ At times, the fishing activities of residents and the ebbing tide added strong, unpleasant odors to the scene. The streets were unpaved, and muddy or dusty as the season dictated; and an 1868 photograph reveals the town's architecture to be a collection of log cabins and rough wooden buildings, some of which, built on wharves and pilings, hung precariously over the water.⁵ Behind the waterfront rose a bluff some seventy to ninety-five feet high, which gave onto a pleasant plateau covered with prairie and trees. This plateau was difficult to reach, however, and ascending its cliff "would make a man, had he the patience of Job, 'wilt,' if he were compelled to travel up and down it more than a dozen times a day."⁶ The mill ports, huddled around their respective sawmills, had great piles of sawdust and noisy machinery.

The towns barely kept the countryside at bay; even in Port Townsend, the largest town in the county, there was a rural atmosphere. A bull might run at large, chas[ing] the school children, [and] badly scar[ing the] ladies." Cows could be found "running around town, eating everything they come across and dipping their noses into everybody's water barrels," or resting in doorways. A pig pen, "directly on one of our main streets and principal thoroughfares [presented] its noxious odors" to passers by; and street-side stables with their attendant manure and mud made it impossible "after a heavy rain ... for people to pass."⁷ A local newspaper editor railed against the "flagrant disregard of the ordinances prohibiting owners of horses and cattle [*sic*] from roaming at large over the city." In addition to the nuisance, "there is great danger therefrom as shown in the recent accident to a little boy ... who was hooked by a cow.⁸

That this rough, frontier appearance coexisted with efforts to replace it with a more genteel, urban facade is evident in James Swan's 1859 appraisal of Port Townsend wherein he describes "the Custom House – a brick building of two stories high and 25 x 40 feet square – the Pioneer Hotel, the large workhouse of Fowler and Co., the Court House and a large building recently used as a theatre," etc. Of themselves, paved streets, lovely homes, brick office blocks, churches, schools, and fraternal-order meeting halls were valued goals for Port

Townsendites, even though it was not until the 1880s that the prevalent frame buildings began to be replaced by brick ones.[9] However, residents also understood the importance of projecting a positive image to outsiders, one that compared favorably to other frontier communities, one that would convincingly demonstrate that Port Townsend was progressing toward urban status as it was understood in the East.

This is not to say that Port Townsend was unique in its rough appearance or in its efforts to project a favorable image to outsiders. Indeed, such efforts were typical of ambitious frontier townspeople: as David Hamer argues, travel writers and authors of emigrant guidebooks – who set the pace for "forming images and shaping perceptions of New World towns" – made comparisons between frontier towns and long-established cities and towns an essential aspect of frontier promotion. Such assessments might be based upon a town's external appearance; and, certainly Jefferson County boosters were concerned with Port Townsend's image – that is, what visitors would see upon arrival in Port Townsend, and how such visitors might interpret that visual image.[10]

Jefferson County residents, however, were focused more nearly on the community's reputation than a visual image, and in the wake of "the Great Port Townsend Controversy," Swan and others tried to erase from the public mind Browne's depiction of the town as disreputable.[11] That Port Townsend warranted a good reputation was arguable though. (See Introduction above for a definition of reputation.) Port Townsend not only looked rough; it was rough, as were the mill ports and logging camps. Browne was not the only person to comment on this. The town's notoriety was an important part of Victor Smith's strategy to remove the Customs House from Port Townsend. Smith hammered home again and again that until Port Townsend became a more *suitable* town for families, the "overdrawn images" of Browne would continue to prejudice investors and immigrants against the community. Its surplus of saloons and lack of schools and churches would, said Smith, continue to "barb the arrows of our up-Sound enemies," and damage Port Townsend's reputation.[12]

There were others who agreed with Browne and Smith. M.V.B., for instance, complained to the *Port Townsend Register* about drinking,

4.1

Chandler and Adams Bar, Port Townsend.
(Jefferson County Historical Society)

gambling, and prostitution in Port Townsend, arguing that they endangered county development. "Who is he, that will expose his child to such ruinous examples" as abound in Port Townsend? "Who is she that will sacrifice her modesty so much, as to dwell in the midst of dissipation and profligacy, [such] essential causes [will] deter emigration, and expel that part of the community which is inclined towards morality."[13]

M.V.B. raised issues that troubled county boosters throughout the nineteenth century. Port Townsend's situation as a shipping center was considered necessary to the county's economic prosperity – present and future. At the same time, it guaranteed that the waterfront district – as a gathering-place for travellers, seamen, itinerant loggers, and mill workers – would be rough: a scene of frequent, public displays of drunkenness, gambling, and violence, where prostitutes openly practised their trade in waterfront brothels and dance houses or on scows anchored in the bay or near the mill ports. As long as Port

Townsend remained a shipping center, such disreputable activities would continue; the town's reputation would remain suspect; and the tension inherent in this situation would be an essential feature of daily living.

Reputation was therefore a powerful, yet equivocal, issue for county residents. Necessary as it was to convince the public of Port Townsend's respectability – to project an image of respectability, as well as economic opportunity and potential – eradicating the town's disreputable aspects was problematic, as it was elsewhere. Violence, drinking, and vice were common in many frontier towns, as was tension over moral reform.[14] Tolerance of vice was certainly not unusual, although the explanations for such tolerance vary. In Butte, Montana, where miners were "wedded to the rough pleasures of a wide-open town," the major employer, Anaconda Mine "did little to alter that," and moral reformers kept a low profile.[15] In the Kansas cattle towns, attempts at moral reform were largely unsuccessful until the cattle drives with their rowdy cowboys waned.[16] In some towns, a disreputable reputation was not an issue, as in mining camps and towns, where "mining-camp democracy meant … wide-open tolerance of drinking, whoring, and gaming." Or, as in Reno, Nevada, where early entrepreneurs saw a "gold mine in the trafficking of vice."[17] On other frontiers, reformers were able to achieve more of their goals, forcing perceived disreputable establishments and groups into sequestered areas of towns.[18] How did Jefferson County residents address this issue?

One way was that over time, the town's "respectable" residents, both working class and middle class, distanced themselves from the waterfront. Roads and a staircase were built from "downtown," as it was called, to the overlooking plateau, or "uptown." Not unlike residents in other frontier towns, respectable Port Townsendites built homes, schools, churches, and shops, but they were built uptown. Downtown continued to be an essential area of economic activity; however, those who lived there were men and women generally considered less reputable. Thus, Port Townsend's geographical division became emblematic of the town's social division, which was based upon respectability rather than economic status, the issue of respectability blurring those class lines based upon income and occupation. This

4.2 *Top*
Adams Street Stairs, Port Townsend. (Jefferson County Historical Society)

4.3 *Bottom*
Residential Port Townsend. (Jefferson County Historical Society)

4.4
Episcopal Church and Manse.
(Jefferson County Historical Society)

solution was a result of the development-based necessity that the disreputable downtown area continue to flourish.

While living uptown protected respectable residents, especially
women and girls, from unnecessary contact with the disreputable
downtown area and maintained the necessary economy of the downtown, it did little to rescue Port Townsend's reputation with outsiders.
How to do so was a knotty problem, and boosters attacked outside
notions about the town's notoriety in several ways. A common practice was for newspapers to report the activities of hard-working, law-
abiding, and sober residents of all classes and the establishment and

maintenance of respectable institutions and events – the reader will remember that the newspapers were aimed, in part, at an outside audience. Some residents worked to eliminate the sale of liquor, prostitution, and gambling from the county through letters to editors and petitions to the city council.[19] More practical, though, were those residents who strove to contain or control drinking and vice through encouraging "respectable" saloon management, and locating brothels and gambling halls where they would be less obvious to public notice. Thus, many Port Townsend residents, while often deploring the reality of downtown, implicitly countenanced the continuation of activities along the waterfront that were assumed to be by-products of economic development, attempting to control and/or contain – rather than eliminate – drinking and vice. Allocation of residential space as linked to respectability rather than economic status was an important aspect of such control and containment of vice, and the privileging of development concerns.

"PORT TOWNSEND IN THOSE DAYS [WAS] SOMETHING OF A TOUGH"[20]

Looking back at Port Townsend's earlier years, Allen Weir, one-time editor of the town's *Puget Sound Argus*, characterized the town as "something of a tough." While saloons were among the earliest businesses in Jefferson County – several were in operation by 1859[21] – schools and churches were established more slowly. It was not until 1867 that Port Townsend school children had a permanent schoolhouse, and school districts were not established in the more rural areas of the county until 1874.[22] A small Catholic church was built in 1859, and an Episcopal one in 1865, but the parishes waited until 1864 and 1871 respectively for resident clergymen; a Presbyterian church was established in 1873 and a Baptist one in 1890. Thus, the spiritual needs of county residents were met by itinerant ministers for many years.[23] The Masons, established in 1859, were the only fraternal order until the late 1860s.[24]

Yet, Port Townsend was one of the most important towns on Puget Sound throughout the region's long frontier period. It was a county seat and location of the Customs House, the Marine Hospital, and a District Court. A city charter established a city board of trustees in January 1860; in 1878, citizens voted to incorporate and replace the trustees with a city council and mayor. Instituted in February 1878 the council continues to govern Port Townsend today.[25] Nevertheless, the functioning of official institutions were relatively unstructured and informal in the frontier period.[26] For several years, Customs affairs were conducted from a small rented office; and in 1862 the entire operation and all the patients of the Marine Hospital were bundled up and removed to a "diminutive" revenue cutter at the whim of a Customs Collector.[27]

That the early application of the law could be carried out in a casual manner is suggested by a burlesque written by a convalescent patient of the Marine Hospital. It tells the story of an Englishman who fled from his residence in British Columbia to Port Townsend to escape his creditors. Upon receiving a writ for the man's arrest, the county sheriff, who was also a "Doctor ... surveyor, dentist, farmer, county commissioner, road surveyor, botanist, chemist and apothecary," went up to the "man in the street, [and] made a 'grab'... to get the man's watch as part of the debt." For his part, the debtor "quickly [made] the claret fly from near the [sheriff's] eye" before being arrested. He came before the court, "a place 20 feet by 16 into which all the town [was] crowded ... a sheet iron stove in the centre, some Indian mats ... laid on the floor and two or three logs sawn off the end of a tree [to] make seats." Chatting away, "the prisoner sat beside the Judge," while courtroom spectators occasionally "went out to liquor." When this happened, "the Judge cocked his leg on the table, took out his pipe and coolly smoked away [sitting] like little Jack Horner ... in a corner, which I suppose he imagined to be the bench of honor. He is a watch repairer, gun repairer, sailor shipping master, clerk of the District Court and squire of the common one, this room serves him for shop, parlor, kitchen and reception room" and is littered with his tools as well as law books.

When "a jury had to be impanelled ... a man on the street was called in and ... sworn in [as] Deputy." He then went into "the different tap-rooms about town to collect the jurymen." As the prosecution and defense presented their cases, "the Court ... puffed away at its pipe, and the spectators laughed and liquored, inside the Court and out of it. The Court was addressed, sometimes as Mister, then as Captain, as Major, worship, and Old Hoss ... This with a little variation is the way the scales of justice are balanced here."[28]

One woman who lived in Port Townsend wrote that the early Puget Sound ports and villages, including Port Townsend and other Jefferson County settlements, had "an excellent class of people ... and [that] the evidences of taste and culture, which are continually seen, are one of the pleasantest characteristics of this new and thinly settled part of the country."[29] Certainly, lyceums, musical societies, and dancing schools of varying longevity and success occasionally appeared in Jefferson County. However, during the long frontier period, such cultural activities were minimal throughout the Puget Sound region.[30] More persistent were less cultured aspects: the easy and public availability of alcohol, gambling, and prostitutes. That it was easy to drink in Jefferson County was undeniable. Saloons, hotel bars, and other outlets were plentiful, and the frequent displays of drunkenness were commented upon by residents and visitors alike. In the words of one resident, it was "a well-known fact that at no time since the settlement of this town" has there been a time but when "our streets have been disturbed, more or less, by drinking men and night made hideous by loud talk and broils of the inebriate." A visiting newspaperman commented on public drinking in Port Townsend – although his tone is humorous rather than outraged – "Every vessel that comes in or goes out ... sends one, two or three men [or more] ashore, [and] the town is frequently enlivened and given a show of business quite exhilarating to see."[31]

By the early 1860s there were several saloons in the county.[32] During the late 1860s and the 1870s, Port Townsend had around ten saloons, and the mill ports had at least one saloon each.[33] In 1887 there were at least twenty-three saloons, and by 1890, at the height of Port Townsend's boom period, approximately thirty-eight, and one or more in each of the mill ports and other villages.[34] Of course, the above figures gleaned from license applications, newspapers advertisements, and city directories refer only to legal establishments. Alcohol was available in brothels and for sale from whiskey peddlers, as well.

Many saloons offered "a type of vaudeville entertainment nightly from nine until dawn." Cards, dice, and other gambling activities were available either in the bars or in separate establishments; and some bars, called madhouses or dance houses, were brothels as well.[35] It is less easy to pinpoint the existence of brothels than that of saloons. Nevertheless, that prostitutes and brothels were common is indicated from several sources. An 1888 fire insurance map designates at least fifteen small houses or shacks in the business section as female boarding houses, a euphemism for brothels, and oral tradition also remembers that there were larger, more expensive establishments in that area. Brothels were sometimes located on scows in the harbor: James Swan commented on the elimination of one in 1877: "the Sheriff and a posse went this afternoon and commenced the [court-ordered] work of destruction and this evening it was set on fire and burned finally."[36] There were dance houses and brothels near the mill ports as well.[37] Incomplete city arrest records also attest to the ubiquitous presence of prostitution within Port Townsend.[38]

Another indication is that on at least four occasions, Port Townsend residents petitioned town officials to bring prostitution under control, citing not only moral concerns, but fears that obvious prostitution would have a negative effect on the town's reputation. In 1879 Port Townsendites asked the city for an "ordinance that shall prohibit Indians and others from encamping inside of the City Limits, as we deem that the presence of Squaw Brothels has hitherto been a nuisance and we desire it to be abated." Around 1885–89, residents "desire[d]" to bring to the attention of the City Council that "on either side of the most frequented thoroughfare in our city, from the low to the upper portion thereof, is a house of evil repute." Such sights, the petitioners said, were "exceedingly distasteful to the virtuous and law abiding portion of our community." They also "familiarize the minds of our children with vice and sin." Further, "such prominence of vicious places gives our city a bad name." Asking that the council take steps to "suppress this great evil," they concluded that "if it must exist at all … let it be only in some retired or unfrequented place." In 1892 some 500 people requested that the council "use its full powers for the enforcement of such laws … as pertain to

Sabbath desecration, gambling, prostitution or other criminal conduct." A fourth petition, circa 1889 or 1900, "earnestly request[ed] to have removed at least from our principal streets all houses of ill fame."[39] Note that the petitioners were variously concerned not just with moral issues but also with Port Townsend's reputation and the *appearance* of immorality.

In 1886 petitioners asked the March-Term District Court Grand Jury to take action against the dance-houses, but the jury reported to the court that even after "careful examination" there was insufficient evidence to make any indictments. "We are satisfied in our own minds that the evils referred to *do* exist and 'flourish as a green bay tree,' and *that* in the very heart of this city, thereby throwing their baleful influence over our homes and hearthstones and contaminating, like a blighting curse, the morality of our youth of both sexes." The jurors regretted that they could do nothing about such "evils," and believed "that it is something which should be taken in hand by the city authorities;" they asked "the Court to so instruct the municipal officers."[40]

Thus, drinking and vice flourished. Violence – usually in combination with drinking – thrived as well. There were at least thirty-four murders in Jefferson County during the territorial period of 1853–89. According to historian Brad Asher, "during the territorial period, there were 34 killings of whites by other whites in Jefferson County ... Fourteen of these defendants were found guilty; one pleaded guilty." Figures for intra-Indian murders in the county are not available. Interestingly, more than half of those charged with violent felonies, regardless of race, went free during the territorial period.[41] In citing Asher, there is no intention to claim that Jefferson County was more or less violent than other Washington towns and seaports, although it would seem to have had a reputation as such. What is intended is to convey that violence was common in Jefferson County.

Murder was only the worst of the violence. In 1877 District Court Judge Lewis reminded the grand jury that two years earlier he had issued a warning that: "'crime has become fearfully prevalent in our midst ... action on the parts of Courts and Juries are necessary to arrest it. The pistol and bowie-knife, and all other instruments of crime are too freely used, and ... until a rigid public sentiment shall demand a strict enforcement of the criminal law, this epidemic of murder and other crime will continue.' This prediction has been in all respects fulfilled."[42]

While by no means a comprehensive collection of data, a random selection of incidents gleaned from the county newspapers[43] supports the judge's contention, attesting to the prevalence – or at least a perceived prevalence – of violence in Jefferson County.[44] For example, in May 1861, three men died in a "drunken frolic" on the beach at Port Townsend.[45] In July 1868 in Port Ludlow, a young man was stabbed. The trouble "started in a chivari, at which liquor figures pretty extensively."[46] In December, "A genius who had been running with John Barleycorn ... made a batter-ram of a cordwood stick and broke in a door, about 2 o'clock this morning."[47] In August 1869, a logging camp near Quilcene was the scene of the murder of Thomas Allen by John Young. According to witnesses, Allen had accused Young of stealing his whiskey; he "drew a knife out of his boot leg and said to Young that he would kill him." Young was convicted of second-degree murder and sentenced to ten years' imprisonment.[48] In October of the same year, one Jerry Boston was murdered, having been stabbed fifteen times in the back, "the second ... murder [of a Native American] which has taken place within a few weeks."[49]

In April 1871, "two soldiers having enjoyed themselves all night on the beach" – in other words, they were drunk – attacked a man who was fishing near a wharf, "throwing down cordwood and coal ... inflicting a severe and painful wound on [the man's] back."[50] In May, at the nearby Kitsap County mill town of Port Gamble, two Chinese men who had been accused of burglarizing houses (although no evidence was found) were taken into custody by the county sheriff who, "brought them down to the Saloon of the Teekalet Hotel, where they were confronted [by saloon customers] with threats and accusations in order to force them ... to a confession of guilt ... One man said ... he 'would fix them,' or make them confess. The officer readily consented and turned them over to the crowd." Eventually, accompanied by the sheriff, the crowd hanged the two men until they ceased to breathe. At this point, the sheriff intervened, and "at last account they were still alive."[51]

In September 1877, "a row [erupted] between Andrew Mathews and one Sullivan, in which the latter was cut very severely in the face ... No arrests were made," however.[52] In one week in early April 1878, two incidents were reported in the *Democratic Press*. One was an altercation between the mate of the ship *Matilda* and a drunken sailor. The sailor pulled a knife, and the city watchman, arriving upon the scene, did the same. The watchman cut the sailor "slightly about the face and in the side." The other was the death of a tugboat crewman named White who "drowned off Union Wharf." White was found wandering "about the streets in a drunken condition," and the night watchman had led him to where his boat was moored, but "he slipped, fell overboard and was seen no more."[53] In September "a sailor ... full of enough tangle-leg to be ugly" refused to go back on his ship. "He was put into a boat by force and pulled off to the ship, swearing vengeance on everyone who had assisted in getting him away."[54] Thus, drinking, gambling, prostitution, and violence were not uncommon features of life in Jefferson County; and Port Townsend was, indeed, "something of a tough."[55]

"IT WASN'T CONSIDERED SAFE FOR A DECENT WOMAN": ESCAPE FROM DOWNTOWN[56]

Some Port Townsend residents dealt with its disreputable features by physically separating themselves from the downtown area. Port Townsend's commercial life was centered along the waterfront, and the first Euro-American residents' homes were there. However, as early as James Swan's visit to the area in 1859, a few homes and the Marine Hospital were on the overlooking bluff.[57] By 1868 there was a division between the two sections, that went beyond the geographical one. A visitor noted that year that:

Port Townsend is a city of two parts. One ... on the sands and the other on the bluffs that overlook them. We may regard these as Port Townsend the Ancient and Port Townsend the Modern. Port Townsend the Ancient ... contains the "rancheree" of the Duke of York [Chet-ze-moka] and his vassals [and]

the customs house, the Good Templars hall, the Masonic hall
... several whisky saloons and other places of business. In Port
Townsend the Modern are the Marine hospital, the schoolhouse, the church, and neat residences.[58]

Downtown Port Townsend was too rough for respectable women
and children. According to resident Florence Pittman, it was a warren
of "laundry houses, chop houses, gambling houses and houses of
prostitution, and a Seamen's Bethel [a chapel for sailors]. Saloons were
numerous, and it was not considered safe for a decent woman."[59]
Visitor Annie Satterlee also found the downtown area unsafe for herself and her children. On their way to Quilcene, she and her family
arrived in Port Townsend at night by sea, and they went to a close-
by hotel or "lodging house." The landlady was "a frowsy woman
dressed in a ragged bathrobe ... surprised to find a respectable family applying for rooms." Once it was daylight, Mrs Satterlee was
"aghast" to observe "that more than half the business places on the
main street were saloons ... Afraid to let [her] children run loose in
this wicked town [she] herded [them] back to the lodging house,"
there to hide until it was time to leave Port Townsend.[60] Indeed, it
was considered remarkable when a "respectable" family did live
downtown, as illustrated by a comment in the *Argus* when the James
Dalgardno family moved uptown in 1879. "A significant fact concerning this matter is that while Capt. Dalgardno's family came here
first some 21 years ago, they never took a residence on the hill until
last week."[61]

Thus, while many people lived downtown, respectable people re-
treated from the flats to make their homes uptown. Respectable men
might very well maintain businesses downtown, and boys did venture
there, but wives and daughters seldom left "uptown." That the schools
and churches were also located uptown kept girls from downtown
influences, and the women who lived on the bluff disliked even shopping in the business area, since "the nature of downtown, saloons,
ships outfitters, meat markets, boarding houses, Chinese community,
bowling alley, stables, blacksmith, etc. offended many." Port Townsend merchants made deliveries to homes on the hill and eventually
many opened shops there. In 1871, there was one store in the upper

part of Port Townsend, but in time it had a "Dry Goods Store, houseware and grocery store, bakery and grocery, a 10-cent store, three millinery shops and the 'Toggery' (women's-wear)," and the uptown area became "the shopping center of choice."[62] Uptown, respectable women and their children were "safe" from contact with the disreputable denizens of downtown, since only rarely did the "rough elements" escape the "diligence and never failing watchfulness [of] our police authorities … and gain a footing in the upper part of town."[63] Thus, geography split Port Townsend into waterfront and plateau, but nature's division had acquired social significance, one determined by respectability rather than economic class.

An examination of residential patterns in Port Townsend during the late 1880s based upon information in city directories, censuses, and maps illustrates this social division.[64] The 1887 city directory lists addresses by cross streets rather than street numbers, which makes it easy to locate on a fire insurance map for the next year where people lived, especially on the long city streets that passed through both the downtown and uptown areas. The city directory also lists people's occupations and whether or not they boarded or lived with family members. The directory only lists heads of families and single men and women, but by cross-checking with the 1889 territorial population census, it is possible to identify where some families lived. By using the 220 names from the 1887 city directory, which matched with names in the 1889 territorial census (817), one sees that twenty downtown residents lived in families – either a married couple or couple with children. Ninety-nine of those living in families lived uptown. Twenty singles lived uptown, while thirty- nine lived downtown. Of course, since city directories only targeted and recorded heads of families and single people, almost all women and children are excluded. Also, since entries were voluntary, some residents are excluded. Nevertheless, it was possible to establish where many individuals lived.

Many people lived downtown. The 1887 city directory lists eighty-six people who can roughly be grouped as businessmen, professionals, and white collar workers – merchants and other businessmen, mostly saloon keepers and hotel owners, and retail clerks and bookkeepers. The businessmen who lived downtown were those who lived on the premises or above their businesses, while the clerks and book-keepers were mostly single men who either lived where they worked or in hotels or boarding houses. Sixty-three skilled workers such as carpenters or tailors lived downtown, either above their shops, or if they were single, in boarding houses or hotels. Most Chinese residents – officially 209 – lived downtown,[65] confined to a two-or-three block area, and after 1871 – when their permanent village was burned (see Chapter 2) – Native Americans often made semi-permanent camps on the beach. The bulk of downtown residents were laborers who were either transients or in occupations considered more or less disreputable. There were seventeen bartenders, twenty-six restaurant workers, fifty-eight sailors, twenty-seven laborers, and nine prostitutes.[66]

There was also a floating population of sailors – sometimes numbering upwards of 400 men – which would have swelled the population of the downtown area. One hundred eighty-two downtown residents listed themselves as boarders. Thus, downtown residents either lived near or where they worked, or were less established (single men who boarded) or were transients or in disreputable occupations. There were few families.

Not all working people lived downtown, however. Thirty-two craftsmen or skilled workers and twenty-three unskilled workers with respectable occupations lived uptown. Skilled occupations included – dressmakers, milliners, a shoemaker, ships' mates and carpenters, printers, a blacksmith, sawyers and a machinist, men in the building trades, a brewer, and a barber. Unskilled workers included teamsters, woodmen, domestic servants, a watchman, a janitor, and men whose occupation was listed as laborer.

A larger number of Port Townsend's business people, professionals, and white collar workers lived uptown rather than downtown: 119 – school teachers, businessmen, ships' captains, pilots, clerks, government officials, and other professionals. More families lived uptown, and only thirty-eight uptown residents were boarders.

Since the city directory only listed widows and unmarried women who listed an occupation or were not living with their families, it is more difficult to identify how many women lived uptown or downtown. However, what numbers there are indicate that fewer women lived downtown than uptown – twenty-three downtown and thirty-seven uptown. These figures suggest that "respectable" people were more likely to live uptown: families with children, married couples, and women who lived in single-family dwellings, men and women with "respectable" occupations.

Thus, Port Townsend's natural division reinforced a social division by which respectable working-class and middle-class residents – those who lived uptown – disassociated themselves from the disreputable aspects of downtown life that were so indispensable to economic development. This division remained effective into the 1920s, by which time the demise of the town as a shipping center had emptied Port Townsend's downtown of all but a few residents and stores, prohibition had driven the remaining liquor trade underground, and the few brothels were discreet operations.[67]

AT WAR WITH NOTORIETY

Although some Port Townsend residents escaped the downtown area, this did not solve the problem of the town's notoriety. As demonstrated by their reaction to the Browne controversy or the scandal attending the impeachment of the gambling judge, Morris Sachs, many county residents were protective of the community's reputation when it was under attack. Indeed, in the case of the Browne controversy, measures were long-lasting; and Browne continued to elicit slurs from county residents and in the county press for many years (see chapter 2). However, boosters were more than defensive. They actively promoted a positive public image of the county, and an important role of the newspapers was to report the activities of respectable county residents and functioning respectable institutions such as churches, lyceums, and temperance organizations. Such stories were intended to salvage the county's reputation with outsiders and encourage respectable townspeople to associate themselves with rehabilitation.

In 1860, when the formation of a Lyceum and Debating Club was announced, the boosterist *North-West* noted "that there are few objects better calculated to wield a lasting beneficial influence in a

community composed principally of young and single men, than such
an organization."[68] The editor also praised the Port Townsend Musical Association, the last meeting of which had been well attended by
"some half dozen ladies and a large number of gentlemen." Such an
organization was of particular importance in a community such as
Port Townsend, since it would "serve to attract young men from the
society of the profligate and by the observance of decorum, compel
the growth of that self-respect and gentlemanly deportment so essential to future social position and advancement. May it increase in
numbers and prosperity until the ribald jest and wicked oath shall
give place to the refinement of thought and expression."[69]

Newspapers made a point of drawing attention to church-related
activities. The "attentive and large" Port Townsend audiences at the
several services held throughout the week-long visit of Bishop Scott
of the Diocese of Oregon and Washington, and Rev. D. Ellis Willes
of Olympia were commended for their attendance by the local press.
"Not withstanding the rain, we counted nineteen ladies present ...
last evening."[70] *The Weekly Message* praised the "rough garbed men
from the logging camps and farms, [their] souls capable of appreciating the harmonies of the children's choir, and hearts big enough to
contribute to the support of the Sabbath School."[71]

In response to a dig in a letter to the editor that Port Townsend
was largely composed of "free-thinking, liberal" non-church goers,
the *Weekly Message* retorted that: "no town on Puget Sound ... has
given more than Port Townsend to religious institutions, [or] been
more humbugged by them. Port Townsend has given sites for three
or four, and built two churches, and it has no resident minister.
[However,] one of our citizens ... holds Divine service every Sabbath
in St. Paul's Church, in this city ... Give us some one capable of
[preaching], and plenty are here who will be [churchgoers]."[72]

When the *Democratic Press* claimed that the citizens of Port
Townsend had cause to feel "encouraged" because church attendance
was at an all-time high, it also noted that "the percentage of church-
going people and stability in a community is a fair index to the prosperity of that community." Thus, according to the *Press*, "it is to the
interest of business men and all who feel an interest in the general

prosperity and good reputation of their town or neighborhood to encourage church work."[73]

Other "respectable" institutions were subjects of comment as well. The opening of "Mrs. G.S. Nunn's Dancing School" was enthusiastically reported as "very largely attended ... everyone ... very highly pleased."[74] The homelike qualities of the Union Hotel, "a 'Haven of rest' ... a genial landlord, good quarters and rich and wholesome food, received praise."[75] And, when "a project [was] on foot to establish a Young Ladies' Select School in Port Townsend," the editor of the *Weekly Message* thought that it was "just the kind of school ... needed here, and if properly conducted will attract attention all along the Sound ... There is nothing that will give more tone and character to a place than well-conducted educational and benevolent enterprises."[76] The formation of a Natural History Society to be headquartered in Port Townsend was announced with hope, too.[77]

Sober election days and orderly celebrations of holidays usually associated with rowdiness were called to readers' attention. Port Townsend's 1868 Fourth-of-July celebration was considered noteworthy because "there was but one arrest for drunkenness – though there were more than two thousand people present in the city." The reporter continued gleefully, "our neighboring town, Seattle, we understand, was not quite so fortunate. We are told the jail was filled before the day was done, and then set on fire by some one outside, and, had it not been for the Olympia Fire Company, it would have been destroyed, and half the town with it ... Have 'em follow our example."[78]

Also reported was a St Patrick's Day in Port Ludlow, which passed without "one drop of blood drawn; not even a single knock-down the whole day." The writer reminisced about the "pleasure and hope ... with which the Lawyers and Coroner would look forward to a Patrick's day or a Fourth of July in Port Ludlow," but times had changed. Now, Port Ludlow could claim to be a respectable town.[79] Election Day, February 1878, was reported with pride, having "passed off quietly and in a manner reflecting much credit upon Port Townsend as a law-abiding community" since the law forbidding the sale of alcohol on voting day was "universally complied with."[80]

While editors praised positive features of county life, they and others worked to alter features perceived to be negative. Drinking, especially excessive public drinking that led to unruly or violent behavior, was a concern for many county residents. In 1855, when the Territorial Legislature produced a referendum for prohibiting the manufacture and sale of liquor in Washington, the measure passed in Jefferson County 46–5, although it lost territory-wide 650 to 546.[81] However, this early vote in favor of prohibition – not to be repeated in Jefferson County – was probably more reflective of a desire to control the sale of liquor to Native Americans residing in or near Port Townsend and Port Ludlow than it was indicative of a temperance movement at this time directed towards Euro-American drinking.[82]

Nevertheless, there were concerns about Euro-American drinking, as reflected by two early groups. The Port Townsend Dashaway Club was an early Alcoholics Anonymous-type organization; James Swan joined in 1859.[83] A similar group, the Port Townsend Independent Reform Club, formed in 1860 and described by a reporter as "a bright star ... which [it is hoped] will be the means of reclaiming many inveterate dram drinkers, men too, of genius and learning who for years have been whirling with delirious apathy, in the frightful vortex of intemperance. May they continue steadfast, and become the principal pillars of society."[84]

Interest in limiting alcohol consumption continued. The Independent Order of Good Templars, one of the foremost American vehicles of temperance reform, was active in Washington by the late 1860s, with lodges in many towns and mill ports; and Templar lecturers – sent by the national organization – frequently spoke to large audiences.[85] Port Townsend's order was formed in 1867, and in the late 1870s the *Argus* maintained a weekly "Good Templar" page that included listings of territorial meetings and lectures, as well as a "Talks on Temperance" section compiled by editor Allen Weir. Port Ludlow and Quilcene also had Good Templars' lodges, and the Templars in Port Townsend and Port Ludlow maintained their own meeting halls. Washington chapters of the Women's Christian Temperance Union were organized beginning in 1874, and in the same year the Washington Territorial Temperance Alliance was established to organize a drive that went beyond individual temperance, as a law prohibiting the manufacture and sale of liquor in Washington was sought. The WCTU and a Blue Ribbon Club for temperance were extant in the mid-1880s in Port Townsend, and there was a Blue Ribbon Band of Hope formed to introduce children to ideas about abstention from liquor, tobacco, and profane language.[86]

Temperance lecturers visited Port Townsend – and occasionally other county towns.[87] During "Temperance Week" in July 1883 – organized by the Washington Territorial Temperance Alliance and including a territorial-wide program through which the WCTU and churches championed prohibition – the "well-filled" Port Townsend Good Templars Hall was the scene of a reception for Frances Willard of the WCTU by "an intelligent and thoughtful audience." Weir, speaking for the press and the local Templars lodge, welcomed Willard, "with earnest heart [and] admiration for your noble service to the cause of Christianity, Temperance and Intelligence." Mrs A.H. Todd spoke for the Port Townsend WCTU, a newly formed organization that was "pledge[d to] a life-long devotion to our holy cause ... encouraged and strengthened by your presence among us, an impetus ... to the temperance cause ... hastening the day of emancipation for all ... in bondage to this giant evil.[88]

During the winter of 1892, many Jefferson County residents were swept away by the "Gospel temperance" lecturer Thomas Murphy, whose scheduled visit of one week in Port Townsend was extended to three weeks. Upwards of 1,000 people in Port Townsend and Quilcene signed a pledge to abstain from drinking liquor, "don[ning] the blue ribbon" as a signal to one and all of their support for temperance. A Gospel Temperance Union was formed in Port Townsend under the auspices of the town's ministers. "There is no denying ... that Murphy's advent here has done a great deal of good," (although long-lasting effects on some converts were judged to be unlikely).

> The admission is made at almost all the saloons in town that the blue-ribbon crusade has been responsible for a falling off of over 20 per cent in the receipts of the various bars ... Among those whom Mr. Murphy has converted are Charley Hawkins, the well-known sporting man, whose skill at mixing a cocktail has become a matter of local pride.[89]

Clearly, there was support throughout the years for the temperance movement in Jefferson County. Yet, Port Townsendites' concern about drinking was influenced also by development thinking. In 1877 "W.L." wrote from Massachusetts to his son William in Port Townsend, lamenting that "Alphonso" (another son) was in "that kind of business [a store which retailed liquor], but he [Alphonso] says everybody sells Liquor out there."[90] Perhaps Alphonso Learned exaggerated, but the sale of liquor was an important business in Jefferson County, one integral to Port Townsend's present and future position as a shipping center. Worries about drinking were often overridden by an understanding that drinking in a seaport town with "great city" ambitions was inevitable. Such thinking was exemplified by Allen Weir, an officer of the Good Templars' territorial organization, but also editor of the *Argus* and a very much involved county booster. While the *Argus* printed a Templars' page, it also carried advertisements for the local peddlers of alcohol; and in 1879 Weir was criticized by some members of the Templars in the *Democratic Press* for working "in the interest of Temperance [but] also aid[ing] the dealers in liquors by ... bring[ing] a good word in behalf of several brands of liquid poison."[91] Weir excused himself by reminding readers that both the Templars and the "liquor dealers" paid him for space in his paper; and that because both were business arrangements, they had nothing to do with his own beliefs about temperance.[92]

In 1886, a controversial territorial local option law was passed, which allowed as few as fifteen residents of towns or voting precincts outside towns to petition their county commissioners to schedule an election to decide whether or not the community would allow the sale of liquor or not.[93] In response to this controversy, Weir offered a more complete explanation of his position on temperance in Port Townsend than he had in 1879, demonstrating with clarity how a "respectable" booster and temperance activist could come to terms with the sale of liquor in Jefferson County.

Weir made a common argument that "the war of Temperance against Rum" would in the end be won by moral suasion rather than by prohibition laws. Although the "traffic" in Port Townsend was great, when "compared with our population," enforcing prohibition would be impossible. "Not because the town is below others in degree of depravity, but because no town as large as Port Townsend and similarly situated [as a busy seaport] would rigidly respect a prohibition law." Weir wrote that "to refuse to grant licenses here, and then try to punish illicit selling of liquor would simply bring the law into contempt, reduce our municipal and school revenues, and fail to reduce crime or immorality." He pointed out that "in other towns and smaller communities – especially inland – it is far different ... Where the temperance sentiment largely predominates, and where the people desire to, and can, enforce prohibition, we believe in allowing them to do so. That is why we favor local option."[94]

However, Weir contended that because the liquor trade was inevitable in Port Townsend, it was more expedient to have some control over those who sold liquor through licensing fees than to unsuccessfully attempt to eradicate the liquor trade. If fees were "high enough to weed out *disreputable* saloons" [author's emphasis], but not so high as to "result in a monopoly of the business for a few rich dealers," or to encourage "adulteration of liquors, gambling dead falls and other thieving devices in order to make enough money to cover license and other requirements," the liquor trade would be more respectable than if prohibition became the law.[95]

Weir assumed that local option would fail in Jefferson County. He did, however, support an election, because he believed a vote would make clear to the city's saloon keepers that there were respectable forces who supported prohibition. It was therefore in the interests of the more "reputable" saloon keepers that they "put down doggeries and places of ill repute, in order that a wave of popular indignation may not strike the whole traffic and wipe it out of existence." Thus, a vote on local option would encourage saloon keepers to remain "respectable."[96] According to Weir, such respectable saloons would be the community's protection against disreputable forces that would flourish without local influence and control.

The notion that some saloons and their keepers were respectable while others were not was a persistent theme in Jefferson County. It was best articulated by Weir, but it crops up in other places. For instance, the Jefferson County Board of Commissioners declared that they would grant licenses to sell liquor only to merchants and saloon keepers who had "proved to the satisfaction of the board that they were men of good moral character."[97] Such a system of licensing, it was said, acknowledged that saloons were "evil," but provided "respectable" people to control drinking establishments. Several years later, when two members of the Port Townsend City Council presented an ordinance to reduce the fee for.local retail liquor licenses from $500 to $300, the mayor vetoed it because the reduction favored "men in one class of business," men who would not care that the loss of revenue to the city ($4,000) would mean a curtailment in the protection offered them by "an efficient police force.[98]"

According to the *Argus*, saloons in Port Townsend were "a necessary evil [which] none know ... so well as the very men who keep them, every one of whom will admit that if he could make money so easily and so fast in any other way, he would give up his present occupation." However, this necessary evil could be controlled through the licensing of saloons, which ensured that "those who carry on the business [will] regard the law more, and be more careful not to violate it in any respect." Those keepers who are "refused licenses know well that they have in many particulars violated the law ... they have no reason to complain of the action of the Commissioners. That this action was for the best interests of society, every one will admit."[99]

Casual, positive references to certain saloons in various newspapers over the years suggests acceptance of such respectable saloons. One saloon was "thoroughly painted and replenished with a fine stock of liquors; also a splendid three-quarter Carrom Billiard Table, just received from San Francisco."[100] Others were "fitted up very tastefully," had a "neat and attractive appearance," had been "overhauled and renovated throughout," or were "resplendent in new paint, paper, &c."[101] A hotel described as "first-class in every respect" had a bar "attached in the new addition at the side of the main building."[102] The Bank Exchange Saloon was "the place where they go who want a high-toned drink, straight or compounded in the highest style of mixology; who want a first class cigar and a game of billiards."[103]

The newspapers praised saloon keepers who were law-abiding: "Mr. Whiting, proprietor of the saloon on Union wharf, deserves to be complimented for generously closing his place of business on Monday last, during the city election. According to the old municipal boundaries he lives outside the city limits, and hence could not be forced by the local authorities to close his saloon during the election."[104] Others were commended by the press for their hospitality: "Messrs Wood and Sterming ... are well known in the business and will be glad to extend to their numerous friends, and to parched and weary travellers generally, the hospitalities of the Union."[105] David Sires "wishes his old friends to give him a call."[106] Another saloon keeper was public spirited: "Mr. C. Louis Schur ... keeps on hand, for the accommodation of those who are too late to obtain from the stores at night a small stock of assorted groceries, tobacco, etc. Don't fail to call and see Louis."[107] A new hotel would be a success since "Mr. and Mrs. Tucker [who] contemplate putting in a bar in connection with their new hotel the 'Tucker House' ... have a great many years' experience in the hotel business."[108] Even the *Democratic Press*, which had castigated Weir for advertising liquor, praised the character of certain liquor merchants and highlighted the importance of the trade to the local economy. The liquor trade "is to a certain extent the business life of our city as those who deal in [it] spend their money here at home, and are ever first and foremost in all enterprises, whether it is for the benefit of our city and the country at large or for charitable purposes. Imagine what would happen if "every house that keeps liquor for sale" were removed from Port Townsend. Without "the money the business puts in circulation ... business would be stagnated and the universal cry of hard times would fill the air."[109]

Thus, while many Port Townsendites considered temperance and even abstinence desirable personal goals, prohibition of the sale of liquor was an unlikely proposition because Port Townsend's situation as a shipping center made the liquor trade inevitable. Essential to the town's prosperity and economic development, it was better to control the trade and encourage respectable saloons.

Community members railed against vice as well as drinking. As with the sale of liquor, there were residents who wanted to do away with prostitution and gambling completely, but there were other, more pragmatic people who only wished vice to be more controlled and less public. In 1890 the *Leader* was eager to close down certain brothels "because it believed that decency and morality are two attributes in which no city of any pretensions should be lacking."[110] However, signers of two of the four late nineteenth-century petitions concerning prostitution in Port Townsend were reluctantly willing to accept discreet prostitution. "Let it be only in some retired or unfrequented place," or be "removed at least from our principal streets," and one also acknowledged that such places gave the city a bad name.[111]

Gambling also roused similar equivocal responses from residents. Resident gambler, John Quayle, known as "Poker Jack," became part of pioneer mythology, eulogized by McCurdy as "of generous disposition and considered a 'square shooter' by his associates and even the better class of citizens regarded him with considerable affection." When Poker Jack was murdered in 1874, Swan considered him sufficiently important to record the details of his murder, as well as information about his estate and heirs.[112] Nevertheless, as early as 1860, M.V.B deplored the presence of gambling – "practised only by cheats and knaves" – in Port Townsend. Thirty years later, in 1890, the *Leader* rejoiced when several "tin-horn ... opium-soaked gamblers" were run out of town; men who not only followed a disreputable calling, but stood "on the street corners and in front of public places ogling respectable ladies and children."[113] And yet, in 1892 the *Leader* reported several complaints about gambling houses that focused on the fact that gamblers "are allowed to ply their demoralizing vocation [on the] ground floor [where] temptations to the young and inexperienced" were within easy reach. The reporter said that "if gambling is to be longer tolerated in Port Townsend a city ordinance should compel the games to be moved upstairs, down in the cellars or somewhere not so easy of access." Later, when a large gambling house was raided and temporarily closed, it was again the openness of the operation that seemed to rouse the reporter's dismay. "If we must tolerate [gambling] let it be regulated and placed where it will do the least harm."[114]

As Hamer and others have noted, ambitious nineteenth-century frontier residents were anxious that their communities project a favorable, progressive image to potential settlers and investors. In Jefferson County, boosters' concerns about image were wedded to improving outsiders' perceptions of Port Townsend's reputation. Subjected early on to derisive comments about Port Townsend's respectability by Browne and others, residents were defensive about their reputation outside the community, speculating that a bad reputation would hinder development. Yet, like many frontier towns, Port Townsend had a rough area in its downtown – one intertwined with the local economy and future prosperity – and its residents confronted this reality in various ways. One response is apparent in the way space was allocated: regardless of economic status, those men and women who laid claim to "respectability" most often lived uptown, where they were separated from the disreputable downtown area. Another response can be seen in the way booster newspapers emphasized the respectable aspects of county life, hoping to convince outsiders and residents that the county was a reputable place. Over the years, some residents also attempted to eradicate drinking, gambling, and prostitution. However, control and camouflage were largely perceived to be more practical responses, since a cure for disreputableness threatened to destroy the patient.

"The Chinese Must Go," but in a Reputable Way: Development, Jefferson County, and Anti-Chinese Activism, 1870–1890

Chinese immigration to Puget Sound began in the late 1850s and by the 1870s there were well-established Chinese communities in Port Townsend, Seattle, and Tacoma, as well as smaller enclaves in mill ports and other towns.[1] Seeking economic opportunity for themselves, Chinese laborers and entrepreneurs also contributed to regional frontier economic development as merchants and labor contractors, laundrymen and fresh vegetable farmers, as laborers in coal mining, railroad construction, logging and lumber mills, fishing, and as cooks, household help, gardeners, etc. Yet, even as Chinese immigrants played useful roles in frontier economies, throughout the American West anti-Chinese thinking, based upon a mixture of racism, cultural tension, and perceived job competition, flourished. Indeed, beginning with the early California Gold Rush, anti-Chinese movements were endemic to the nineteenth-century American West, and mid-century anti-Chinese activism culminated in the Chinese Exclusion Act of 1882, which prohibited the immigration of Chinese laborers to the United States.[2]

In the immediate wake of the Exclusion Act, Puget Sound anti-Chinese forces were pleased, yet Chinese immigration to the United States continued illegally, especially in Washington, whose shared northern border with Canada made illegal entry relatively easy. Conveniently situated across the Strait of Juan de Fuca from Vancouver

5.1
Three unidentified men. (Jefferson County Historical Society)

Island, Jefferson County was a destination point for many such immigrants, and during 1883 and 1884 *Puget Sound Argus* editor Allen Weir led a call for stringent enforcement of the Exclusion Act. (See discussion below.) However, by 1885 his efforts were overshadowed as agitation throughout Puget Sound to expel all Chinese residents from the territory captured the imagination of many non-Chinese.

The new movement was led in part by Knights of Labor members who used anti-Chinese rhetoric as a means to organize and unify laborers in the Puget Sound region.[3] There was, however, important middle-class support as well.

Organizers' efforts were aided not only by resentment of illegal immigration and racism, but by a nation-wide depression, exacerbated in the region by recent completion of the Northern Pacific railroad, which had released Chinese and non-Chinese laborers into a tight labor market.[4] Fastening upon Chinese labor as an important factor in wide-spread unemployment, non-Chinese labor interests argued that employers, especially large corporations such as the railroads and coal companies, favored Chinese who were willing to work for much less than non-Chinese. They claimed that without the Chinese, regional non-Chinese would better be able to find work.[5] This combination of employment anxieties with racism, cultural tensions, and resentment over illegal immigration would create a potent anti-Chinese movement.

Until the fall of 1885, activities of the movement were directed towards generating public support for expulsion.[6] In September, however, the expulsionists were inspired by the example of a riot on September 4, 1885 in Rock Springs, Wyoming, during which a Euro-American mob killed twenty-eight Chinese miners, wounded others, and drove hundreds more from their encampment. After the Rock Springs riot, the Puget Sound movement entered a new phase. Three days after the Wyoming massacre, a group of non-Chinese hop pickers fired into the tents of some thirty Chinese pickers at Wold Brothers Farm in Squak Valley, Washington Territory – now Issaquah. Three Chinese were killed and four were injured.[7] The next expulsions were aimed at Chinese who were employed in nearby Cascade range coal mines. At the Newcastle mine at Coal Creek, on September 11, thirty-seven workers were driven from their quarters, which were then burned. On September 17, nine were forced to flee from the Black Diamond Mine, and September 29 saw a similar incident at the Franklin mine. Such relatively spontaneous expulsions were followed by more organized efforts that led to the violent expulsion of hundreds of Chinese residents from Tacoma, Seattle, and other Puget Sound towns between October 1885 and March 1886.[8] During this period anti-Chinese feelings ran high in Jefferson County, but there were no attempts at violent expulsion of the approximately 300 Chinese residing there in the fall and winter of 1885–86.[9] Instead, there was a short-lived boycott of Chinese labor and services in the spring of 1886, one that fizzled out through lack of support.

A large body of literature addresses the Puget Sound expulsion movement,[10] and several historians have questioned why there was no violent expulsion in Jefferson County. Two have concluded that a lack of job competition between local Chinese and non-Chinese laborers and the importance of Chinese merchants to Port Townsend's economy explain the failure of expulsion in Port Townsend.[11] Similarly, another scholar argues that the Chinese were too well integrated into the local economy for expulsion to appeal to sufficient numbers of Euro-American residents.[12] However, while such explanations of events in Port Townsend may suggest why the economic boycott failed, they do not account for the decision by local anti-Chinese activists to attempt expulsion through a non-violent boycott rather than by force.

Port Townsend was similar to other Puget Sound towns in the virulence of its anti-Chinese thinking, economic competition between white labor and Chinese workers was an issue, and the town's Chinese residents were castigated for characteristics stemming from perceived ethnic flaws. Further, much of the invective flung at Chinese in Jefferson County cast them as a serious block to development because of supposedly disreputable features of their culture. In addition, county residents were ideally situated to be well aware of illegal entries by Chinese into the United States. Nonetheless, violent anti-Chinese activities such as arose in other Puget Sound communities failed to develop in Port Townsend. Blunted by residents' concerns that violent expulsion would damage the county's reputation, the town's anti-Chinese movement culminated in the non-violent boycott. Thus, Euro-American residents were inflamed against their Chinese neighbors by racism, ideas about job competition, concerns that the Chinese would impede development, and resentment over illegal immigration. Yet their impulse towards violent resolution was mitigated by anxiety about the county's reputation and the important link between economic development and reputation. Some Euro-

Americans sought "to rid" the community of its Chinese, but they tried to do so through a boycott of Chinese labor and services, a non-violent expulsion they hoped would protect that reputation.

While concerns about development had a significant effect upon the expulsion movement locally, the character of the Chinese community was also important. Port Townsend's Chinese enclave, well established by the mid-1880s, functioned as the community center for Lower Puget Sound Chinese. Its merchants, labor contractors, and other businessmen were powerful leaders within that fairly populous community;[13] further, those leaders had a well-established economic relationship with many non-Chinese residents, and there is evidence that suggests they responded to the expulsion crisis from this position of strength from within and without their community, making a determined and successful stand against leaving.

JEFFERSON COUNTY'S CHINESE COMMUNITY

During the late nineteenth and early twentieth centuries, Jefferson County was home to a sizable Chinese population, which peaked at approximately 450 in 1890.[14] The majority lived in Port Townsend – approximately 340 in 1890 – although there were smaller enclaves in the mill ports.[15] Officially, Chinese immigration to Puget Sound began in the 1860s.[16] However, it is likely that Chinese laborers and businessmen made their way to Jefferson County in the years immediately after the Gold Rush, since there was frequent traffic by sea between the county and San Francisco. References to Chinese in the county begin in early 1860 and increase throughout the decade. The *Port Townsend Register* refers to a Chinese labor contractor and laundryman resident in Port Townsend in 1860. Several Chinese are known to have contracted to work at the Puget Mill Company in nearby Port Gamble in 1857, and the Amos, Phinney and Company mill at Port Ludlow employed at least one Chinese cook on its lumber vessels as early as 1862.[17]

In the early years Chinese residents in Jefferson County were dispersed throughout the county, living in approximately even numbers in Port Townsend, Port Discovery, and Port Ludlow. Most were cooks on ships, in private homes, in lumber mill cookhouses, and logging camps, or they operated or worked in laundries in Port Ludlow and Port Townsend.[18] By the 1870s, however, the Chinese had established an enclave in Port Townsend's downtown area. There were three laundries, including the long-established one owned by Sam Sing.[19] In 1878, a Chinese merchandising family – Ng Soon and his brothers Ng Jay and Ng June[20] – started the Zee Tai Company,[21] and by 1880 some numbers of county Chinese were working as contract laborers.[22]

The Chinese who settled in Jefferson County were part of a large-scale migration to North America from Guangdong Province that began following the discovery of gold in California and continued into the twentieth century.[23] Although scholars have traditionally seen this migration as a desperate response to widespread socioeconomic disturbances, more recent scholarship indicates that immigrants "were [not necessarily] totally impoverished" and that many, especially those of middle or lower-middle class status were motivated by a desire for upward mobility.[24] The Ng brothers, Sam Sing, and other Port Townsend Chinese businessmen may have fallen into this category. Impoverished or not, tens of thousands of Chinese immigrated to North America,[25] and some made their way to Puget Sound. Few immigrants planned to settle permanently in the United States; immigration by male family members was a traditional response to economic necessity or ambition, but wives and children ordinarily remained with the patriarchal family.[26] By intent, such immigrants were sojourners rather than settlers, and, although in the end many Chinese did remain in the United States, ties to China remained strong, the Chinese American community being transnational in character.[27]

Some immigrants were entrepreneurs – merchants and labor contractors, laundrymen, restaurateurs, or truck farmers. Others were laborers, often contracted to Euro-American employers by Chinese merchants such as Ng June of the Zee Tai Company.[28] Chinese immigrants pursued many avenues of employment, especially mining and railroad construction,[29] often, although not always, working for minimal wages. Few immigrants had the luxury of being picky about what work they did or what wages they earned. By the time an immigrant started working in the United States he may have incurred

5.2
Charlie Tze Hong, agent for the Zee Tai Company.
(Jefferson County Historical Society)

approximately $200 or more in debt for entry papers and passage
money. In addition, the average immigrant sent from $30 to $40 a
year to his family in China, and many immigrants saved money for
their return to China. Such pressures would have necessitated immediate employment, so it is hardly any wonder that many Chinese were
willing to work for the low wages on offer. The average Chinese railroad worker might earn $30 a month. In 1883, Chinese laborers
working for the Washington Mill Company earned $30 per month;
in 1890, $35. Not all Chinese were paid the same, though. Port Lud-
low's Admiralty Hotel paid some of its Chinese employees $60 a
month and others $15.[30]

In Jefferson County, all the lumber mills[31] employed Chinese laborers at one time or another, where they performed unskilled tasks
in the sawmill, worked the lath mill, were cooks and cooks' helpers,
or built roads for logging operations.[32] The Puget Sound Iron Company employed Chinese labor; laborers were employed as cooks,
servants, laundrymen, gardeners, and casual laborers by the military
at Fort Townsend, 1856 to 1895; they were favored as cooks and
stewards on shipping vessels and tugboats, working also in many of
the county's private homes, restaurants, hotels, and brothels.[33]

As well, Chinese were employed within the Chinese community,
which included several successful businesses. The most prominent
were the merchants' stores (see discussion below), but Chinese businessmen also operated truck gardens, laundries, and restaurants.
There were two Chinese-run truck gardens located outside Port
Townsend that monopolized the local market for fresh vegetables
from at least the late nineteenth century and shipped produce to
Seattle and other Puget Sound points.[34] There were several Chinese-
operated laundries in the county. Port Townsend, which had a Chinese laundry as early as 1860, had eight or more in the early 1890s,
and there was usually one laundry in each of the mill ports. Several
laundries remained in business for many years: Sam Sing, Wah
Chung, Lee Hop, Wa Hong, Yee Chung, and Wing Sing.[35] Thus, the
county's Chinese businessmen and laborers fulfilled a necessary economic function within the county.[36]

Chinese immigrants established close-knit communities throughout the West. While such enclaves varied in size and location – from
Chinatown in San Francisco to a single merchant's store in a mining
camp – they provided leadership, institutional structure, and a sub-
stitute for home.[37] The Port Townsend community functioned as such
for Chinese living throughout the Lower Puget Sound.[38] In Port
Townsend there were fellow immigrants with whom to socialize;
the stores carried familiar and necessary Chinese merchandise; and
restaurants served traditional food. Chinese New Year was celebrated
with strings of firecrackers and burning sandalwood, while the merchants distributed free cigars, wine, candy, and lychee nuts to their
customers, both Chinese and non-Chinese.[39]

Opium, alcohol, and gambling were available in the merchants' stores and perhaps prostitutes also.[40] Merchants who sold opium had backrooms with bunks where "there were always at least one or two men in there [in] sessions [which] lasted from four to five hours or all night."[41] Some merchants' stores – Zee Tai and the Wing Sing Company – were also gambling establishments. Men "gambled three or four times a day. At night was [sic] their big games. Every three or four hours, they had a game going. At night, when everybody was off work, they had big games. They played all night."[42]

While gambling and the use of opium excited negative reactions amongst Euro-American residents;[43] another Chinese pastime, kite flying, did not. Kite flying was an adult activity that often included gambling large stakes on which kites could stay in the air the longest. Competition was intense, and often ground glass, glued to the cord ten to twelve feet below the kite all the way to the ground, assisted flyers' attempts to cut rivals' kites loose. From ten to forty feet long – memories differ – the kites were made of rice paper, covered with designs and often shaped like caterpillars. Once in the air a bamboo reed attached to the tail hummed loudly. The kites were so heavy, it could take several men to pull one in.[44]

Some nineteenth- and early twentieth-century North American Chinese communities included brothels,[45] but it is impossible to verify their existence in Port Townsend. There are no specific references to prostitutes in local sources, and the census is inconclusive. The very few resident Chinese women are listed as housewives except for one woman in the 1880 census, a "housekeeper" who lived alone with a female child.[46]

The excavation in 1990 of the sites of nineteenth and early twentieth-century Chinese-occupied buildings in Port Townsend yielded perfume bottles mixed with other, predominately Chinese artifacts. Since one of the buildings was designated as a "female boarding house" – a euphemism for brothel – on an 1891 fire insurance map, the bottles may contribute to a conclusion that there was a brothel on the site. However, since the Chinese community was located in the "disreputable" area of Port Townsend, the building may very well have been a non-Chinese brothel or dance house, rather than a Chinese brothel.[47] An incident that suggests Chinese relations with non-Chinese prostitutes occurred in November 1889, when a Chinese man and an Euro-American woman, "the latter a member of the soiled dove fraternity," were arrested while smoking opium together.[48]

Although most Chinese immigrants in Port Townsend were single, there were a small number of Chinese families, only two or three at any one time in Jefferson County. A few wives and concubines did emigrate to the United States from China, and some men married Chinese prostitutes after purchasing their freedom or helping them escape prostitution. Some married or formed alliances with Native American women.[49] Chinese men and women also fell in love with non-Chinese, although such relationships were frowned upon.[50] Eng Ah Dock and a Miss Sherlock of Port Townsend were one such couple. In April 1895, Charles Sherlock, father of Miss Sherlock, instigated legal action against Ah Dock, charging that he was insane

5.3
Man and child. (Jefferson County Historical Society)

because he gave gifts to Miss Sherlock and wished to marry her. However, according to the testimony of Ah Dock's friend, Mon Yik, Miss Sherlock had given Ah Dock cake and talked of marriage with him. Mon Yik said that Ah Dock "acted very foolish [and] had a great deal of thought about matrimony." When Ah Dock wrote to Miss Sherlock formally proposing that they marry and flee to California, her father found out; a dramatic scene ensued, and Ah Dock was arrested. Mr Sherlock spoke for his daughter – she did not testify – insisting that she had never wanted anything to do with Ah Dock; and at the trial Ah Dock denied any interest in Miss Sherlock. In the end, two medical doctors testified that Ah Dock appeared to be mentally sound, and he was released on bonds of $500 to keep the peace, with Eng Ting and Ng Soon of Zee Tai Company acting as sureties for him. It is difficult to know for certain what happened between Miss Sherlock and Ah Dock, although Mon Yik's testimony does suggest a romance.[51]

Chinese communities were also headquarters for traditional social organizations that accompanied immigrants to North America. An essential part of the social structure of the North American diaspora, they were controlled by the merchants. In Port Townsend, there were clan organizations and one chapter of the Zhigongtang – known to Euro-Americans as the Chinese Freemasons[52] – was organized by at least 1883.[53] For many years, this was Port Townsend's only social organization, excepting the clans. Its Chinese Consolidated Benevolent Society (CCBS) was not established until 1894, a second Zhigongtang was founded in 1902.[54] While the Zhigongtang had connections to the anti-dynastic Triad Society in China, in small frontier towns such as Port Townsend it likely functioned as an umbrella organization – much as the CCBS did later – serving the needs of the Chinese community but also helping to secure the power of merchants.[55] In this early North American West incarnation, anti-dynastic ideology was less important than providing a social structure for its members and a power base for merchant leaders.[56]

Organizations such as the Zhigongtang, the clans, and the Six Companies or Chinese Consolidated Benevolent Society provided the institutional structure necessary for communities that were particularly isolated from American society by language, cultural barriers, and racism. In large communities such as San Francisco, there were numerous social organizations. However, in smaller communities the separate roles of such organizations might be united in one or more groups centered in local merchants' stores. Large or small, they were dominated by the merchants, and such organizations exercised great influence in the lives of Chinese residents in North America.[57]

At one level, these organizations were mutual protective associations similar to those established by other ethnic immigrant groups, but the Chinese organizations were often more complex. The leaders of such organizations represented the Chinese community before official and unofficial American groups, often standing in the place of Chinese consular and diplomatic officials. Their representatives met incoming ships, arranged for housing, work, and necessary medical treatment. They also shipped the bones of the dead back to China – a traditional practice for the Chinese diaspora – and settled arguments between members. Representatives also attended the departure of any ships bound for China, made certain that members paid their contribution to the welfare funds of the organization, and collected debts owed to the merchants. Because of the sojourning nature of the Chinese American community, this system was fairly effective in insuring that merchants collected their debts and community leaders did not have to fund welfare activities themselves.[58]

In Port Townsend, as elsewhere, the merchants were the leaders of the Chinese community, a community that may have been perceived by Euro-Americans to be without structure, but was in fact well organized. As heads of clans and the Zhigongtang, as labor contractors, and as providers of necessary supplies, opium, gambling, and perhaps prostitutes, the merchants were powerful figures within the community. Descriptions of the partners in the Zee Tai Company confirm their status. They wore distinctive Chinese-style clothing of expensive silk while the average Chinese, "the common scrubs ... just wore anything, half Western and half Chinese." The merchants also ate separately from the others and were the authorities within their clans. "When ... talking business of any kind among their clan[, if] there were any arguments over anything, they had the most say."

And, Ng Soon – or Zee Tai, as he was often called by Euro-Americans – always walked in the front of the other men, who trailed single-file behind him.[59] Ng Soon's prestige reached into the Euro-American community as well, for he was respected for his wealth and the trade he brought to Port Townsend.[60]

Most of the Port Townsend Chinese were members of the Eng or Ng clan, although there were representatives of the Wong, Lee, Jong, Mar, and Chung clans.[61] Chinese Americans usually patronized and worked for those merchants who represented their own clan and regional ties.[62] The Zee Tai Company was the headquarters for the Eng clan in Jefferson County and the Lower Puget Sound.[63] Three other merchant stores stand out as possible clan headquarters, although only the clan name of the partners in the Wing Sing Company – Mar – is known.[64]

The Yee Sing Wo Kee Company, owned by Jay Ah Kly and established by at least 1887, did labor contracting and was for many years the largest Chinese merchant's store in Port Townsend. The Wing Sing Company was well established by 1892. A Customs inspector claimed that few goods were sold from Wing Sing, although there was a great deal of gambling, and one Mar Get was arrested for smuggling Chinese into the United States in 1899.[65] However, its longevity – into the second decade of the twentieth century – suggests that it was more than just a cover up for illegal activities.

The Hong Kee Company, established by at least 1890, was another merchants' store that contracted labor – Fung Chong supplied the Washington Mill Company with laborers between at least 1900 and 1903. Yip Fang, also connected to the store, was the founding president of the 1902 Zhigongtang chapter, and his leadership of the tong suggests that the Hong Kee was a clan headquarters.[66]

Thus, Port Townsend's Chinese community not only provided area Chinese with goods, services, and recreation; it was also the locus for community social organizations and leadership, and its merchant leaders, whose influence reached throughout the Lower Puget Sound, held positions of power with their community. Its members were employed in the area's lumber mills, and as cooks, stewards, servants, and casual laborers by a variety of employers. Both the status of the merchants within their community and the economic position of the

Chinese within the larger county population had an important effect on the 1885–86 crisis.

"THE CHINESE INVASION"[67]: EXCLUSION LAWS AND ILLEGAL ENTRY

The Exclusion Act of 1882 was the result of efforts by anti-Chinese activists to prevent the immigration of Chinese laborers. However, the act and its successors failed to stifle either immigrants' desires to enter the United States or their creativity in achieving that end. Prior to the first exclusion act, most Chinese immigrants entered the United States through San Francisco, although in the 1870s direct steamship routes between China and the Northwest increased entries through Puget Sound.[68] Overall Chinese immigration peaked in 1882 with 39,579 arrivals; thereafter, official figures decline sharply. In 1883, 8,031 arrivals were recorded, but only 279 for 1884, and during each of the years between 1884 and 1889 there were fewer than 50 official new arrivals as opposed to re-entries.[69] These figures suggest that Chinese immigration had almost ceased, but it had not. Rather, immigration continued through illegal means, which Customs was too poorly staffed and funded to effectively control.[70]

Illegal entry occurred along the West Coast or on the borders separating the United States from Canada and Mexico, at points where secret entry could be made and where there were accessible Chinese communities to aid and absorb the newcomers. Puget Sound, where there was an established tradition of smuggling wool, whiskey, and opium from British Columbia,[71] became a major point for illegal entries; and Jefferson County became an important destination for immigrants who were brought by boat across the Strait of Juan de Fuca from Vancouver Island. Sheltered bays provided safe landings in rough weather, the beaches were sparsely populated, and Chinese settlements at Port Discovery and North Beach near Port Townsend, as well as the larger community in Port Townsend, were often within walking distance. The *Argus* speculated that in the space of just one week in 1883, twenty-five to forty Chinese had landed at Port Discovery, disappearing into the Chinese community,[72] or entered through the Puget Sound Port of Entry at Port Townsend with false papers. Although numbers are difficult to estimate, government officials at the time suggested that from 300 to 2,000 Chinese per year illegally entered the Puget Sound Customs District during the remainder of the nineteenth century.[73]

Illegal entry papers were also used. Some were genuine certifications of American residence purchased from the previous owners; some were simply falsified.[74] Other papers were obtained through "doubling up." Portland Chinese would go to Victoria, sell their certification papers to newly arrived immigrants, and then go to the United States consul in Victoria, claiming to have lost their papers. Since they were able to prove their American residency, the Consulate would issue them emergency certification.[75] Similarly, certification might have been forged papers such as those provided by Port Townsend attorney John Trumbull, who was arrested and brought to trial in 1891 for selling forged entry papers – seventy between January 1 and April 20 – to Chinese in Victoria. Investigation into the matter indicated an active operation that may have included Customs officials – at least one was dismissed from his position.[76] Certification might also have been obtained from Port of Entry officials if the entrant provided reliable witnesses to his or her previous residence in the United States. Chinese who had left the United States before the Exclusion Act of 1882 and therefore had no certification of their American residence often enlisted the help of Euro-Americans who knew that they had been resident in the United States to testify on their behalf. James Swan was often hired to aid Chinese in this process.[77] Unknown numbers of Chinese also hid themselves on boats and ships travelling between Victoria and Vancouver, British Columbia and Washington ports.[78]

Allen Weir, editor of the *Argus*, had championed exclusion, arguing that although it was useful to look at all sides of "the Chinese question" some method should be found that would "open the way for a mitigation of the evils of unlimited Chinese immigration to this country."[79] However, when the Exclusion Act was passed, he predicted that "the prohibited race would find ways of evading its provisions from our northern boundary."[80] Congratulating himself on his perspicuity, Weir led a regional campaign in 1883 against illegal immigration, arguing that violations occurred frequently, and that officials were remiss in their performance or in need of reinforcements.[81] Notwithstanding the campaign for more effective enforcement of the Exclusion Act, by the fall of 1885 disappointed anti-Chinese activists were reaching for new solutions to the perceived "Chinese problem," and in Jefferson County – as elsewhere throughout Puget Sound – "getting rid of the Chinese" became a topical issue.

"THE DIFFICULTIES ... IN GETTING RID OF THE CHINESE"[82]: ANTI-CHINESE IDEOLOGY AND DEVELOPMENT THINKING IN JEFFERSON COUNTY

By the 1880s, Chinese residents had created a strong community in Port Townsend. However, the community – like all Puget Sound Chinese communities – was established and maintained amid an atmosphere of racism and anti-Chinese thinking. In 1880, Jefferson County's Immigration Aid Society published *North-Western Washington: Its Soil, Climate, Productions and General Resources*.[83] Prepared by members of the Immigration Aid Society and edited by Allen Weir, its purpose was to attract immigrants and investors to the Lower Sound. Prepared with the support and input of community residents, and intended to project a favorable public image of Jefferson County and the Lower Sound, the booklet is at least partly representative of county Euro-American thinking about Chinese residents. Believing that the area's Chinese community might deter Euro-American immigrants, the authors attempted to explain why the county had Chinese residents and what could be done to get them to leave, and their prose runs the gamut of anti-Chinese stereotyping. They argued that "white laborers and the country have suffered" from Chinese immigration; defined the Chinese and their culture as alien – "not of us, from us, or for us"; described their living conditions as dirty and crowded, "without furniture or other similar comforts." Not only did Chinese immigrants fail to contribute to the local economy – "importing most of what they eat from China while they hoard their earnings" – they carried local wealth to China when they returned home. The pamphlet continues, saying that no Euro-American laborer "can begin to compete with these leprous creatures because they cannot, will not, and OUGHT [sic] not live as they do." Arguing that the Chinese had for years been taking jobs that should have been filled by settlers, the authors argued for an exclusion act lest the Chinese take all employment, displace employers, and come to control the entire Pacific coast. Although making a strong argument for exclusion, the authors suggest that Euro-American immigration is the best hope for destroying the influence of the Chinese. "There is a growing determination to be rid of them, and the change will be effected as soon as acceptable white men and women can be had to take their places."[84]

Port Townsend's newspapers expressed similar anti-Chinese senti-ments, which given the frequency of such expressions and the lack of any articulated disagreement from readers suggests a general agree-ment.[85] Politics reflected anti-Chinese thinking, as when the editor of the Democratic Press urged voters to reject Ben Miller who was run-ning for county sheriff: Miller was the man "who furnishes employ-ment to more Chinamen than any other one man in the county, in preference to giving the same employment to honest, hard working men who glory in the boasted title of 'I am an American citizen.'" The county's electorate was asked to "pronounce to the world that the 'Chinese Must Go,' by voting against the Great Mongolian Contrac-tor, Ben S. Miller." Miller won the election, but editor Meyers praised Port Townsend voters for electing Charles Eisenbeis – a local baker – as mayor. "Our citizens did the correct thing ... Mr. Eisenbeis does not employ Chinamen nor does he import them ... and thereby de-prive needy white men and women of their daily bread." Both Meyers and H.L. Blanchard, the previous editor of the Press, applauded in-stances where Chinese were denied employment or replaced with Euro-American employees. They also criticized the reverse.[86]

While the Press ranted against Chinese immigrants in general, other Port Townsendites campaigned for a city tax to be levied on the town's Chinese laundries.[87] However, when an ordinance, "taxing very moderately all wash-houses, Chinese or otherwise, within the city limits," was passed, it was declared unconstitutional in the District Court. Townspeople lamented the decision, and Francis James, a city councilman, complained that the Chinese "reside and carry on their business here; they use our roads, receive the benefit of the city improvements, appeal to our laws, and drain this city and county of its gold which they remit regularly to China, yet they utterly refuse to pay a tax or work on public roads." James declared himself quiescent for the time being, but he said that "before many years have passed it will become an imperative necessity on the part of civilized nations to pass laws ... discriminating against those people compared to which this city's simple ordinance would seem but a bagatelle."[88]

The Chinese laundries attracted continuing censure. In his "Health Officer's Report" of July 30, 1879 – addressed to the Board of Trustees of Port Townsend – Dr Thomas Minor reported his "inspection of those localities [the laundries] in which I have reason to believe disease germs were liable to arise from noxious odors and prevalent filth." Minor cautioned the trustees that if Chinese laundries were to continue to operate within the city limits, then "the question of proper sewers and drains ... must command the early attention of your body ... The reputation this place now justly enjoys for health, can, in one season, be destroyed for years [by the laundries], if proper means are not provided to carry off pollutions that we permit in our midst."[89]

Several months later, the *Argus* raised an outcry against laundries, opium parlors, and fires in the Chinese section of Port Townsend. Although no such action was taken, the *Argus* reported that townspeople hoped "that the grand jury will pronounce the celestial abodes a nuisance – and thus authorize their removal to some place outside of the city limits."[90] The subject was raised again in 1883. The *Argus* mourned the absence of a "white labor laundry," which forced residents to patronize Chinese-run laundries.[91] A fire in one of the laundries – which was put out with little damage done – prompted the *Argus* to report that unless the authorities take notice there would be complaints about the "nuisances to the next grand jury ... Let the wash-houses be segregated from the business part of town."[92]

In a letter to the *Argus,* "X" complained about the laundries and clearly made the connection between anti-Chinese and development thinking:

The whole of the back premises of such "rookeries" should be visited by the City Fathers in their official capacity and such measures taken that strangers will not be disgusted with loathsome sights and foul stenches, which ... may ... burst forth into typhoid and other deadly diseases. Citizens, your property is at stake, for capitalists will fight shy of you if these things be not righted. Inhabitants, your lives are in danger![93]

Euro-American reaction to the Chinese was not always negative. Even the *Press* might praise Chinese for growing "1200 bushels potatoes ... on two acres of land."[94] Further, violence against Chinese residents was deplored in the local press.[95] An attack that resulted in a man's queue being pulled from his head was denounced. "The perpetrators of the outrage ought to be punished to the full extent of the law. Such brutal maltreatment of poor heathens is cowardly, malicious and criminal in the extreme."[96] The editor of the short-lived *Port of Entry Times* said that the Chinese were "an inoffensive race of people ... and have as much right to the protection of the laws of the country as any other foreigner or indeed, native."[97]

The *Argus*, under the editorship of the anti-Chinese Allen Weir, might defend the Chinese upon occasion, as in 1879 when the paper denounced the "roughs and hoodlums [who] hooted at and hunted down" the Chinese. The paper argued that rather than "idle, criminal, incapable of civilization, &c.," Chinese were frugal, dependable, and hardworking; there were fewer Chinese than any other nationality in California prisons, hospitals, and alms houses and fewer Chinese sold opium than Euro-Americans sold liquor. Further, whites gambled away more in a single day than all the Chinese living in the United States. However, even while defending their character, the *Argus* cautioned that it was not trying to "champion the Chinese, but to do them simple justice ... those who are with us have a right to live and be protected." Nevertheless, Americans should "check the influx ... the Chinaman is a detriment to America."[98]

Weir's *Argus,* however, was usually stridently anti-Chinese, and such thinking was closely connected to Weir's commitment to development. This is demonstrated by his call for the city council to force the removal of Chinese laundries to the town's perimeters, claiming they detracted from the advantages of Port Townsend's healthful location by habitually dumping dirty water into the streets.[99] Further, according to Weir, the opium smoking associated with all Chinese businesses implicitly affected the town's reputation through the danger it posed to the children of respectable families.[100] Port Townsend was entering a new phase in its development and would require all available land downtown for the expansion of industry and business. Yet, Chinese laundries, other businesses, and lodgings occupied some of the most desirable land in town. It was necessary to ensure that they did not damage Port Townsend's potential since, according to Weir, the "race not only unfits property they inhabit for the occupancy or use of white people ... they gradually drive out adjacent whites; a Chinatown ... becomes a hotbed of vice." Let us stop "this celestial colonization" before it is too late. "The remedy is obvious; let it be applied while it can be carried into effect."[101] Soon, however, it was deemed that removal outside the city limits was insufficient.

"OUR CITY IS PROSPEROUS AND WE INTEND TO KEEP IT SO"[102]: THE FAILURE OF EXPULSION BY BOYCOTT, 1885–1886

As Puget Sound anti-Chinese thinking coalesced into an anti-Chinese movement in the fall of 1885, Euro-Americans – led by the Knights of Labor – gathered throughout the region in groups large and small to plan and put into effect the expulsion of all Puget Sound Chinese residents. In a crisis period, which lasted from September 1885 to March 1886, several Chinese died or were injured, and many hundreds more were driven – with violence or threat of violence – from mining camps, villages, and towns by anti-Chinese mobs – the largest and most complete expulsion occurring in Tacoma. As well, many other Chinese left the region voluntarily.

For a time, it seemed that Port Townsend would follow the example of Tacoma. In late September, a Port Townsend Knights of Labor assembly – organized in the spring of 1884 – pressured the Port

Townsend Mill Company to replace its Chinese workers with non-Chinese. The mill complied,[103] and by December expulsion was a primary topic of conversation in the county. The *Argus* was in favor of pushing the Chinese community from the county; "if permitted to flourish here ... [the Chinese will] work untold injury."[104] However, Weir worried about the form expulsion might take. It was essential that "the better class of people take the matter in hand [before] hoodlums ... get to working dynamite plots." It would be preferable if a group "composed principally of those who *have permanent interests here*" (Weir's emphasis) seize control of the situation, taking it out of the "hands of irresponsible persons who are always likely to adopt rash and impracticable measures, to the detriment of public welfare and the injury of the cause abroad." In other words, Weir feared that unless those who were sensitive to development issues controlled the anti-Chinese movement, less-reputable forces would try to expel the Chinese through violence – as had been done in numerous other locations throughout Puget Sound. Such disreputable means would damage "the public welfare," and jeopardize prospects for development by damaging Port Townsend's reputation.[105]

Aware that Tacoma had become a byword for mob action following expulsion by Euro-Americans of the city's Chinese, Weir feared a similar fate for Port Townsend. Much better would be a non-violent economic boycott of Chinese labor and services. Support for a boycott and opposition to any other means of expulsion remained the position of the *Argus* throughout the crisis, and judging from events, it was shared by much of the Euro-American community. The "Chinese Evil" was a problem that "must be solved," but those "who apply the remedy of force and mob law [while] their intentions are in the main good ... their methods are wrong."[106] A boycott would "rid the county of the Asiatic pests, if energetically applied."[107]

The *Argus* also thought that violent expulsions threatened negative consequences to the entire territory. Its bid for statehood might be denied, and its wide disorders put Washington "on a par with mining towns and cowboy ranges where vigilance committee and Judge Lynch proceedings hold sway." Further, "political economists are apt to argue that when the present irritating cause [the Chinese] is re-

moved, the same spirit of lawlessness will find other evils upon which
to vent itself."[108] Closer to home, feared Weir, violent behavior might
result in immediately stopping the construction of a new Federal
Building in Port Townsend.[109] Weir praised peacekeeping efforts:
"our city authorities are made of the right kind of pluck, [the] few
cranks" who would make trouble were being kept under control.
"Our city is prosperous and we intend to keep it so."[110]

Port Townsendites, both Chinese and non-Chinese, were alarmed
when ninety-six Chinese refugees from the expulsion in Seattle[111] arrived in Port Townsend on February 12, 1886 to wait for passage to
San Francisco. Euro-American residents, fearing an incident, provided them a safe place to wait for the steamer. Apparently, Port
Townsend Chinese were worried by the event as well, but "a few of
leading [Euro-American] citizens assured the Chinese living here that
the newcomers ... were on their way out of the country," and that
presumably the local Chinese were safe from violence.[112] When the
ninety-six men sailed two days later on the *George Elder*, James
Swan commented with relief to his diary that "everything passed off
quietly and satisfactory."[113] Pleased with the restraint shown by Port
Townsendites – and even more pleased that expulsion had brought
martial law to Seattle – he wrote to a friend, "there is a class in Seattle
ready at any time for plunder ... and until they are driven out stock
and fluke ... capital will be timid of investing in property there."[114]

Soon after this event, however, local Chinese residents were
warned that they would be wise to leave town; and the *Argus* concurred. We "unite in encouraging them to go [although] no violence
or threats of violence will be tolerated."[115] However, the Chinese
were "apparently disposed to remain"; and Euro-American residents
believed that the town's Chinese population was actually swelling
through an influx of refugees.[116] Fearful of a violent outbreak, Euro-
American Port Townsendites began to cast about for non-violent solutions to the town's own anti-Chinese crisis. The *Argus* reported that
some residents proposed forming a town militia since "there is abundant material here for a good strong company," and the city could
hire "a little extra help on the police force." Together, a militia and
more lawmen "would be amply sufficient to quell any disturbance

that may occur" to blight development.[117] A week later, Weir reiterated the danger violence posed to the local economy and development:

> Business is on a healthful basis, new blood and new capital are being added ... to swell the forces that are impelling us toward a larger and more prosperous municipal growth ... our own capital is fully employed, and we have yet other openings for industries that will bring both money and people here ... While our neighbors are wasting their energies in fruitless domestic quarrels over the Chinese we are gathering our strength for onward strides.[118]

Nevertheless, Weir promoted the boycott, which he hoped would effect a peaceful expulsion with no damage to county development. In early March, he prepared a formal petition for the boycott, the signatories of which would be published in the *Argus*.[119] There was some opposition to the idea of a boycott, although not because it might force the Chinese to leave town. Some Euro-American residents – characterized by the Blaine *Journal*, as "'I want the-Chinese-to-go-the-right-way'" – thought even a boycott might be considered unlawful by some members of the public. Weir was accused of "becoming an agitator and favoring lawlessness."[120] The *Port Townsend Call* also criticized the boycott as a possible threat to law and order, although it agreed that the Chinese should go and, in the end, it supported the boycott.[121]

Whether lawless or not, the boycott was a failure. The *Argus* reported that employers had difficulties in replacing Chinese workers. For instance, one county landowner claimed to have refused an offer from a Chinese contractor to clear land for $20 an acre and tools supplied. He preferred to hire "white men [and offered] $25 and tools found." However, the work "has been looked at by white laborers, 'anxious to get work,' but they decline[d] it." In another story, the *Argus* told about a Port Townsend brick maker who said if he fired his reliable, skilled Chinese workers, he would have to charge considerably more for his bricks, and have to deal with "white men ... often intemperate and unreliable." One letter writer took a different view point: "mills and factories that were running and paying employees fair wages, because of the employment of cheaper Chinese help in some of the ruder forms of labor, have been compelled to cease work entirely or to run on half time. As a consequence many persons are out of employment and without means of support."[122]

Throughout the boycott, Port Townsend's Chinese community remained intact and vital, although some servants and laborers lost their jobs and the laundries some custom. Such losses were of short duration, however, because Chinese labor and services filled a need in the county, and there was some popular understanding of this.[123] In the end, the boycott demonstrated that non-violent expulsion was more complicated than anti-Chinese rhetoric would allow. Weir blamed the failure on "white labor" refusing to work for lower wages: "There are altogether too many men hunting for work and praying they may not find it."[124]

Actual competition for jobs throughout the crisis period may have been less intense in Jefferson County than on the east side of the Sound, however. Certainly, the county's lumber mills – the Port Discovery Mill and the Puget Mill at Port Ludlow were joined by the Washington Mill Company at Port Hadlock in the fall of 1886 – were busy throughout the 1880s, their businesses maintained by Pacific Rim markets in Australia, Southern California, and Chile.[125] The Puget Sound Iron Company was in operation; and shipping was sustained by lumber. As for the laundries, the cooks, and the other domestic workers, they replaced the female workforce missing in a frontier society that still had an unbalanced sex ratio.[126] Thus, Chinese labor and services were actually needed in the community. The economic aspects of their anti-Chinese ideology had proven false: the Chinese did not in reality compete with Euro-American labor. This blunted – if not racism – some of the importance of job competition, an important element in the success of the Puget Sound Chinese Expulsion movement elsewhere on the Sound.

Further comparison with Puget Sound's east side is illuminating. By the mid-1880s, the economic downswing of that period and the completion of the Northern Pacific Railroad had brought thousands of wage workers to Seattle and Tacoma seeking employment. According to historian Carlos Schwantes, these working men became desperately disenchanted with the Pacific Northwest when "reduced incomes and unemployment ... snuffed out their dreams of a good life in a promising new land." Class polarization resulted and was a potent aspect of the expulsion movement in both Tacoma and Seattle.[127]

In Jefferson County, however, some resident wage workers – mostly employed in the logging and lumber industry – owned property, especially small farms. Such laborers would likely have perceived a connection between their individual prosperity and successful development in the county. Other wage workers would have seen the chance of social mobility in small-scale entrepreneurial opportunities that development might make available in shipping, shipbuilding, shop-keeping, logging, and so on. The establishment of the Knights of Labor in Port Townsend in 1884 certainly indicates a conscious working-class presence, but the failure of the expulsion movement in Jefferson County suggests that there was not a level of class polarization such as existed elsewhere on Puget Sound.

Also interesting are certain details of the expulsion crisis as it played out in Seattle. Here, there were people who – while they still expressed anti-Chinese thinking – argued against violent expulsion because they feared the negative impact such violence would have on regional development and the territory's timely promotion to statehood.[128] These people, known variously as: the Opera-House gang, white Chinamen, and the Law and Order group,[129] in alliance with leaders of the Seattle Chinese community, were able to block total expulsion in Seattle.[130] Significantly, the "Opera-House gang," was composed of long-term residents of Seattle with a history of interest in development, and legal and business ties to Chinese merchants.[131]

In Tacoma and other eastern-shore towns, working-class interests, bolstered by some middle-class support, were able to effect nearly total expulsion – and partial expulsion in Seattle – yet it never seemed to have stood a chance in Port Townsend. Perhaps the anti-Chinese working class was silenced – still clinging to its anti-Chinese position; nevertheless, the outcome of the movement locally argues for the importance of development thinking within the community.

The boycott may also have failed simply because of its non-violent nature. The expulsions in other towns succeeded because a critical mass of anti-Chinese agitators supported violence. However, in Port Townsend such violence was stifled in part because concerns about the town's reputation limited the numbers of people willing to effect a violent expulsion. Thus, the failure of expulsion may demonstrate most clearly how development remained an issue with broad community relevance into the late-nineteenth century.

The character of the Chinese community may also have had an effect on Port Townsend's attempted expulsion. According to the *Argus*, in March 1886, when they were ordered to leave, the Port Townsend Chinese declined to do so. Perhaps the leadership of this well-established community – aware of their strong economic position and of Euro-American concerns about preventing violence – preferred to risk staying. There is but the one *Argus* article that gives a clue as to what the Chinese did during the crisis of 1885–86, but there were other incidents in which community leaders and members defended their own and the community members' interests in the face of anti-Chinese thinking. For instance, Mon Yik was willing to defend his friend Ah Dock in court when he was charged with insanity by Mr. Sherlock; Ng Soon and Eng Ting of the Zee Tai Company were willing to stand surety for his good behavior. During congressional debate for the passage of the 1892 Exclusion Act – known as the Geary bill – a *Leader* reporter interviewed leading members of the Port Townsend Chinese community. They did not mince words about what they thought of the Geary bill. "Zee Tai" said he thought the bill was unjust:

> If the Chinese are excluded from the United States I think the Americans will be excluded from China. There is no doubt but that the bill, if it becomes a law, will make trouble between China and this country. I doubt if the Chinese government will be entirely able to protect the Americans who are now in that country.

Ah Ge, another merchant agreed with "Zee Tai," and "Wing Sing" claimed that nothing could stop the hundreds of Chinese immigrating illegally to the United States every day from coming.[132]

An incident involving Chinese laundries and a man suspected of having leprosy, demonstrates not only anti-Chinese thinking but also the outspokenness of one Sam War. In March 1892, when a Chinese resident was discovered to have leprosy, it invoked a great deal of rancor against Chinese laundries. Citing several supposedly verified cases in which Chinese laundries had spread leprosy, the *Leader* said that "the one way to prevent the spread of this disease is to keep clear of Chinese laundries, as you cannot tell but what your clothing may become infected with the germ of this disease while patronizing this class." In the face of a series of editorial comments such as this, Sam War, who had been accused of employing the leper in his laundry, nevertheless wrote to *The Leader* to complain against such maligning of his laundry.[133]

There were numerous other incidents in which Chinese men preferred to settle their differences with Euro-Americans assertively. Some used their fists, but Ah Ham, who had been shoved off the end of a wharf by a "young Napoleon of rowdyism," took his assailant to court. Judge Oliver Wood fined the rowdy $25, and when he spoke rudely to the judge, he was sentenced to twenty days in jail for contempt of court.[134]

Chinese merchants and laundrymen also made a friendly practice of including Euro-Americans in their New Year's celebrations, especially through gift-giving of silk handkerchiefs, china dishes, or potted lilies, all of which furthered positive relations between Chinese and non-Chinese. The merchants also gave coconut candies, sugared ginger root, and lychee nuts to Port Townsend's children during the Chinese New Year.[135]

Such activities argue for significant Chinese pro-activism or resistance in their relations with Port Townsend's non-Chinese.[136] Thus, if development thinking tipped the balance against violent expulsion, the Chinese themselves also influenced the outcome. Their community had a well-developed structure of merchant leadership, which, having been established in the county for many years, stood to lose a great deal if they were forced to leave the area. As well, community members were well entrenched in the county's economy. Thus, leaders' status and prosperity and the economic niche many laborers filled may have provided Chinese leaders and community members with the resolve to stay. Throughout the rest of the 1880s Port Townsend's Chinese community grew in numbers, peaking at 453 in 1890.[137] Its gradual demise in the early twentieth century resulted from economic changes that would affect all Jefferson County residents.

"Times [Got] Worse Instead of Getting Better"[1]:
The End of Frontier Boosterism

Nearly thirty years elapsed between Isaac Stevens' railroad survey and the completion of the Puget Sound's first transcontinental connection, celebrated when Henry Villard hammered the final spike for the Northern Pacific Railroad on September 8, 1883. The connection between Puget Sound and St Paul, Minnesota – via Portland and Tacoma – was followed rapidly by other lines in what would be the greatest period of railroad building in the Pacific Northwest. Of particular importance to Puget Sound was the Northern Pacific's Cascade Division – from the Columbia River through the Yakima valley and across the Cascade Mountains – to Tacoma and Seattle. This line began service in the summer of 1887. In the same year the Southern Pacific completed a line between Portland and San Francisco, which linked the Pacific Northwest with New Orleans. Seattle acquired a connection to the transcontinental Canadian Pacific in 1885, and its own transcontinental connection to St Paul with the completion of the Great Northern Railroad in 1893.[2] Thus, the Pacific Northwest and Puget Sound's "era of isolation" came to an end as the long journey between East and West shrank to a five- or six-day trip.[3] Washington Territory boomed: the population increased – more than tenfold, from 25,000 to 300,000; between 1880 and 1889 the value of real and personal property went from $62,000,000 to $760,000,000, and the assessed valuation of property and value of manufacturing increased tenfold.[4] The territory became a state on

November 11, 1889, as a result of the "great burst of immigration" which followed the 1887 completion of the cross-Cascade line. [5] Washington's long frontier period was drawing to a close.

"CHICAGO WILL BE ASHAMED:" BOOM IN
JEFFERSON COUNTY[6]

Following the completion of the transcontinental railroads, most of the new arrivals to Puget Sound were absorbed by the east side of Puget Sound, especially by Seattle and Tacoma,[7] which quickly "solidified [their recently] won stature as [Western Washington's] dominant urban areas."[8] However, Jefferson County's population grew as well – between 1880 and 1890 from 1,712 to 8,368 – and residents continued to be optimistic about the county's future.[9] Port Townsend continued as Port of Entry to Puget Sound, and throughout the 1880s commercial opportunities for Port Townsendites increased as the shipping industry grew. In 1885, 582 cargoes of lumber, coal, and wheat – totalling 456,134 tons – were exported from Puget Sound, more than ever before. Other exported goods were canned salmon, large shipments of oats, and other "products of the surrounding country."[10] During the 12 months ending June 1, 1888, the number of vessels entering Puget Sound through the port of entry was 971, tonnage 834,104, and 954 vessels, tonnage 804,853 leaving.[11] In 1890 there were 430 cargoes of lumber – 120,000,000 board feet – and during the 12 months ending June 30, 1890, 2,598 vessels entered Juan de Fuca Strait and Puget Sound. The reader will recall for comparison's sake that in 1858 there were approximately twenty sailing vessels that averaged six trips a year each in and out of Puget Sound.[12]

In general, the 1880s were a prosperous decade for Puget Sound lumbering,[13] and Jefferson County's lumber industry expanded. Amos Phinney, owner of the Port Ludlow mill, had died in 1877; however, the Puget Mill Company purchased the mill in November 1878, making improvements and increasing the mill's capacity. It reopened October 18, 1883.[14] The Port Discovery mill had likewise changed hands due to the deaths of its first owners, S.L. and Levy

Mastick. Here again, the new owners, Moore and Smith of San Francisco, made improvements and increased the mill's capacity.[15] By way of comparison, between June 1859 and January 1860, the Port Discovery mill had shipped 2,420,716 feet of lumber and 7,000 feet of piles. In 1885, the mill shipped 28,000,000 feet of lumber, 10,000,000 laths, 215,000 feet of piles, and 200,000 feet of pickets.[16]

Further, the Western Mill and Lumber Company constructed a new mill at Port Hadlock. It was completed in June 1886, and a party of seventy people, which included James Swan, the mayor of Port Townsend, and the city council, travelled to Port Hadlock by steamer to watch the machinery put into operation. On July 15, Swan dined with J. Kennedy, the mill superintendent, and then joined approximately 200 other county residents to see and celebrate the first logs milled into lumber. This event featured band music, and was described by Swan as "a most memorable event for Port Townsend. Everybody was delighted and the day will be long remembered."[17] The mill was then purchased by the Washington Mill Company, whose Seabeck mill had burned to the ground in August 1886. Their operations began in Hadlock in October.[18]

Over time, the county press had called for the establishment of a sawmill in Port Townsend,[19] and in 1881, "the people of Port Townsend formed a stock company and raised about $20,000" to establish the Port Townsend Mill Company. While it did not rival the larger cargo mills – it employed about approximately thirty men in this period, while the other county mills employed 100 or more each – it was a going concern during Port Townsend's 1880s building boom.[20]

County residents were encouraged not only by the new county sawmills and the iron mill at Irondale – at the time the largest on the West Coast[21] – but by other smaller manufacturing firms: a sash and door factory, a foundry, several machine shops, a brewery, a cigar factory, and brick works which were located in Port Townsend. Port Townsend's first bank, the First National Bank of Port Townsend, was established in 1883. It initially capitalized with $50,000, which increased to $75,000 in 1885. By December 1889, during the real estate boom, its deposits on hand were $403,617.22. Commented one observer: "its large and substantial stone building indicates a healthy and solid business basis."[22]

The face of Port Townsend had begun to change, as stone and brick buildings replaced wood frame storefronts, and new homes were built uptown. Although Port Townsend's building boom did not peak until 1889–91, nineteen new commercial buildings, several wharves, and eleven homes were built in 1885, at a total cost of $66,700. Repairs and improvements to existing buildings totalled $75,000. There was also a new waterworks, a telephone exchange, a new school building "erected on the latest improved plans" and run by a principal and four teachers – "for common school training our facilities are the best"[23] – and "three street railways were running to full capacity."[24]

Optimistic promotion of county development continued. The *Argus* printed portions of a promotional address given by territorial governor Watson Squires in which he described Jefferson County as "one of the most important counties in the whole territory." Port Townsend, "one of the leading towns on Puget Sound," was also "one of the healthiest, prettiest and most prosperous towns in the Territory." Said the governor, its spacious, "beautiful bay [was] neither too deep or too shallow [with] room for the entire navy and merchant marine of the United States to ride in safety at the same time ... the immense maritime business transacted here ... brings an excessive local trade with shipping." It was also a "natural center of trade and travel, having mail routes and lines of travel radiating in all directions." Port Townsend was "located just inside of the line of fortification proposed for the defense of [Washington's] inland waters";[25] the area's increasing military importance would add to its commercial prosperity.

Squires pointed to the recent construction of "magnificent brick and stone buildings, indicating a solidity and stability seldom noticed among the young and growing towns of the west ... fine public schools, her opera house, her four churches, all indicate intellectual culture and literary privileges." All of which, he said, "bespeak a city here in the near future, teeming with a hardy, industrious people and buzzing with manufacturing industries."[26]

Such rhetoric aside, the county's economy *was* expanding, and residents had cause to be hopeful that such expansion would continue. In December 1887, the Seattle *Post-Intelligencer* reported that there had been more business transactions, especially in real estate, in Jefferson County than "in any previous year, not excepting the railroad boom experienced in 1870–71." The influx of new settlers made it difficult to find a place to live, and rents were especially high in Port Townsend. "Outside capital and the investments thereof" were responsible for rising real estate prices, and soon outside investments in business "will be brought into prominence." According to the *Post-Intelligencer*, "the old pioneers are regarding the [situation], especially in the port of entry [Port Townsend] as the dawn of a new era of prosperity for the commercial centre of the lower Sound."[27]

County boosters, however, were interested in Port Townsend becoming more than the "commercial center of the lower Sound." Still dreaming of "great cities," they sought to effect the long-sought connection to one of the transcontinentals – if not the Northern Pacific, then the Union Pacific. On August 19, 1887, a group of county residents joined together to incorporate the Port Townsend Southern Railroad Company.[28] Their purpose: to start construction of a railroad from Port Townsend south through Quilcene and along Hood Canal to Olympia, but more importantly, to attract outside capital to the venture.[29] In doing so, they joined other Puget Sound towns in an intensifying interest in building small railroads designed to connect Puget Sound towns to one or the other of the transcontinentals – interest which resulted in the construction of more Washington railroads during the 1880s than in any other period. Certainly in Jefferson County, boosters had decided that this was the time to make another determined bid for a connection to a transcontinental railroad,[30] and they hoped to "see a city here [in Port Townsend] that will make Chicago ashamed of herself." The enthusiasm of the original PT Southern Railroad stockholders was matched throughout the county as land for the right of way to Quilcene and along Hood Canal was acquired through subscriptions from local property owners.[31]

While the company sought funds locally to begin construction, they knew that they would need to interest "outside capital" in the venture. James Swan travelled to New England in 1888 to deliver to Charles Francis Adams, president of Union Pacific, a chart and detailed report that listed the advantages of a line running west of Puget Sound with Port Townsend as its terminus. Encouraged by Adams'

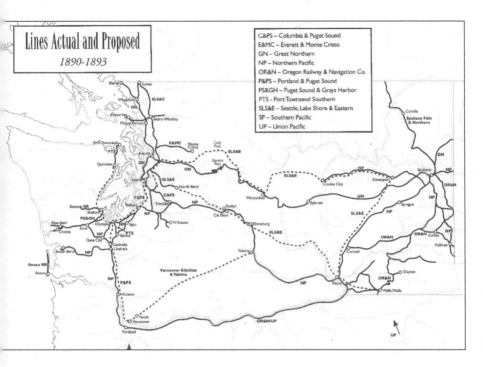

Lines Actual and Proposed 1890-1893	C&PS – Columbia & Puget Sound E&MC – Everett & Monte Cristo GN – Great Northern NP – Northern Pacific OR&N – Oregon Railway & Navigation Co. P&PS – Portland & Puget Sound PS&GH – Puget Sound & Grays Harbor PTS - Port Townsend Southern SLS&E – Seattle, Lake Shore & Eastern SP – Southern Pacific UP – Union Pacific

6.1

Railroad lines actual and proposed, 1890–1893.

(Washington State University Press)

response, Swan wrote in July to J.A. Kuhn, president of the Port Townsend Southern. He reported that Adams said he was "'much obliged ... for the information ... I shall go next month to Portland and Port Townsend and when I am there I will study up the whole question'."[32]

By the end of the year, however, nothing had come of efforts by Swan and others to secure outside backing.[33] According to McCurdy, "a number of railroad men drifted into town from time to time, but no definite tie-up resulted."[34] The, by now desperate Port Townsend Southern trustees decided to seize the bull by the horns: on March 23, 1889, they called for bids to lay the first six miles of track. Local builders who won the bid understood that as soon as funds became low, the work would stop. A ground-breaking ceremony was held two miles west of Port Townsend on property owned by Albert

Briggs, one of the original donation land claimants. Briggs turned the first spadeful of dirt, and Ben Pettygrove and Ben Hammond – sons of town founders, Francis Pettygrove and T.M. Hammond – each plowed a few furrows. Notwithstanding the great interest in the project – as demonstrated by a photograph taken of the crowds of people at the groundbreaking event – the track was extended only a mile before funds gave out.[35]

Then, on July 31, 1889, an agent of the Union Pacific approached the Port Townsend Southern trustees. He proposed that the Oregon Improvement Company, a subsidiary of Union Pacific, would construct a railroad from Port Townsend, via Quilcene, along the west side of Hood Canal, from whence it would connect with a transcontinental line. The Port Townsend Southern was asked to assign all its rights of way to the Oregon Improvement Company and raise and give $100,000 to Oregon Improvement. At a public meeting on February 18, 1890, the Port Townsend Southern agreed to the proposal, and the $100,00 for the OIC was raised locally through subscriptions from county residents ranging from as little as $50 to as much as $6,000.[36] The transaction was finalized on March 15, 1890. The company retained its original name, the Port Townsend Southern Railroad.

By May, there was a large workforce engaged in construction, and by September about one-half of the 26.2 miles between Port Townsend and Quilcene was covered by track and in operation servicing the construction crews. In the meantime, the Oregon Improvement Company had purchased a fifteen-mile line that ran from Olympia to Tenino on the Northern Pacific line. Its narrow gauge track was converted to standard gauge, and the new company operated it as the Southern Division of the Port Townsend Southern – the line from Port Townsend to Quilcene was the Northern Division.

Nevertheless, by September 1890, over seventy miles still separated the two divisions, and construction had stalled. The Oregon Improvement Company also owned a line near Anacortes, Washington, which – according to McCurdy – was receiving the company's attention to the exclusion of the Port Townsend Southern's best interests. "The speculation bug had caught the officials ... and they had become more intent upon selling land than in building railroads."

6.2
Dedication of the Port Townsend Southern Railroad, March 23, 1889.
(Jefferson County Historical Society)

The county had been booming, but local growth began to slow down.
The real estate boom had preceded the Port Townsend Southern venture, but it gathered momentum with the possibility of a transcontinental railroad connection. By summer 1889, the town's population
was over 7,000, and there was a record high of 2,209 county real
estate transfers for 1890, valued at $4,594,695.93.[37] However, when
railroad construction came to a halt, real estate sales slowed down,
although residents continued to be hopeful.

In any case, there were growing rumours that the Union Pacific and
the Oregon Improvement Company were having financial troubles,[38]
which proved to be true. On November 25, 1890, the Oregon Improvement Company went into receivership, never to recover its financial equilibrium.[39] For several months county residents maintained
some optimism. C.J. Smith, general manager of the Oregon Improvement Company, periodically issued encouraging statements, promising
that when the track was completed to Quilcene, ferries would trans-

TERMINAL DOCKS AND WAREHOUSES PORT TOWNSEND SOUTHERN RAILROAD.

6.3
Drawing of Port Townsend Southern Railroad: Terminal Docks
and Warehouses. (Jefferson County Historical Society)

port freight and passengers across Hood Canal from Quilcene to
Union City, where docks and further lines would be built.⁴⁰

On February 23, 1891, the line to Quilcene was completed, and
residents' hopes there were revitalized. The *Quilcene Queen* wrote,
"there is a time coming, and that within a very few months, when
the value of property will double in Quilcene ... there is no power we
know of that can prevent this place from becoming a large and thrifty
city of several thousand inhabitants." Also, aside from "superior advantages for manufacturing ... the vast farming territory ... tributary
to this place ... will alone build up a large town."⁴¹

When nationwide customs statistics were released for the first
quarter of 1891, the *Leader* wrote that the report was "such as to
rouse the drooping spirits of those whom dull times have tended to
discourage." In this quarter, more vessels had entered and cleared
from the Puget Sound port of entry than anywhere else, "not excepting New York, which so long headed the list." Three hundred and

forty-nine vessels had cleared from Port Townsend, 232 cleared from New York; entering Port Townsend, 320; and 248 entering New York. The *Leader* prophesied that the next quarter's report would show Port Townsend still in the lead, since "there has been a large increase in the shipping since then." Port Townsend was and would hopefully continue to be the New York of the West, said the editor.[42]

Promotional efforts continued. In June 1891 Swan wrote a pamphlet for the recently established Port Townsend Chamber of Commerce,[43] 5,000 copies of which were printed for distribution. It set out in meticulous detail hoped-for plans by which the Union Pacific and Northern Pacific railroads would develop and expand their operations to include Port Townsend. According to Swan, the Union Pacific was going to make Port Townsend "their great wheat shipping point." The company also intended to develop the fisheries of the North Pacific and Puget Sound, in order to ship fresh fish such as halibut, cod, salmon, etc., in refrigerator cars to the rest of the United States from Port Townsend. The North Pacific whaling fleet would then also be serviced from Port Townsend rather than San Francisco.

Swan wrote that the Pacific Mail Steamship Company of San Francisco would also headquarter steamers engaged in the "China and East India trade" at Port Townsend once the railroad connection was completed. Further, he said the Northern Pacific Railroad was known to have surveyed a route from Tacoma to Port Townsend whereby railroad cars would travel by a combination of track by land and ferry boats over the intervening bodies of water – Point Defiance Narrows and Hood Canal – to reach Irondale where it would connect with the Port Townsend Southern Railroad. Swan also claimed that the Canadian Pacific Railroad was willing to establish a steamer route to Port Townsend once the transcontinental line was completed. In this way, immigrants who came west on the Canadian Pacific would be able to settle "along Hood canal and to the Chehalis river district ... Dungeness, Port Angeles, Quilleute and other places along Fuca strait and the interior" of the Olympic Peninsula.

Swan argued that because all railroads approaching Puget Sound came from the east, "it is but a logical conclusion that the cities on the eastern side of the Sound, being first reached, would be the first to be developed and built." However, he reasoned, "when speculating employees of various railroad companies shall have unloaded the wild cat lands on the eastern shores of Puget sound which they are fast doing, they will be willing and zealous to tell the truth about Port Townsend and announce the fact, already well known here, that these very railroad companies will build [here] the largest city on the Pacific Coast."[44]

Swan continued his efforts to catch the interests of a railroad company in creating this "largest city on the Pacific Coast" on Port Townsend Bay. In August 1896 he wrote the Northern Pacific directors; and in June 1899 he wrote Charles Francis Adams and James J. Hill of the Great Northern Railway trying to draw their attention to Jefferson County. He received polite refusals.[45] Swan's "long-cherished hope of being able to board a train in Port Townsend and ride to Boston to see his children" was not to be.[46]

THE END OF FRONTIER BOOSTERISM

Swan's determined optimism had been misplaced. By 1891 Jefferson County's "boom" was coming to a close. Once the Oregon Improvement Company went into receivership, the real estate market in Port Townsend declined and collapsed. The town's population dropped from 7,000 to 2,000, and most of the boom land sales were defaulted upon, the property returning to the original owner or going to the county for back taxes.[47] For example, James Swan, who owned acreage just outside Port Townsend, had sold it in the spring of 1890 to T.J. Pearce for $100,000, payable in six months. In a common tale, the sale was never finalized, and the property reverted to Swan, who had difficulty paying the taxes. When he died in 1900, there was a claim of more than $2,000 against the property, and his executor was unable to sell it even for its appraised value of $352.[48]

The financial institutions of which county residents had been so proud suffered as well. In October 1889 there had been five banks in Port Townsend – First National Bank, Merchants Bank, Sisley and Bell, Jarvis-Conklin Mortgage and Trust Company, and Puget Sound Loan and Investment Company.[49] However, in the real estate crash,

three of the banks "passed out of existence," and deposits in the First
National Bank went from the December 1889 high of $403,617.22
to $48,000.[50]

Other facets of the county's economy were in trouble as well. The
Puget Sound Iron Company at Irondale had closed down in 1889.[51]
More importantly, by 1890 the lumber industry also faced hard
times. The 1880s had been a period of prosperity such as the cargo
mills "had not known since the days of the Gold Rush." A large part
of this 1880s lumber boom had been the business generated by Pacific
Rim markets in Southern California, Australia, and Chile. However,
these markets were down by 1890, as was the market provided by
Pacific Northwest railroad construction. In Jefferson County, the Port
Discovery mill closed for good in the spring of 1891,[52] and the whole
lumber industry was retrenching when the Depression of 1893–97
thrust it into "a desperate struggle for survival."[53]

The troubles in the lumber industry necessarily affected shipping
as well, and the depression brought it almost to a standstill. James
Griffiths, a shipping agent in Port Townsend from 1885 to 1898, remembered that "the years 1893 and 1894 were the most trying in
our business experience. The U.S. financial panic of 1893 caused endless failures, and Banks all over the country closed, also 80% of the
mills on Puget Sound were shut down."[54]

By the time the depression began to recede in 1897, both the
lumber and shipping industries had changed in ways that drastically
affected Jefferson County's economy and prospects of further development.[55] By 1905, Washington led the nation in the production of
lumber.[56] However, the Puget Sound cargo industry that had been
dominated by westside lumber mills was no longer viable. San Francisco had been the "heart" of the cargo industry, but by 1897 the
lumber needs of the city and its hinterlands were often met locally
or by southern Oregon lumber companies who were able to ship
lumber to California on the Southern Pacific Railroad.[57] Foreign
markets remained, and indeed, they kept the cargo industry alive in
the late 1890s and early 1900s, including the Washington Mill Company in Port Hadlock and the Puget Mill Company at Port Ludlow
and Port Gamble.[58]

However, the development of eastern markets in the interior of the United States – serviced by the transcontinental railroads – accounted for most of the phenomenal growth in the Washington lumber industry. By 1906 the rail trade was taking as much lumber as the cargo trade. A few of the old cargo mills were situated to take advantage of the rail trade while continuing to participate in the cargo trade – for instance, the Tacoma Mill Company and the Perry mill at Cosmopolis on Grays Harbor. However, the westside Puget Sound cargo mills were unable to do this, since they had no ready access to the railroads.[59] Also, technological changes in both milling and shipping lumber made competitive modernization very expensive for the older cargo mills; even as early as 1891, such costs were part of what drove the Port Discovery Mill out of business.[60]

Thus, "the old cargo trade ... d[ied]."[61] In Jefferson County, once so central to the Puget Sound lumber industry, only one mill remained in operation after the Washington Mill Company closed in 1908.[62] The Port Ludlow mill continued to mill lumber off and on until 1938, and logging has continued in importance to this day. However, the demise of the cargo industry nearly destroyed Jefferson County's industrial base for years to come.

By the end of the depression, accumulated changes in the shipping industry affected Jefferson County as well, and Port Townsend's important role as a shipping center disappeared. During the 1890s steamships began to replace sailing vessels in Puget Sound shipping, and while abandonment of sailing vessels was gradual,[63] the advent of change lessened Port Townsend's key position in the shipping industry. The prevailing winds made it difficult for sailing vessels to manoeuver once they sailed into Admiralty Inlet, and there were few harbors past the inlet that could "be approached by sailing vessels without having to resort to towing very frequently during the year."[64] This fact had created an advantage for Port Townsend when most shipping was carried on sailing vessels. But the steamships cruised past Port Townsend.

In 1899, Puget Mill Company executive Edwin Ames wrote that "a great deal of shipping goes by Port Townsend, going direct to Seattle or Tacoma, the sub-ports of entry, and making a direct entry or clearance ... at those ports. As a result, where there used to be from ten to twenty ships at anchor [in Port Townsend,] there are seldom more than one or two, and oftentimes [*sic*] none at all."[65] Ames said that a Port Townsend shipping agent estimated that as little as one-fourth of Puget Sound shipping stopped at Port Townsend by 1899, and he characterized it as a "very dead town."[66]

While Port Townsend declined, Seattle and Tacoma continued to grow. In 1910 when Jefferson County's entire population had fallen to 8,337, Seattle's had grown to 237,194; Tacoma's was 83,743.[67] As Seattle and Tacoma grew into large manufacturing cities and shipping centers, they demanded and received sub-ports of entry.[68] No longer the key to Puget Sound shipping, its viability as a shipping center was gone; Port Townsend lost the Customs Port of Entry in 1911.

Further, although the iron and steel industry was revived at Irondale between 1901–04 and 1907–13, its operation was sporadic and ultimately unsuccessful, unable to compete with iron and steel products sent to western markets from the east.[69] The construction between 1898 and 1902 of Fort Worden, Fort Flagler, and Fort Casey brought a fleeting advantage to Port Townsend; and while in operation Fort Worden and Fort Flagler provided some economic benefit.[70] Fish and vegetable and fruit canneries brought employment as well; and the First World War was a period of some little prosperity.[71]

The war, however, was followed by an economic downturn that was "intensified" when the Port Townsend lumber mill and the fruit and vegetable cannery failed. It was not until 1927 – when "the future looked the darkest"[72] – that the National Paper Products Company built a pulp and paper mill on the site of Albert Briggs' homestead, and Jefferson County could lay claim to any significant industry in the county beyond the Port Ludlow mill and logging.[73] Thus, in the words of one local historian, "after being jilted at the church door again and again, Port Townsend finally made it to the altar in 1927." A paper mill was a far cry from great-city status, but it was better than nothing.[74]

EPILOGUE

Thus, Jefferson County settled into rural obscurity. Several factors in the 1890s brought an end to the hopeful boosterism of the frontier period: the last, failed attempt at securing a connection to one of the transcontinental railroads and the real estate crash in 1891; the take-off of the "railroad" lumber industry on the east side of Puget Sound and the demise of the "cargo" lumber industry; the impact of steam on Port Townsend's pre-eminence in the shipping industry; and the economic devastation of the depression of 1893–96. As "times [got] worse instead of getting better," residents' ambitions for significant development in the county dwindled and eventually disappeared.[75] A loser in the rivalry for great-city status, no longer an essential player in either the lumber or shipping industries, its population in decline, Jefferson County could no longer inspire any hopes of greatness.

How different this was from the dreams of those early settlers who had been drawn to the county because of its prospects in lumber, shipping, and other businesses. Optimistic about western development, confident in their assumptions that the land would and should provide them with economic opportunity, they attached their own desires for prosperity to the perceived economic potential of Jefferson County. They believed that more immigrants would come and Port Townsend would link the wealth of Asia by sea and rail to the eastern United States and Europe. Natural resources, manufactured goods, and agricultural products would flow from county hinterlands, towns, and mill ports – and beyond – to the rest of the world. Their own security assured by the county's economy, residents dreamed that they would be able to lead prosperous, happy lives. These were high stakes, making economic development an important community issue, one sought or worked for by many county residents.

Many names stand out as active boosters for Jefferson County: Isaac Stevens, territorial governor, who first proposed a railroad terminus for Jefferson County and inspired James Swan's move to Port Townsend; Lafayette Balch, sea captain, who like Stevens and Swan, predicted commercial importance for Jefferson County; H.C. Wilson, who brought the Port of Entry to Port Townsend; Francis Pettygrove,

Loran Hastings, Alfred Plummer, T.M. Hammond, and Albert Briggs, donation land claimants and town-builders; Travers Daniel, John Damon, Al Pettygrove, H.C. Blanchard, Frank Meyers, and Allen Weir, newspaper editors; D.W. Smith, president of the Immigration Aid Society; and last but not least, James Swan. While not all county residents worked as hard at development as those mentioned above, nevertheless, many were boosters in that they identified their own economic prospects – as shipping agents, shopkeepers, and saloon keepers, as loggers and farmers, as mill workers and other laborers who were often small producers, as shipbuilders and other craftsmen – with the county's economic prospects. Direct interest in development can be seen not only through the large-scale county development projects devised and financed by county residents – and the perceived individual economic opportunities stemming from them – but in the many letters about development concerns to local newspaper editors over the years; in the continued support for those very development-focussed newspapers; in the small and large local investments of money and land made in significant industrial development by residents (especially the Port Townsend Mill and Port Townsend Southern Railroad); in the demand of local landholders that the iron ore taken from their property be milled locally; in the gatherings of local residents to celebrate breaking ground for the Port Townsend Southern railroad or the first lumber milled at a new sawmill, and so on.

Concern for development can be seen as expressed in less direct ways as well: the tension surrounding county development and reputation throughout the nineteenth century; certain aspects of relations between Euro-American settlers, resident Native Americans, and Chinese immigrants; the course of the Chinese Expulsion Movement in Port Townsend. All suggest the importance of development to the culture of this "commercial place."[76] During the early settlement period, concerns about the county's wild reputation became closely linked to development thinking; and throughout the rest of the nineteenth century, reputation, because it was perceived to have an influence on county development, remained an important community issue. Not only was it essential to promote county development, it was also necessary to establish an image in the public mind of Jefferson

County as a community of law-abiding, orderly, industrious, sober men and women. Development and reputation were key reference points in public discourse in other ways. For instance, during "the great Port Townsend controversy," the town's reputation was bound up with that of the S'Klallam, and many of the settlers defended S'Klallam reputation along with their own. Relations between settlers and S'Klallam were also influenced at times by the frequent dovetailing of the two groups' economic agendas. Similarly, the struggle over Victor Smith's campaign to remove the Port of Entry to Port Angeles was motivated by imperatives of development. Further, because Victor Smith reiterated J. Ross Browne's interpretive view of Port Townsend as a battle tactic, reputation was an important element in that conflict.

Although economic interests and reputation were integral aspects of county development, there was unavoidable tension between the two concerns. County residents sought to project a image of respectability to the outside world. Many county features were perceived to be disreputable, yet drinking, vice, and violence were inevitable accompaniments to Port Townsend's highly desirable position as a shipping center. On a lesser scale, this was true of the mill ports, too. Over the years there were many calls to clean up the county, but county residents made compromises over what many saw as moral issues. In the end, it was better to control drinking and vice through licensing supposedly respectable saloonkeepers, and through camouflaging as much as possible other more disreputable activities. Because Port Townsend's downtown was considered disreputable but necessary, respectable Port Townsendites created a haven for themselves uptown, building homes, schools, churches, and retail shops on the plateau that overlooked downtown. The escape to uptown of respectable working-class and middle-class residents reinforced the softening of economic-based class divisions associated with development thinking and is therefore representative of the development culture.

Some residents thought that certain groups of people jeopardized the county's reputation and potential development. For instance, over the years there were demands to force the S'Klallam to move to their reservation, or at least outside the city limits. However, such ideas stumbled against the economic role played by the S'Klallam, their connection with the county's reputation, and their own refusal to leave the county. If some residents thought the S'Klallam pulled the county's reputation down, others were inclined to defend them. Further, the act of removal itself could be seen as a potential danger to the county's reputation. This was also true when anti-Chinese activists sought to remove the Chinese from Port Townsend during the winter of 1885–86. Caught up in the Puget Sound expulsions, a movement based upon a mixture of racism and conflict over jobs, some Port Townsendites called for expulsion, and in 1886 there was an organized effort to expel Port Townsend Chinese. An important aspect of local anti-Chinese rhetoric was the idea that the supposedly disreputable Chinese threatened the county's reputation and, hence, its economic development. However, the force of the expulsion movement in the county was mitigated by fears that a violent expulsion of itself would damage that self-same reputation; hence, an economic boycott – meant to effect expulsion non-violently – was instituted. When it failed, expulsion became a dead issue.

The cause and culture of development in nineteenth-century Jefferson County did not survive the debacle of the Port Townsend Southern Railroad and the Oregon Improvement Company episode, the economic downturns and depression of the 1890s, the changes in the lumber and shipping industries, and the obvious pre-eminence acquired by Seattle by 1900. Notwithstanding these specific factors, however, it was unlikely that the county's ambitions would have come to fruition. Ironically, the completion of the Northern Pacific railroad – which, beginning with Isaac Stevens and James Swan, had been perceived as essential to Port Townsend's development as a great city – destroyed any possibility that the town would become a metropolis. During the early settlement period, most settlers arrived on Puget Sound by ship. Coming into Puget Sound from the Pacific Ocean, many of the early lumbermen and other settlers, drawn by the safe harbors and extensive forests of the western Puget Sound shoreline, perceived those shores as the primary site for future development. However, when the transcontinental connections were completed to the east side, they brought thousands and thousands more settlers and investors to that area. The ever-increasing population and economic development of the east side of Puget Sound – especially, the railroad lumber industry – soon overshadowed development on the west side.

Further, Jefferson County's development culture was shaped by frontier thinking about economic growth. Arguably, only on the frontier, perceived by settlers to be undeveloped, could such boundless optimism exist. Once significant development occurred and the frontier closed, such thinking changed, becoming more practical and far less expansive. Indeed, as pointed out by historian Earl Pomeroy, attitudes about development throughout the Far West changed dramatically between the frontier period (up to the 1890s) and the twentieth century. By the turn of the century, "expectations of development [were] lowered." Yet, in the earlier period settlers had believed that development would provide them with significant individual economic rewards.[77] Thus, as the century turned, and the frontier closed, dreams faded away not only in Jefferson County, but elsewhere as well.

Ironically, ideas about Port Townsend's reputation shifted as boosterism declined. In 1937, when James McCurdy wrote *By Juan de Fuca's Strait*, he celebrated the settlers for their "big hearts and broad sympathies ... rugged, fearless nature ... achievements and successes ... the culture and refinement found prevailing in the homes of the pioneers." But he also took delight in recounting that "it was a common saying that the odour of whiskey permeated the soil along Water Street [the main street downtown] to a depth of ten feet." Of its struggles to appear respectable, McCurdy says nothing. His writing fits within a regional literature of pioneer reminiscences that is inclined to emphasize the challenges and danger of the settlement period.[78] However, the tendency to find the disreputable elements of the county's past more interesting and worthy of note than townspeople's desire to be considered respectable has continued. Since the latter part of the twentieth century, Port Townsend has been a popular tourist destination point, and its surviving Victorian architecture and the beauty of the surrounding land and seascapes draw many visitors each year. In recent years, Port Townsend guides have taken tourists on an evening round of once-disreputable sites in the old downtown and present-day night spots located in still-standing nineteenth-century buildings; thus, participants can vicariously experience rough, frontier Port Townsend. Another example of the proclivity to romanticize disreputableness was an exhibition at the Jefferson County Historical Society museum. Entitled "Bars and Bordellos," it highlighted drinking, gambling, brawls, and prostitution.[79] The exhibit certainly would have displeased Swan, but Browne would have felt quite vindicated.

Statistical Information

Table 1. Port Townsend: 1860 and 1870

	1860[1]	1870[2]
Shipping-related occupations[3]	114	190
Farmers and farm laborers	36[4]	20[5]
Women	39	85
Children	85	160
Professionals	11	18
Laborers	–	19
Craftsmen	13	38
Construction	16	15
Miscellaneous	25	49[6]
Total	339	594

1 Total population: 339. All figures from United States Census, Federal Population Census Schedules, Jefferson County, Washington Territory, 1860, National Archives.

2 Total: 594. United States Census, Federal Population Census Schedules, Jefferson County, Washington Territory, 1870.

3 Includes merchants and their clerks, bakers, butchers, hotel and saloon-keepers, stewards and cooks, boatbuilders, boatmen, sailors, sea captains.

4 For the 1860 Census this figure includes the Chimacum Creek valley, which was the principal farming area of the county.

5 The 1870 Census does not include Chimacum, which in 1870 included
  38 farmers and farm laborers.
6 Includes 28 British Columbia Indians who were camped on the beach
  and 8 household servants.

Table 2. Port Ludlow and Port Discovery: 1860 and 1870

PORT LUDLOW	1860	1870
Lumber	86	79
Maritime	7	63[1]
Shipbuilding	14	–[2]
Native Americans (B.C.)	–	38[3]
Women	5	25
Children	5	35
Farmers and Farm Laborers	1	–
Miscellaneous	6	14
Total	124	254

PORT DISCOVERY	1860	1870
Lumber	51	72
Maritime	7	21
Shipbuilding	–	–
Native Americans (B.C.)	–	–
Women	1	14
Children	–	17
Farmers and Farm Laborers	10	3
Miscellaneous	–	25[4]
Total	69	152

1 This census included 6 ships in port.
2 It would appear that there was a lapse in shipbuilding at the time of the
  census. The ship carpenters in the census would appear to be mariners,
  and there are no ship joiners or shipwrights listed. However, this was a
  state which did not last. Hall Bros. began operating their shipyard there
  in 1874.

3 There were 17 Haida men listed in this census for Port Ludlow. Some of them may have been millworkers.

4 Includes 7 laborers.

Table 3. Quilcene: 1870

Lumbermen[1]	70
Farmers[2]	9
Women	14
Children	30
Other[3]	6
Total[4]	129

1 This figure includes: resident lumbermen: 12, camp cooks: 8, and men working in the logging camps: 50.

2 Farmers often worked in the woods as well.

3 Fishermen: 4, Shoemaker: 1, Merchant: 1.

4 1870 Manuscript Census for Quilcene.

INTRODUCTION

1 In this work, the term frontier refers to a place, but also the process by which diverse peoples come together, often in conflict, but nevertheless engaged in the creation of new societies. For discussion of this often controversial term, see Gitlin, Berglund, and Arenson, "Introduction," 3, 210n7; Hine and Faragher, *Frontiers*, 5–6; *Port Townsend Leader* (hereinafter cited as *Leader*), Mar. 5, 1891

2 Ibid., Feb. 19, 1891.

3 Ibid., Mar. 5, 1891

4 Ibid., Mar. 2, 1891.

5 Ibid., Mar. 5, 1891.

6 Ibid.

7 Hamer, *New Towns in the New World*, 7.

8 There had been earlier frontier boosters. See Bartlett, *The New Country*, 401–5; Reps, *The Making of Urban America*, 349–60; Taylor, *William Cooper's Town*; Wrobel, *Promised Lands*, 4–5, n. 10–14, 202–3.

9 Glaab, "Jesup W. Scott and a West of Cities," 3, 6. According to William Cronon, "although Jesup W. Scott and William Gilpin were better known than most who wrote about urban growth in the West, no one person could claim authorship of the booster

theories themselves, which quickly became the common intellectual property of speculators, newspaper editors, merchants, and
chambers of commerce throughout the West" (Cronon, *Nature's
Metropolis*, 34); Hamer, *New Towns in the New World*, 40–3.
Ideas about urban frontier development have been promulgated
on many frontiers. See Hamer for a comparative treatment of
urban frontier development and boostering in Australia, New
Zealand, Canada, and the United States. See also Owram, *Promise of Eden*; Stelter and Artibise, *Shaping the Urban Landscape*.

10 Cronon, *Nature's Metropolis*, 34. See also Hamer, *New Towns in
the New World*, 1–2. For a global analysis of such thinking, see
Weaver, *The Great Land Rush*, 3–43.

11 See Cronon, *Nature's Metropolis*, especially the section, "Booster
Dreams" (31–41), in

12 Ibid., 46; Wrobel, *Promised Lands*; Worster, *Dust Bowl*, 7. See
Steinberg, *Down to Earth*, for a history of how since 1790,
Americans have "harness[ed] the natural world into an instru-
ment of economic gain"(57).

13 Earl Pomeroy points to a shift in Far Westerners' attitudes towards development between the frontier period (up to the 1890s),
as opposed to the twentieth century. He notes that by the turn of
the century westerners looked for less from development. Yet, in
the earlier period settlers had believed that development would
provide them with significant individual economic rewards
(Pomeroy, *The American Far West*, 14–19).

14 See Henry Nash Smith's discussion of Thomas Jefferson's interest
in this topic as well as discussion of the significance of a passage
to India in expansionist thinking. (Henry Nash Smith, *Virgin
Land*, 15–51).

15 Ibid., 36; Richards, *Isaac I. Stevens*, 47; Chambers, *Old Bullion
Benton*, 83–7.

16 Brown, "Asa Whitney," 209–24, 211; Schwantes, *The Pacific
Northwest*, 171, 173. For a discussion of the planning of the first
transcontinental railroad, see Meinig, *The Shaping of America*, 4–
19. See also, Schwantes and Ronda, *The West the Railroads Made*.

17 Goetzmann, *New Lands, New Men*, 169, 285.

18 For a discussion of the importance of Pacific ports to nineteenth-

century expansionism, see Graebner, *Empire on the Pacific*, v–vii, 2–9, 22–42, 123–49, quotation, 105.

19 Cronon, *Nature's Metropolis*, 398–9, n. 79.

20 Wrobel, *Promised Lands*. 2; Cronon, *Nature's Metropolis*, 36–41, quotation, 36; Abbott, *Boosters and Businessmen*.

21 Glaab, "Jesup W. Scott and a West of Cities," 12; Scott, "Our Cities – Atlantic and Interior," 383, quoted in Glaab, 7.

22 Abbott, *Boosters and Businessmen*, 112–25; Cronon, *Nature's Metropolis*, 34; Morrissey, *Mental Territories*, 62–3; Wrobel, *Promised Lands*, 58.

23 White, *"It's Your Misfortune: and None of My Own": A History of the American West*, 209, 181–211. See also Limerick, "Haunted by Rhyolite," 18–39.

24 Hamer, *New Towns in the New World*, 40–64.

25 Ibid., 40–1, 52–3.

26 Wrobel, *Promised Lands*, 2–3, quotation, 2; Hamer, *New Towns in the New World*, 41. Schwantes writes that in the Pacific Northwest, "state and territorial governments ... let [others] advertis[e] the region's resources" (*The Pacific Northwest*, 227). Post-frontier promotion was more likely to be institutionalized, carried out by the Chambers of Commerce, which proliferated in the 1890s and early twentieth century (Pomeroy, *The American Far West*, 16–17).

27 Frederick Jackson Turner, *The Frontier in American History*, 11–22, 30–2. See Findlay, "Closing the Frontier in Washington," 59–69, and Cronon, *Nature's Metropolis*, 46–54, for discussions of how Turner's rural frontier differed from urban and industrial frontiers. Robert E. Lang, et al., "'Progress of the Nation'," 289–307, gives a critique of Turner's definition of "frontier" as opposed to that used in the Census. For discussion of the differences between new Western History and Turner, see Deverell, "Fighting Words," 185–205; Limerick, et al., *Trails*; Steiner, "From Frontier to Region"; and Wunder, "What's Old about the New Western History ... Part 1" and "What's Old about the New Western History ... Part 2."

28 Elkins and McKitrick, "A Meaning for Turner's Frontier," 321–53, 565–602; Boorstin, *The Americans*, 51–62, 65–72, 113–23; Dykstra, *The Cattle Towns*.

29 Glaab, *Kansas City and the Railroads*, preface to 2nd ed., xi–xxi, for a discussion of frontier urban history; quotation, xvi; also, Hamer, *New Towns in the New World*, 2–4; Glaab and Brown, *A History of Urban America*, 25–51; Bartlett, *The New Country*, 401–40; Doyle, *The Social Order of a Frontier Community*; Wade, *The Urban Frontier*.

30 Cronon, *Nature's Metropolis*, xiv–54, quotation, xiv. See also Abbott, *How Cities Won the West*, and Abbott, *Boosters and Businessmen*; Moehring, *Urbanism and Empire*; Robbins, *Colony and Empire*, 162–83.

31 Abbott, *How Cities Won the West*, 5; Bartlett, *The New Country*, 419; Hamer, *New Towns in the New World*, 57; Wrobel, *Promised Lands*, 23; White, *It's Your Misfortune*, quotation, 417.

32 Cronon, *Nature's Metropolis*, 46.

33 Wrobel, *Promised Lands*, 8–9, n. 26, 204. See Emmons, *Garden in the Grasslands*; Robbins, *Colony and Empire*; Blodgett, *Land of Bright Promise*.

34 Wrobel, *Promised Lands*, 9.

35 Cronon, *Nature's Metropolis*, 34; Hamer, *New Towns in the New World*, 11; Abbott, *How Cities Won the West*, 4,10; Moehring, *Urbanism and Empire*, xxvi; Mahoney, *River Towns in the Great West*, 89. See Wills, *Boosters, Hustlers, and Speculators*, for her work on the importance of entrepreneurs to frontier development, particularly in the establishment of political links between boosters and local, state, and federal governments.

36 Mahoney, *River Towns in the Great West*, 279.

37 Goldfield, *Cotton Fields and Skyscrapers*, 15.

38 Emmons, "Constructed Province"; and Jenson, et al., "A Roundtable," 437–59, 461–86; Robbins, *Colony and Empire*, 162–83, and *Landscapes of Promise*; Van West, *Capitalism on the Frontier*, 4, 183–213. Carol Lynn MacGregor argues that Boise, Idaho, although limited by its isolation, prospered without attracting large-scale investment. See MacGregor, *Boise, Idaho*, 1, 39–79.

39 Bunting, *The Pacific Raincoast*, 1–2, 39–40, 72; Robbins, *Landscapes of Promise*, 14, 179–204, 181. For a concise discussion of development culture as the culture of capitalism see Worster, *Dust*

Bowl, 3–8. See also Robbins, "In Pursuit of Historical Explanation," and Steinberg, *Down to Earth*.

40 Morrissey, *Mental Territories*; Abbot, *How Cities Won the West*, 1–15; Boag, *Environment and Experience*.

41 Moehring, *Urbanism and Empire*, xxvii, xxix, 314–16.

42 Wrobel, *Promised Lands*, 4, 194–9. Wrobel includes pioneer reminiscences in his argument about the construction of popular ideas about the West.

43 There are certainly exceptions; see Boag, *Environment and Experience*; Harris, "Industry and the Good Life Around Idaho Peak," in *The Resettlement of British Columbia*, 194–218; Moehring, *Urbanism and Empire*; Morrissey, *Mental Territories*; Wrobel, *Promised Lands*. See also Engle, "Benefitting A City," for a discussion of the links between boosterism and female progressive reform thinking in late nineteenth- and early twentieth-century Spokane, Washington.

44 See Abbott, *How Cities Won the West*, 4; Cronon, *Nature's Metropolis*, 31–41; Emmons, *Garden in the Grasslands*; Robbins, *Colony and Empire*, 162–83, and *Landscapes of Promise*, 118–21; White, *It's Your Misfortune*, 417.

45 See Weaver, *The Great Land Rush*, for a discussion of the role squatters played in "the great land rush."

46 Historian David Wrobel has noted that "contradictions and variations [in] "European American thinking about race" are often reflected in booster literature (*Promised Lands*, 15, 157–80).

47 As demonstrated by several historians, members of any group are likely to have multiple identities, which derive variously from class, race, ethnicity, gender, sexuality, religion, and/or family. See, for example, Emmons, *The Butte Irish*; Jameson, *All That Glitters*; Johnston, *The Radical Middle Class*. The influence of development in community relations in Jefferson County suggests that commitment to development may have been one of such multiple identities.

48 Daly, "The Legal Creation," in *With Pride in Heritage*, 4–10.

49 Fletcher, "Valley of the Hoh," in *With Pride in Heritage*, 216–38.

50 Newell, *Ships of the Inland Sea*. By the closing years of the nineteenth century Seattle was the premier city on Puget Sound.

Nevertheless, its future status was not apparent in the early period. Then, the primacy of water-borne travel and trade (in that most travelers approached Puget Sound from the Pacific Ocean on sailing ships), the initial economic dominance of the western-shore "cargo" lumber industry (see Chapter 1) and that industry's dependence upon San Francisco capital and Pacific Rim markets, all argue for the early importance of the lower Sound and the western shore. It is therefore important to utilize Newell's defini-tion of a larger Puget Sound.

51 Jefferson County's current population is approximately 30,000; there is one larger, incorporated town (Port Townsend) and sev-eral smaller towns and villages. Paper milling, logging, assorted small businesses, tourism and boating, commuter and retirement communities, and construction sustain the local economy.

52 *Leader*, Aug. 27, 1891. See also Simpson et al., City *of Dreams*, 100.

53 Cox, *Mills and Markets*; Ficken, *The Forested Land* and *Wash-ington Territory*.

54 Isaac I. Stevens, *Report of Explorations for a Route for the Pacific Railroad*, 469.

55 H. Wilson to J. Wilson, Apr. 24, 1853, quoted in Cox, *Mills and Markets*, 60.

56 Wood, *The Freedom of the Streets*, quotation,13; Weaver, *The Great Land Rush*, 43; Armitage, "Are We There Yet?" 70–3, quotation, 73.

57 See Ficken, *Washington Territory*, 1–3.

58 Browne, "The Coast Rangers," 289–301, and *Crusoe's Island*.

59 How to delineate important themes in booster rhetoric and litera-ture has been explored by several historians. For instance, David Hamer uses the term *image* and emphasizes that the appearance of a town – that is, what the visitor saw upon arrival – and how that appearance or image might suggest the potential for individ-ual economic opportunity was an important theme for boosters (Hamer, *New Towns in the New World*, 40–64). Alicia Barber's study of the history of Reno, Nevada boosterism covers the city's promotional activities over many decades, and she argues for a more complex terminology in defining boosterism. Barber sees

"promoted image" combining with "civic reputation" and "sense of place" to create a "place identity." Sense of place is "the attachment of individuals … to specific locales and regions … [It may be] inspired by the natural environment, but … it can just as easily be rooted [in an urban setting]." Opposite this is "the promoted image … aspirational and idealistic, embodying how officials [want] a place to be perceived." Reputation, for Barber, is the governing impression of a city or town from the outside (Barber, *Reno's Biggest Gamble*, 1–8, quotations, 5).

For Jefferson County boosters or residents, reputation, or establishing that county residents and their life styles were respectable, was a key component of booster literature. Certainly boosters insisted that Port Townsend was bound "to be [and was already becoming] a place of commercial importance" (Swan, "Washington Sketches" 4–5), and they promoted images of busy entrepreneurial activity, emphasizing the growing commercial aspect of the county's landscape. Nevertheless, reputation, or respectability, remained key, and, in reading county booster literature, it would be difficult to separate image – as defined by either Hamer or Barber – from the concern for reputation. Interestingly, Jefferson County was, and is, a location of great scenic beauty, but commercial development, economic opportunity and reputation or respectability were the key terms in promotion of the benefits of settlement or investment in the county.

60 *Oxford Encyclopedic English Dictionary*, s. v. "boost," "development."

CHAPTER ONE

1 Binns, *The Roaring Land*, 51, quotation; Cox, *Mills and Markets*, 59.

2 Important sources for early Puget Sound settlement are: Berner, "The Port Blakely Mill"; Buchanan, "Lumbering and Logging"; Donald Hathoway Clark, "An Analysis of Forest Utilization"; Coman and Gibbs, *Time, Tide and Timber*; Cox, *Mills and Markets*; Ficken, *The Forested Land* and *Washington Territory*; Ficken and LeWarne, *Washington*; Gleason, *The Voyages of the*

Ship Revere; Gedosch, "Seabeck"; Griffiths, *Shipping Reminiscences*; Wright, *Lewis and Dryden's Marine History*; McCurdy, *By Juan de Fuca's Strait*; Newell, *The H.W. McCurdy Marine History*; Prosch, *Reminiscences of Washington*; Tattersall, "The Economic Development of the Pacific Northwest"; Tulloch, *Diary*; James G. Swan Papers; Pope and Talbot Papers; Washington Mill Company Papers; Washington Pioneer Project; United States Censuses, Federal Population Schedules and Manufactures; and City Directories.

3 *Port Townsend Register* (hereinafter cited as *Register*), Mar. 7, 1860.

4 The agreed boundary actually runs along the 49th Parallel from the crest of the Rocky Mountains to the middle of the Strait of Georgia, then dips south to the middle of the Strait of Juan de Fuca in order to include Vancouver Island in what was then British territory.

5 For further discussion, see Schwantes, *The Pacific Northwest*, 19–24, 41–79, 91–100, 110–25 133–4; Ficken and LeWarne, *Washington*, 3–22; Ficken, *Washington Territory*, 15–21. For discussion of the United States's acquisition of the trans-Mississippi West, see White, *"It's Your Misfortune and None of My Own,"* 61–84.

6 See Henry Nash Smith's discussion of Benson in *Virgin Land*, 19–34; Chambers, *Old Bullion Benton*; also, Emmons, *Garden in the Grasslands*, 7–9.

7 Richards, *Isaac I. Stevens*, 96. After serving as territorial governor, Stevens had two terms as territorial delegate to Congress, 1857–61. He lost the nomination for delegate in 1860; whether he could have rebuilt his Democratic Party political base in Washington is unknown. As Major General Stevens of the Union army, he was killed at the Battle of Chantilly, Virginia, Sept. 1, 1862 (384–7). See also William L. Lang, *Confederacy of Ambition*, 136–42.

8 Richards, *Isaac I. Stevens*, 103, 109.

9 Ibid., 326.

10 Isaac I. Stevens, *Report of Explorations*, 469.

11 Ibid., 114–16.
12 Richards, *Isaac I. Stevens*, 362. See also Johansen and Gates, *Empire of the Columbia*, 305–15; Meinig, *The Shaping of America*, 69–89; Schwantes, *Railroad Signatures*.
13 *Register*, Mar. 7, 1860.
14 Ibid., Jan. 25, 1860.
15 Cox, *Mills and Markets*, 57; Ficken and LeWarne, *Washington*, 21–3; *Eighth Census of the United States*, Washington Territory.
16 Ficken and LeWarne, *Washingon*, 20. Phoebe Goodell Judson writes of Puget Sound's farming frontier in her engaging *A Pioneer's Search for an Ideal Home*.
17 See May, *Three Frontiers*, for an exploration of the differences in motivational factors for migration per various settler groups.
18 Ficken, *The Forested Land*, 34, 39.
19 Cox argues that the California Gold Rush was "the Golden Catalyst" to the West Coast lumber industry (*Mills and Markets*, 46–70). Robert Ficken describes the lumber industry as the impetus to settlement and economic development of Puget Sound and Western Washington as well (*The Forested Land* , xiii–xiv, 19–26). For a discussion of how the west side of the Sound dominated the frontier lumber industry, see Ficken, *Washington Territory*, 14–15.
20 Cox, *Mills and Markets*, 6, 9–11, 25. For a discussion of the pre-Gold Rush West Coast lumber industry, see 3–35.
21 Ficken, *Forested Land*, 21; Cox, *Mills and Markets*, 46–8, 51.
22 Cox, *Mills and Markets*, 55.
23 Ibid., 63, Ficken and LeWarne, *Washingon*, 30–1; Buchanan, "Lumbering and Logging," 35.
24 "Early Days in Quilcene," Washington Pioneer Project, quotation 1–2; Cox, *Mills and Markets*, 57–60; Buchanan, "Lumbering and Logging," 34–5; Coman and Gibbs, *Time, Tide and Timber*, 34; Ficken and LeWarne, *Washington*, 21; Meinig, *The Shaping of America*, 81.
25 In 1843, before British and American claims to Oregon had been settled, American residents of Oregon formed a provisional government, which in 1844 authorized land claims of 640 acres to

males over eighteen on condition that the claimant occupy and improve the land – the acres could be two non-contiguous parcels of 600 acres of prairie and forty of timber.

Through the 1850 Donation Land Claim Act, Congress acknowledged these claims and established generous encouragement to new claimants. Any white – or half Indian – male settler who was a citizen – or who declared his intention to become a citizen by Dec. 1, 1851 – over eighteen years of age, and residing in Oregon Territory on or before Dec. 1, 1850, and would cultivate and live upon it for four years would receive 320 acres of land. If married he would receive another 320 acres. (The provision allowing half Native-half Euro-Americans and prospective citizens to claim land was meant to encourage employees of the Hudson's Bay Company to stay in the territory, and many did.)

Second, any white male citizen over twenty-one years of age settling in Oregon Territory between Dec. 1, 1850, and Dec. 1, 1853 – later amended to Dec. 1, 1855 – would receive 160 acres of land. If already married or married within one year of arriving in the territory, he would receive another 160 acres. During the five years this act was in effect some 8,000 people claimed approximately three million acres of land, most of it in the Willamette Valley (Yonce, "Public Land Disposal in Washington," 102–29; Schwantes, *The Pacific Northwest*, 121).

26 Cox, *Mills and Markets*, 57–60; Ficken and LeWarne, *Washington*, 22; Coman and Gibbs, *Time, Tide and Timber*, 6–7, 33–5, 64.

27 Prosch, *Reminiscenses of Washington*, 7, 11.

28 Coman and Gibbs, *Tide, Time and Timber*, 34; McCurdy, *By Juan de Fuca's Strait*, 12–13.

29 By 1860 Puget Sound's lumber industry was out producing Oregon two to one (Ficken, *Washington Territory*, 14).

30 H. Wilson to J. Wilson, Apr. 24, 1853, qouted in Cox, *Mills and Markets*, 60.

31 McCurdy, *By Juan de Fuca's Strait*, 11–18, 21–35; Simpson et al., *City of Dreams*, 96–100.

32 McCurdy, *By Juan de Fuca's Strait*, 12–13.

33 Ibid., 17–18; *The Weekly Message*, Oct. 24, 1867; Mar. 3, 1868.

34 *Register*, June 27, 1860.

35 The original Jefferson County claimants were: John L. Tukey at
    Port Discovery, 1850, 1852; Alfred A. Plummer and Charles
    Batchelder – Batchelder did not perfect his title – at Port
    Townsend and Rueben Robinson at Chimacum, 1851; John R.
    Thorndyke at Port Ludlow, 1852; and H.C. Wilson, Francis W.
    Pettygrove, Loren B. Hastings, J.C. Clinger, Albert Briggs and
    Ruel W. Ross, Thomas M. Hammond, John Harris, and Ben-
    jamin Ross at Port Townsend, 1852 (McCurdy, *By Juan de Fuca's
    Strait*, 28–32; W.J. Daly and V.J. Gregory, "Port Townsend," in
    With Pride in Heritage, 64; Arthur Swanson, "High Tide at Lud-
    low," in *With Pride in Heritage*, 180; Simpson et al., *City of
    Dreams*, 48–9; United States Census, Federal Population Census
    Schedules, Jefferson County, 1860, 1870; *Register*, Feb. 20, 1861;
    The Weekly Message, May 21, 1868; July 23, 1868; Sept. 1,
    1869; Feb. 18, 1870; see also, "Map of Quimper Peninsula."

36 Briggs, Pettygrove, and Hastings each had farms located outside of
    Port Townsend, and in 1860 Pettygrove had eighty-one acres in
    hay, wheat, potatoes, vegetables, and fruit (Swan, *San Francisco
    Evening Bulletin*, May 19, 1859, and *The North-West*, Oct. 25,
    1860. See Chapter 3 for a discussion of Puget Sound agriculture.

37 McCurdy, *By Juan de Fuca's Strait*, 13, 28; Gregory, "Profiles of
    Pioneers," in *With Pride in Heritage*, 125–6; Meany, *History of
    the State of Washington*, 227. Wilson is not listed in the 1860 or
    any subsequent census for Jefferson County.

38 McCurdy, *By Juan de Fuca's Strait*, 12–14, quotation 13; Cox,
    Mills and Markets, 59–60.

39 Throckmorton, *Oregon Argonauts*, 34, 36, 40, 58–9, 61, 90,
    quotation 58; Cox, *Mills and Markets*, 21, 30–3, 60; Gregory,
    "Profiles of Pioneers," in *With Pride in Heritage*, 400–2; also
    Snyder, *Early Portland*, 35–46.

40 Gregory, "Profiles of Pioneers," in *With Pride in Heritage*, 351,
    373–4; McCurdy, *By Juan de Fuca's Strait*, 11–14, 21–8; Simp-
    son, et al., *City of Dreams*, 96–8. Charles Batchelder had drink-
    ing problems and after a time was asked to leave the partnership.
    He sold his interests to Pettygrove for $300 and moved to Port
    Ludlow, where he died soon thereafter (Simpson, et al., 98; Gre-
    gory, 351). Pettygrove left the partnership on Feb. 28, 1854, but

continued to develop his property. (*Pioneer & Democrat*, Feb. 17, 1855; see "Map of Quimper Peninsula").

41 McCurdy, *By Juan de Fuca's Strait*, 31; Donald Hathaway Clark, "An Analysis of Forest Utilization," 35–6; Cox, *Mills and Markets*, 60; Simpson, et al., *City of Dreams*, 46.

42 Information on Thorndyke and the fate of the partnership is scant. Lucile McDonald says Thorndyke also filed a claim at Whidby Island, Washington, in Sept. 1853. However, Thorndyke is listed in the Port Ludlow 1860 census as a lumberman, with real property valued at $20,000 and personal property valued at $1,000. Sayward appears on the same census, living in the same household as Thorndyke, with $15,000 in real property, but neither appears on any subsequent county census. It is not clear what position, if any, Thorndyke had in Sayward's milling and shipping enterprises. (Lucile McDonald, "A Seafaring Visit," 5; United States Census, Federal Population Census Schedules, 1860.

43 Lucile McDonald, "A Woman's Views," 2, and "Life in Puget Sound Ports," 11; Cox, *Mills and Markets*, 62; Ficken, *Forested Land*, 28.

44 *Pioneer & Democrat*, Feb. 17, 1855; Cox, *Mills and Markets*, 117, 135, 109; United States Census, Federal Population Census Schedules, 1860; *Democratic Press*, Feb. 19, 1880; Swanson, "High Tide at Ludlow," in *With Pride in Heritage*, 180; Lucile McDonald, "A Woman's Views," 2.

45 See Birder, "Expanding Creative Destruction," 45–63, for a discussion of the importance of entrepreneurship to the development of the West.

46 McCurdy, *By Juan de Fuca's Strait*, 13.

47 Goodman, *A Western Panorama*, 58–9; McCurdy, *By Juan de Fuca's Strait*, 51–3, 98–101; Ficken and LeWarne, *Washington*, 23.

48 *Weekly Message*, May 28, 1868.

49 Wright, *Lewis and Dryden's Marine History*, 77–8, 89, 142, 165–7; *Weekly Message*, May 28, 1868.

50 Tulloch, *Diary*, 21.

51 Swan, *San Francisco Evening Bulletin*, May 10, 1859. In 1860

there were 338 Euro-Americans living in Port Townsend, a figure that includes the county's principal farming area in nearby Chimacum Valley (United States Census, Federal Population Census Schedules, 1860).

52 Ibid.; *Register* Jan. 18, 1860; Jan. 25, 1860; Feb. 13, 1861; Feb. 20, 1861; "An Outline of the History of Jefferson County," Washington Pioneer Project, 5–6.

53 "Old Pilot Notes," Archival Collections, McCurdy Historical Research Library; "Randall Dalgardno," Washington Pioneer Project, 1–2; Simpson, et al., *City of Dreams*, 35; Griffiths, *Shipping Reminiscences*, 10–11; Plum, "Diary of Ida Plum Wife."

54 *Register*, Jan. 18, 1860.

55 Ibid., and Aug. 21, 1861; *Weekly Message*, May 21, 1868; Sept. 1, 1869.

56 *North-West*, May 9, 1861.

57 Ficken and LeWarne, *Washington*, 23.

58 Clark, "An Analysis of Forest Utilization," 48; *Weekly Message*, Jan. 14, 1870.

59 Swan, *San Francisco Evening Bulletin*, June 17, 1859.

60 The first local steamer, the small sidewheeler *Fairy*, was brought from San Francisco in 1853 to run between Seattle and Olympia. Although her exact dimensions are not known, she was small enough to be carried to the Sound on board a bark, the *Sarah Warren*. By 1890 the *City of Kingston*, 246 feet long, with "three decks and ... elegantly fitted up with stateroom accommodations for over three hundred passengers," was running between points on the Sound and Victoria (Wright, *Lewis and Dryden's Marine History*, 45, 374; Newell, *The H. W. McCurdy Marine History*, 14, 47). See also Schwantes, *Long Day's Journey*, 327–34.

61 Wright, *Lewis and Dryden's Marine History*, 129–30, 155–7. The lumber schooners also continued to carry some passengers and consumer goods (Gleason, *The Voyages of the Ship Revere*, 85–94).

62 Tulloch, *Diary*, 21.

63 See Appendix I, Table 1.

64 In 1860 the cut was worth $154,000 – with 108 employees; in 1870, $326,050 – with 120 employees. Kitsap County's 1860 production totaled $694,000 – with 348 employees; in 1870

$1,108,000 – with 125 employees. King County's in 1860 was $36,000; in 1870 $169,000. There were three cargo mills in Kitsap County: Puget Mill Company (the largest), the Washington Mill Company, and the Port Madison Mill Company. The three King County mills were smaller and little involved in the cargo industry (*Eighth Census of the United States: Manufactures*, 1864, 671; *Ninth Census of the United States: Manufactures*, 1872, 741).

65 *North-West*, Nov. 22, 1860; *Puget Sound Argus* (hereinafter cited as *Argus*), Dec. 31, 1885. See also Ficken, *Washington Territory*, 14–15, for a discussion of industry dominance by lumber mills on the west side of Puget Sound.

66 Cox, *Mills and Markets*, 117.

67 For comparison's sake, the Puget Mill Company at Port Gamble, whose production far outpaced all other mills on the Sound at this time, shipped altogether 13,091,845 feet of lumber, as well as: 2,517,000 feet in laths; 200,000 in pickets; 800,000 in shingles; approximately 80,000 feet in piles; 22,000 in large masts; 91,000 in spars (*Register*, Jan. 18, 1860).

68 *Washington Standard*, Feb. 17, 1866; Lucile McDonald, "A Woman's Views," 2.

69 Lucile McDonald, "Events of 1853," 7; Swan, *San Francisco Evening Bulletin*, June 17, 1859; Gleason, *The Voyages of the Ship Revere*, 81; *The Northwest*, Nov. 22, 1860; *Register*, Feb. 15, 1860.

70 Cox, *Mills and Markets*, ix, 125–6; Perry, *Seabeck*, 51.

71 Swan, *San Francisco Evening Bulletin*, May 10, 1859; McCurdy, *By Juan de Fuca's Strait*, 80.

72 Ficken and LeWarne, *Washington*, 33–7; Ficken, *Forested Land*, 56; Cox, *Mills and Markets*, 25.

73 For instance, see Edwin Ames to Messrs. Pope & Talbot, San Francisco, California, ls, Edwin G. Ames Papers.

74 Coman and Gibbs, *Time, Tide and Timber*, 14, 33–4.

75 Cox, *Mills and Markets*, 62.

76 Talbot was partnered by Andrew J. Pope, Josiah P. Keller, and Charles Foster (Coman and Gibbs, *Time, Tide and Timber*, 46).

77 Cox, *Mills and Markets*, 117; "Port Gamble sawmill."

78 Cox, *Mills and Markets*, 62.

79 Ficken and LeWarne, *Washington*, 29–38; Cox, *Mills and Markets*, 108, 110; Ficken, *Forested Land*, 28; McCurdy, *By Juan de Fuca's Strait*, 76–7.

80 Cox, *Mills and Markets*, 123–5.

81 In its first full year of operation, the Puget Mill Company, which had been built to supply the San Francisco trade, sent one third of its 3.6 million board feet of lumber to foreign markets (Cox, *Mills and Markets*, 75).

82 Ibid., 71–100. According to Cox, the Puget Mill took the lion's share of Pacific Rim markets (120), although the Washington Mill Company at Seabeck and later Port Hadlock consistently looked beyond San Francisco markets (88). To my knowledge, for neither the Port Ludlow Mill – under Sayward and Phinney – nor the Port Discovery Mill are there surviving company records, although there are indications that both mills participated to some extent in Pacific Rim markets. Port Ludlow sent at least one cargo to China (*Weekly Message*, Mar. 3, 1868), and the Port Discovery Mill sent cargoes to Southern California and Hawaii (Cox, 119–20).

83 Wright, *Lewis and Dryden*, 77–8, 89, 142.

84 Ficken, *Forested Land*, 34, 39; Tattersall, "Economic Development," 43, 67.

85 See Appendix I, Table 2.

86 Gedosch, "Seabeck," 139–40.

87 Buchanan, "Lumbering and Logging," 34–5; Cox, *Mills and Markets*, 228–9; Geodosch, "Seabeck," 143; Rajala, "The Forest as Factory," 77; *Puget Sound Herald*, Apr. 23, 1858.

88 Holbrook, *Holy Old Mackinaw*, 101,163–5; Buchanan, "Lumbering and Logging," 34–5; Cox, *Mills and Markets*, 228–9; Gedosch, "Seabeck," 142.

89 United States Census, Federal Population Census Schedules, 1870, 1880.

90 More often than not in the early years, logs were simply taken from public lands. See Ficken, *Forested Land*, 40–51, Yonce,

"Public Land Disposal," 225–68, for a discussion of the legal and illegal ways the cargo mills acquired logs and eventually timber lands.

91 Gedosch, "Seabeck," 139–41; Berner, "Port Blakely Mill Company," 159–60; Coman and Gibbs, *Time, Tide and Timber*, 68–9; Ficken, *Forested Land*, 32.

92 Gedosch, "Seabeck," 143–51, quotation, 151; John McReavy to Richard Holyoke, Apr. 4, 1876, Washington Mill Company Papers, Coman and Gibbs, *Time, Tide and Timber*, 147–8; Berner, "Port Blakely Mill Company," 159.

93 Gedosch, "Seabeck," 151.

94 "Early Days in Quilcene," Washington Pioneer Project, 1–2.

95 Ibid., 1; "History of Quilcene," McCurdy Historical Research Library; Eva Cook Taylor, "Quilcene," in *With Pride in Heritage*, 162–9; Simpson, et al., *City of Dreams*, 211.

96 See Appendix I, Table 3.

97 See chapter 3 for discussion of farmers who worked in mills or "in the woods."

98 United States Census, Federal Population Census Schedules, Jefferson County, 1870; Gedosch, "Seabeck," 149.

99 Initially, it was thought that Douglas fir, the most abundant timber on Puget Sound, was unsuitable for shipbuilding, especially of large ocean-going craft. (Native Americans made their canoes from cedar logs.) However, experimentation with Douglas fir at the Mare Island Navy Yard established Puget Sound fir to be of sufficient strength for shipbuilding (*Democratic Press*, Sept. 25, 1879; Cox, *Mills and Markets*, 244–5), and West Coast shipbuilders found that it was durable "if cut in winter, seasoned, and salted."

An inquiry into the reliability of Douglas fir by the Board of Marine Underwriters of San Francisco in 1867 sanctioned its use (Coman and Gibbs, *Time, Tide and Timber*, 150); and in 1875 the board published specifications for vessels built of it that "won first-class ratings and lowest insurance rates" (Cox, 245). In the late 1870s Puget Sound shipyards began producing large vessels such as the 694-ton *Kitsap* launched from Port Ludlow in 1881 (Cox, 149).

100 United States Census, Federal Population Census Schedules, 1860, 1880.

101 From 1856 until 186l, William F. Thompson launched several small vessels from Port Ludlow (*Register*, Feb. 15, 1860; June 13, 1861; Greene, "Early Shipbuilding," 12). Franklin Sherman's "Shipyard and Boat Builder's Shop," launched a sloop and a schooner from Ludlow in 1855 and 1856, but relocated at Port Townsend in the early 1860s (*Register*, Jan. 18, 1860; Greene, 11). Thomas J. Smallfield advertised from Port Townsend, and Charles Brown launched small schooners from Port Ludlow, later moving his operations closer to Port Townsend (*Register*, Jan. 18, 1860; Feb. 13, 1861; Greene, 12). William Hammond employed several ship's carpenters, a joiner, a caulker, and a laborer at Port Ludlow in 1860 (*Register*, Jan. 18, 1860; United States Census, Federal Population Census Schedules, 1860). Calhoun Bros. at Chimacum and George Middlemas of Port Ludlow were county shipbuilders in the late 1860s (*Weekly Message*, Nov. 14, 1867; Aug. 6, 1868). Hall Bros. which employed approximately thirty men operated from Port Ludlow between 1874 and 1880, and other builders continued to launch ships from there until at least 1890 (Greene, 5–6, 11–12).

102 Cox, *Mills and Markets*, 68–9, 109, 113, 116. This was not uniformly true. The *Revere,* which carried lumber for the Port Discovery mill for many years, was owned by Levi Mastick, one of the mill partners, and the John Kentfield Company, San Francisco lumber dealers who also owned a lumber mill in California (Gleason, *The Voyages of the Ship Revere,* 85).

103 Coman and Gibbs, *Time, Tide and Timber,* 117–26. Some lumber companies had vessels constructed for their use in the East also.

104 As early as 1861, Amos and Phinney Company commissioned a 185-ton schooner from William Thompson of Port Ludlow (*North-West,* June 13, 1861).

105 The Washington Mill Company's shipbuilder was Hiram Doncaster, who had been employed by William Hammond at Port Ludlow in 1860 (*Register*, Jan. 18, 1860; Greene, "Early Shipbuilding," 16–17; Gedosch, "Seabeck," 22; Cox, 115; Coman and Gibbs, *Tide, Time and Timber,* 149–52, 163, 179–80).

106 Swan, *San Francisco Evening Bulletin*, May 10, 1859.

107 Important sources about James Swan are: James G. Swan, Diaries; James G. Swan Papers; Swan, *The Northwest Coast*; *San Francisco Evening Bulletin*, May 10, 19, 1859; Swan, "Washington Sketches; Swan, *Almost Out of This World*; Lucile McDonald, *Swan among the Indians*; Doig, *Winter Brothers*; Jane Turner, "Inventory of James G. Swan Papers."

108 William A. Katz's introduction to Swan, *Almost Out of the World*, x; also, Cole, *Captured Heritage*, 9–47.

109 Swan, "Washington Sketches," 4–5, quotation, 5; James G. Swan to Thomas H. Canfield, Esq., General Agent Northern Pacific Rail Road Co, No 54 Broadway, NY, ls, Feb. 27, 1869, James G. Swan Papers.

110 Swan, *The Northwest Coast*, 25–33, 30.

111 Ibid.; "Washington Sketches," 5.

112 *The Northwest Coast;* "Washington Sketches"; *San Francisco Evening Bulletin*, May 10, 1859.

113 *Register*, July 26, 1860; Nov. 14, 1860.

CHAPTER TWO

1 "Report on the Conditions of the Indian Reservations in the Territories of Oregon and Washington, from J. Ross Browne," 7–8. The report was released Jan. 25, 1858.

2 Ibid.

3 Browne, *J. Ross Browne: His Letters*, quotation, 182; Letters to *San Francisco Bulletin* and *San Francisco Globe* reported in *Pioneer and Democrat*, May 7, 1858.

4 Browne, "The Coast Rangers," 289–301.

5 *Washington Standard*, Nov. 22, 1862; Winthrop, *Canoe and Saddle*, v–xii, 2–12, quotation, 2; *North-West*, Nov. 16, 1861; Letter to *Overland Press*, reported in *North-West*, Jan. 25, 1862. The Euro-American settlers, who followed the practice of Hudson's Bay Company employees in naming Indian leaders after European and American public figures, called Chet-ze-moka, the Duke of York. See Isaac I. Stevens, *Report of Explorations for a Route for the Pacific Railroad*, 429–31.

6 Browne, *Crusoe's Island*, 170–83, 270, quotation; Nordhoff, *Nordhoff's West Coast*, 219.

7 See Hamer, *New Towns in the New World*, 40–64, for his detailed discussion of the importance of image and travel literature to Western development.

8 See Harmon, *Indians in the Making*; Thrush, *Native Seattle*; Naylor, "Chet-ze-moka," 59–68. See also Van West, *Capitalism on the Frontier*, 7–52, for a discussion of exchange relations between the Crows and settlers in Yellowstone Valley; and Lutz, "After The Fur Trade," 69–94, for a discussion of the important economic role played by aboriginal laborers in nineteenth-century British Columbia. Also, an important reference is Witgen, "'An Infinity of Nations.'" Witgen's work is focused on the complex relations between Native peoples of the Great Lakes and the interior West and Europeans and Euro-Americans and demonstrates the importance of Native Americans to non-Indian endeavors in that region from the seventeenth century through the nineteenth century.

9 *Puget Sound Herald*, Apr. 12, 1858.

10 My understanding of S'Klallan coexistence with Euro-American settlers in Jefferson County (and between Puget Sound Native Americans and Euro-Americans settlers in general) is based, in part, on primary material cited in the text. See also Eells, *The Twana*; Gibbs, "Tribes of Western Washington," 157–242; Menzies, *Rainshadow*; Swan, *San Francisco Evening Bulletin*, May 10, 19, 1859; Swan, Diaries; Port Townsend newspapers; Asher, "'Their Own Domestic Difficulties'"; Barsh, "Ethnogenesis and Ethnonationalism"; Gorsline, ed., *Shadows of Our Ancestors*; Harmon, "A Different Kind of Indians"; Ruby and Brown, *Indians of the Pacific Northwest*; Suttles, ed., *Northwest Coast*, 169–72; Thrush and Keller, Jr., "'I See What I Have Done'," 168–83; Valadez et al., "The S'Klallam," 17–63.

11 Ruby and Brown, *Indians of the Pacific Northwest*, 3–4; Gibbs, "Tribes of Western Washington," 167–77; Gorsline, ed., "Prelude," in *Shadows of Our Ancestors*, xv.

12 Ruby and Brown, *Indians of the Pacific Northwest*, 3–4; Swadesh, "The Linguistic Approach to Salish Prehistory," 165;

June M. Collins, "Distribution of the Chemakum Language," 149–50. By the 1850s the Chimakum had been much weakened, probably by smallpox and warfare with other tribes – according to local tradition they were almost totally destroyed in a battle with another tribe around 1857. Their traditional territory had been between Point Wilson and Port Gamble, their main village near modern Port Hadlock. In the 1850s they had a small village site on the beach at Port Townsend near the S'Klallam. The Chimakum often spoke S'Klallam Salish rather than their own Chemakuam (Swan, "Washington Sketches," 8).

13 Gibbs, "Tribes of Western Washington," 177–8, 191; Eells, *The Twana*, 12–13; Simpson et al., *City of Dreams*, 211–12; Ruby and Brown, *Indians of the Pacific Northwest*, 64. S'Klallam oral historian Mary Ann Lambert Vincent writes that the Quilcene are extinct (*Dungeness Massacre*, 20). Myron Eells, missionary for the Skokomish, S'Klallam, and Chimakum from 1874 to 1907, mentions their late nineteenth-century presence on the Skokomish Reservation and integration with the other bands who lived on that reservation (Eells, *The Twana*, 12).

14 Gibbs, "Tribes of Western Washington," 178; Swan, "Washington Sketches," 8.

15 Gibbs, "Tribes of Western Washington," 167, quotation; White, "Treaty At Medicine Creek," 31.

16 Gibbs, "Tribes of Western Washington," 193–97; "The Prince of Wales: Present Chief of the Clallams," Washington Pioneer Project, 2. Vegetables traditionally made up about 10% of the Juan de Fuca Strait Native American diet (Collins, "Subsistence and Survival," 191, n7). See also Rivera, "Diet of a Food-Gathering People," 22, 19–36; Valadez et al., "The S'Klallam," 5.

17 Some of these techniques would eventually clash with the interests of settlers and the lumber industry (Gorsline's "Introduction" in Menzies, *Rainshadow*, 14–15, 20–1; White, *Land Use, Environment, and Social Change*, 14–34).

18 Gibbs, "Tribes of Western Washington," 192.

19 Ibid., 197.

20 Bunting, *The Pacific Raincoast*, 8, 20–1. See 5–21 for discussion of the pre-contact forest ecosystem.

21 Gorsline, "Prelude," *Shadows of Our Ancestors*, xv–xvi; Ruby
    and Brown, *Indians of the Pacific Northwest*, 4.

22 Gorsline's "Introduction" in Menzies, *Rainshadow*, 25; Menizes,
    Rainshadow, quotation 39; Ruby and Brown, *Indians of the Pa-
    cific Northwest*, 9; White, "Treaty at Medicine Creek," 6.

23 The maritime fur trade was inaugurated by Russians in the mid-
    eighteenth century, the British and Americans becoming involved
    after 1778. It continued into the first decade of the nineteenth cen-
    tury, when over-hunting shifted focus to development of the conti-
    nental fur trade in the Northwest, which lasted into the 1840s
    (Schwantes, *The Pacific Northwest*, 19–24, 41–79, 114–19).

24 Harmon, "A Different Kind of Indians," 51–3, 124–5, 131; Ruby
    and Brown, *Indians of the Pacific Northwest*, 27–66; Langness,
    "A Case of Post Contact Reform Among the Klallam," 167–71.

25 Harmon, "Lines in Sand," 443–50, quotation 444–45; Barsh,
    "Ethnogenesis and Ethnonationalism," 215–43, especially 216–
    23. For a discussion of a similar "flux of peoples" among the
    Coast Salish of lower British Columbia, see Harris's chapter "The
    Making of the Lower Mainland," in *The Resettlement of British
    Columbia*, 69–76, quotation 73. Also see Witgen for his discus-
    sion of the fluidity of group formation among Indian peoples of
    the Great Lakes and interior West. Here, too, identity often re-
    flected a reality far more complex than "tribal."

26 Harmon, "A Different Kind of Indians," 6–10; White, *Land Use,
    Environment, and Social Change*, 14.

27 Harmon, "A Different Kind of Indians," 10, 47–50, quotation
    61, 23, 36.

28 Chet-ze-moka quoted in Gates, ed., "The Indian Treaty of Point
    No Point," 55.

29 "Treaty with the S'Klallam, 1855," 674. The treaties were to pro-
    vide annuities of useful goods; furnish teachers, doctors, farmers,
    blacksmiths, and carpenters to aid in the "civilizing" process;
    prohibit war between tribes; end slavery; and halt the liquor
    trade. For a discussion of developing federal reservation policy in
    the Far West, see Findlay, "An Elusive Institution," 13–37; and
    Prucha, *American Indian Treaties*, 381–409. See also Harmon,
    ed., *The Power of Promises: Rethinking Indian Treaties in the*

Pacific Northwest, a collection of essays written for the sesqui-
centennial commemoration of the Washington Territory Indian
treaties, also known as the Stevens treaties, especially Harmon,
"Introduction," 3–31, especially, 8–11. Also see Wilkins and
Lomawaima, *Uneven Ground*.

30 Richards, *Isaac I. Stevens*, 202; Harmon, "A Different Kind of
Indians," 210.

31 Richards, *Isaac I. Stevens*, 201; Harmon, "A Different Kind of
Indians," 245; Langness, "A Case of Post Contact Reform," 199;
White, "Treaty at Medicine Creek," 53–4.

32 "Treaty with the S'Klallam, 1855."

33 Harmon, "A Different Kind of Indians," 114, 145.

34 Only one treaty – the Medicine Creek Treaty – was immediately
ratified, the others not until late in 1859 (Ficken and LeWarne,
Washington, 26; Richards, *Isaac I. Stevens*, 191–2).

35 The Twana and Skokomish lived along Hood Canal.

36 Chinook was a mixture of three to four hundred Indian, English,
and French words; one word might convey several meanings depending upon emphasis, pronunciation and the use of hand signs.
Describing Chinook, William Sayward used as an example, the
word "Siyah," which means distance. According to Sayward, if
a place was close by, it was described simply as "'Siyah;' if it is
farther off, 'Siyah' prolonging the last syllable and giving a little
more emphasis; if it is farther still, 'Siyah,' more prolonged and
more emphatic, and if it is a great distance 'Siyah,' greatly prolonged, and very emphatically spoken, the [speaker] rising on his
toes and swinging his arms to give greater expression to the language" (Ficken and LeWarne, *Washington*, 26; Sayward, "Additional Statement of Capt. Wm. T. Sayward," 4).

37 Benjamin Shaw, the interpreter, was adept at using jargon, and
Michael Simmons, one of the first Americans to settle on Puget
Sound, had been in the region since 1844. Further, George Gibbs
was a student of Northwest Indian language and customs, eventually writing extensively about their culture (Richards, *Isaac I.
Stevens*, 197–8), although this "did not temper in the slightest his
desire to remove the Indian and open the territory for white settlement" (White, "Treaty at Medicine Creek," 52–3). According

to White, Simmons had contempt for Indians, but saw the value
of Indian labor to the Puget Sound economy (Ibid., 53–4).

38 Che-lan-teh-tat, Shau-at-seha-uk, Nah-whil-uk, and Hool-hol-tan
quoted in Gates, ed., "The Indian Treaty of Point No Point," 55;
Gorsline, "Pioneer Existence," in *Shadows of Our Ancestors*, 37;
Harmon, "A Different Kind of Indian," 263, n50).

39 Chet-ze-moka, quoted. in Gates, ed., "The Indian Treaty of Point
No Point," 55.

40 Ibid. Stevens was pleased with the rapid execution of the treaties,
but up-river Puget Sound Indians – those who were dissatisfied
with the lack of grazing land for their horses on their reservations
– and tribes in Eastern Washington were not. Arguably, the
treaties provoked a war (Harmon, "A Different Kind of Indians,"
222). The S'Klallam were not hostiles (see Chapter 3). There was
a volunteer battalion under Major J.J. Van Bokkelin at Port
Townsend, but the settlers were more afraid of the periodic raids
by northern Indians – as those peoples from Vancouver Island
were called – than they were worried that the war would reach
Jefferson County (Richards, *Isaac I. Stevens*, 262–63, 268). For
discussion of the war, see Richards, 211–312; Harmon, "A Different Kind of Indians," 222–40; White, "Treaty at Medicine
Creek," 89–136; Schwantes, *Pacific Northwest*, 147–8; Ficken,
Washington Territory, 43–52, 55–9.

41 Richards, *Isaac I. Stevens*,195, 198–9; Harmon, "A Different
Kind of Indians," 215.

42 Harmon, "A Different Kind of Indians," 284–6, 291–3.

43 Ibid, 299, 283. quotation.

44 Chet-ze-moka quoted in Gates, ed., "The Indian Treaty of Point
No Point," 55; Harmon, "A Different Kind of Indians," 197,
241–5, 300, quotation

45 Eells, "Ten Years of Missionary Work Among the Indians, 82–3;
Eells, *The Twana*, 13–14; Harmon, "A Different Kind of Indian,"
147–8, 245, 287–8, 474–7; *Puget Sound Herald*, Apr. 23, 1858;
The Puget Sound Argus (hereinafter cited as *Argus*), Oct. 15,
1875; June 2, 1876; Sept. 15, 1876; Oct. 20, 1876; *Democratic
Press*, July 4, 1878; *Leader*, Aug. 27, 1891; Swan, Diaries, Sept.
25, 1872; Oct. 5, 1872; June 12, 1873; Feb. 14, 1875; Jan. 9,

1876; Mar. 14, 1883; Mar. 17, 1883; Apr. 12, 1884; Aug. 14, 1884; Sept. 27, 1885; Jan. 22, 1886; Jan. 8, 1889; July 13, 1889; Oct. 6, 1889; Mar. 19, 1894; Sept. 2, 1895.

46 The census does not list any Native Americans other than the women living with Euro-American men, the children of these relationships, and the British Columbia men and women living in the beach settlements, except for an 18-year old Native American man in Port Discovery listed as a mariner. The total county population in 1870 was 1,268 (United States Census, Federal Population Census Schedules, 1870).

47 See Harmon, "A Different Kind of Indians," 153–5, 162–3, 246, 287, 317–23. For a discussion of the response of California Indians to reservations, see Findlay, "An Elusive Institution," 28–32, and Benson, "The Consequences of Reservation Life," 221–44.

48 McCurdy, *By Juan de Fuca's Strait*, 26.

49 "The Prince Of Wales: Present Chief of the Clallams, Jefferson County," Washington Pioneer Project, 1–2; Gregory, "The Duke of York," in *With Pride in Heritage*, 131. See Harmon, "A Different Kind of Indians," 153–5, for a discussion of Native American willingness to accept settlers as fellow residents.

50 Harris, "Voices of Smallpox around the Strait of Georgia" in *The Resettlement of British Columbia*, 20–3. In 1859 James Swan numbered the S'Klallam approximately 1,000 and the Chimakum 100 (*San Francisco Evening Bulletin*, May 19, 1859); by 1880 Myron Eells estimated that 485 S'Klallam lived on the Olympic Peninsula, although his figures exclude S'Klallam living elsewhere (Eells, "Ten Years of Missionary Work," 92–3). The Chimacum had declined to ten (Eells, "The Twana," 607, cited in Boyd, *The Coming of Pestilence*, 169).

51 See Harris, "Voices of Smallpox," in *The Resettlement of British Columbia*, 3–30, and Boyd, *The Coming of Pestilence*, 21–60, for discussion of the debates about dating of epidemics. See also, Fenn, *Pox Americana* 224–58. Fenn, who favors the 1782 dating, discusses the Northwest Coast epidemic within the context of the North American continental smallpox epidemic of 1775–82.

52 Harris, "Voices of Smallpox," in *The Resettlement of British Columbia*, 10–14.

53 Boyd, *The Coming of Pestilence*, 145-71.

54 Ibid., 262-78, 5.

55 Gorsline's "Appendix A," in *Shadows of Our Ancestors*, 235. Gibbs mentions potato grounds as a defining characteristic of the winter villages (Gibbs, "Tribes of Western Washington," 197).

56 The dogs became so mongrelized that their wool was no longer suitable for weaving (Simpson, "We Give Our Hearts To You," 133-4).

57 For discussion, see Asher, "Their Own Domestic Difficulties," 189-209.

58 McCurdy, *By Juan de Fuca's Strait*, 13-14, 38-9; "Washington State, Believe It or Not, Has Its Own 'Royal Family' of the Olympics," Washington Pioneer Project, 1-2.

59 McCurdy, *By Juan de Fuca's Strait*, 38; Harmon, "A Different Kind of Indians," 156-7.

60 *Pioneer and Democrat*, Mar. 11, 1854; Mar. 25, 1854; Dec. 9, 1854; Simpson, "We Give our Hearts to You," 133; Harmon, "A Different Kind of Indians," 203, 256 n15; White, "Treaty at Medicine Creek," 47-9.

61 Weir, "Roughing It on Puget Sound," 75. In this case the opposing parties settled the matter in a traditional way through "the principle of kin-group responsibility," which meant that damage or death visited upon an individual required compensation be paid to his or her kin-group by the perpetrator or his kinsfolk. Negotiation might settle the matter, but if it did not, retaliatory violence, which often led to long-standing feuds could follow (Asher, "Their Own Domestic Difficulties," 193).

62 *Register*, Mar. 28, 1860.

63 Ibid.

64 Ibid., June 27, 1860. Also passed was an ordinance which prohibited drunk and disorderly behavior, "shouting, singing, quarreling, discharging of firearms, or ... any other rude and boisterous manner," within the city limits by any residents whether Euro-American or Native American.

65 "A Portfolio of Klallam Photos," in Gorsline, ed., *Shadows of Our Ancestors*, 101-20. The photographers were Joe McKissick (1869-1939) and William Wilcox (?-1940), 101.

66 *North-West*, May 24, 1862. See also Mar. 1 and Mar. 29, 1862.

67 "Petition to Honorable Mayor and Common Council," Jan. 3, 1879; *Democratic Press*, May 20, 1879.

68 *Leader*, May 11, 1890; Delanty, *Along The Waterfront*, 102–5.

69 Lettter. from James Swan to Hon. Edward R. Geary, Superintendent Indian Affairs, Portland, Oregon, Oct. 26, 1860, Swan Papers, 1852–1907.

70 Swan, Diaries, June 14, 1870.

71 *Weekly Message*, Nov. 14, 1867.

72 Vincent, *Dungeness Massacre*, 19–20. Chet-ze-moka's son Lach-ka-nim – the Prince of Wales – lived there as well, dying in the 1930s; grandson David Prince moved to Jamestown ("Washington State, Believe It Or Not, Has Its Own 'Royal Family' Of The Olympics," Washington Pioneer Project, 2).

73 The right-to-fish clause of the 1854–55 treaties has been used to the present day by Washington tribes to protect their rights to fishing – both for individual and commercial purposes – from state attempts to prohibit or limit Indian fishing. In a series of cases stretching from 1904 to 1979, the United States Supreme Court: ruled that Washington Indians could not be barred from their usual and accustomed sites for fishing and could access those sites through either public or private lands (1904); ruled that the state could not regulate off-reservation Indian fishing (1942); reaffirmed the right of Indians to fish from accustomed sites and declared that since nets had been used and since there had been commercial aspects to Indian fishing at the time of the treaty, such aspects of modern Indian fishing were legal (1968); ruled that tribes could fish steelhead with nets but must follow state conservation measures (1973); reaffirmed rights of Indians to fish at "all usual and accustomed grounds and stations," subject to conservation regulation by the state (1977); ruled that Indians had right to a fair share of fish, to be calculated as 50 percent of the catch (1979, 1974 Boldt Decision in U.S. District Court) (Prucha, *American Indian Treaties*, 402–6; Gorsline, "The New Federalism," in *Shadows of Our Ancestors*, 230). Also see Barsh, "Ethnogenesis and Ethnonationalism," 215–43; Boxberger, *To Fish in Common*.

74 Eells, "Ten Years," 76; Gorsline, "Jamestown," in *Shadows of Our Ancestors,*164–6.

75 Eells, "Ten Years," quotation 82; Gorsline, "Jamestown," in *Shadows of Our Ancestors,* 164–6; Harmon, "A Different Kind of Indians," 315–6, 358, 427 n22; Langness, "A Case of Post Contact Reform," 166–200.

76 *Argus,* Sept. 14, 1876; *Democratic Press,* May 17, 1878.

77 *Argus,* June 2, 1876.

78 See Jamie Valadez et al., "The S'Klallam," 17–63, for a discussion of how the Elwha, Jamestown, and Port Gamble S'Klallam tribes gained federal recognition and their own reservations.

79 Browne, "The Coast Rangers."

80 *American National Biography,* 758–60; Browne, *J. Ross Browne: His Letters,* 181–2, xiii, 159–60; Goodman, *A Western Panorama,* 1 and 17, quotations 51, 127–37.

81 Goodman, *A Western Panorama,* 121–2.

82 "Letter from J. Ross Browne." See Wrobel, "Global West, American Frontier," 1–26, for a discussion of travel writers who "could be forceful critics of empire" (5), especially with regard to the consequences of expansion for Native Americans. Certainly, Browne and James Swan, while proponents of American expansion, were aware of the negative aspects of such for Indians.

83 Browne, "The Indians of California" in *Crusoe's Island,* 286–7, 291, 295. For a discussion of developing federal reservation policy in the Far West, see, Findlay, "An Elusive Institution," 13–7, and Prucha, *The Great Father,* 381–409.

84 Browne, "The Indians of California, 288–89; Browne, "The Conditions of the California Indian Reservations, 1856–57," quoted in Goodman, *A Western Panorama,* 118–19. Browne had an idealized understanding of missions; for a more realistic approach, see Sandos, "Between Crucifix and Lance," 196–229.

85 Browne to William P. Dole, Dec. 27, 1863, quoted in Findlay, "An Elusive Institution," 28.

86 "Report on the Conditions of Indian Reservations," 2.

87 Tribal leadership was advisory, rather than absolute, and dependent upon tribal acquiescence. Governor Stevens had appointed "chiefs" – in the political sense – because he wanted political

leaders with whom to negotiate treaties, but the position was not
traditional (Gibbs, "Tribes of Western Washington, 184–5; Simpson, "We Give Our Hearts to You," 125–6.

88 "Report on the Conditions of Indian Reservations," 7–8.

89 Stevens had been anxiously awaiting the report on Indians and
reservations, but more especially the companion report "Origin
of the Indian War of 1855–57." General Wool, commander of the
U.S. Army Department of the Pacific, had been very critical of the
conduct of both Stevens and the Territorial Volunteer forces during the war, suggesting that the civilian authorities had made war
"for the sake of plundering the national treasure." The Interior
Department had appointed Browne to look into the causes of the
war, one of two investigations required by Congress before it
would appropriate the funds necessary to pay the territorial debts
encountered during the war. Browne's report was seen to exonerate Stevens, and Congress eventually made restitution for the territorial debts (Lucile McDonald, *Swan among the Indians*, 31;
Richards, *Isaac I. Stevens*, 238, 333–42).

90 *Puget Sound Herald*, Apr. 23, 1858.

91 Letter to *San Francisco Bulletin*, reported in *Pioneer and Democ-
rat*, May 7, 1858. The other signatories were Washburn &
Wheele, J.G. Clinger, Thomas S. Russell, A. McLean, Fowler &
Co., A. Hibbard, J.J.H. VanBokkelin, G.H. Gerrish, and John
Price.

92 Letter to *San Francisco Globe* reported in *Pioneer and Democrat*,
May 7, 1858.

93 Ibid.

94 Browne, "The Great Port Townsend Controversy" in *Crusoe's Island*, 282–3.

95 *San Francisco Bulletin*, reported in *Register* Feb. 22, 1860.

96 *The North-West*, Aug. 30, 1860.

97 *Register*, May 22, 1861. According to one of Browne's biogra
phers, "for years afterwards particularly vile liquor was apt to be
referred to as 'Port Townsend whiskey'" (Browne, *J. Ross
Browne: His Letters*, 187).

98 *Weekly Message*, Nov. 21, 1867. The writer is probably also referring to Winthrop's *Canoe and Saddle*.

99 *The Weekly Message*, July 9, 1868; Oct. 6, 1869. See also: *Alta California*, Mar. 26, 1858; *Weekly Message*, Oct. 3, 1868; Feb. 24, 1869; Apr. 21, 1869.

100 Lucile McDonald, *Swan among the Indians*, quotation, 60; Swan, "Washington Sketches," 8.

101 Katz's introduction to Swan, *Almost Out of the World*, x.

102 *San Francisco Evening Bulletin*, May 10, 1859.

103 Bishop, "Why the 'Duke of York' Was Friendly to the Whites," Washington Pioneer Project, 1–2; *San Francisco Evening Bulletin*, May 19, 1859; McCurdy, *By Juan de Fuca's Strait*, 38. Similarly, in 1856 Michael Simmons tried to get Governor Stevens to send "six of the principal and 'most intelligent'" Puget Sound chiefs to Washington, D.C., and in 1859 several defeated chiefs from Eastern Washington and Oregon were taken to Portland (Ruby and Brown, *Indians of the Pacific Northwest*. See also Harmon "A Different Kind of Indians," 199, 254, n4).

104 *San Francisco Evening Bulletin*, May 10, 1859.

105 See Morgan, *The Last Wilderness*, 39–43. Other writers who comment upon the controversy are Goodman, *A Western Panorama*, 130–1; Dillon, *J. Ross Browne*, 73–84, 175; and McCurdy, *By Juan de Fuca's Strait*. McCurdy says that Browne "gave considerable offense" to townspeople; but missing the irony in Browne's apology, he suggests that townspeople forgave Browne after he claimed that the controversy actually promoted settlement by making Port Townsend "one of the best known towns on the Coast" (218).

106 See Hamer's discussion of the importance of a good image to nineteenth-century boosters, *New Towns*, 40–64.

107 *San Francisco Bulletin* quoted in *Pioneer and Democrat*, May 7, 1858.

108 *Bulletin*, May 10, 1859.

109 Swan, "Washington Sketches," 8.

110 "Report on the Conditions of Indian Reservations," 7–8.

111 Browne, "Controversy," in *Crusoe's Island*, 270–1.

112 Ibid., 273, 280.

113 Ibid., 273, 275.

CHAPTER THREE

1 H. Wilson to J. Wilson, Apr. 24,1853, Bushrod W. Wilson Papers, quoted in Cox, *Mills and Markets*, 60.
2 Swan, *San Francisco Evening Bulletin*, May 10, 1859.
3 McCurdy, *By Juan de Fuca's Strait* 102–10, 113, 119; Harmon, "A Different Kind of Indians," 238–40, 274 n100; Simpson et al., *City of Dreams*, 77–8.
4 Ficken, *Washington Territory*, 35–6.
5 Ficken, *The Forested Land*, 34, 39; Tattersall, "The Economic Development of the Pacific Northwest," 43, 67.
6 United States Census, Federal Population Census Schedules, 1860, 1870.
7 Geodosch, "Seabeck," 4,18; Cox, *Mills and Markets*, x, 96, 114; Ficken and LeWarne, *Washington*, 33.
8 Tattersall, "The Economic Development of the Pacific Northwest," 44, 76; McCurdy, *By Juan de Fuca's Strait*, 128.
9 Tattersall, "The Economic Development of the Pacific Northwest," 44–5, 68.
10 Harmon, "A Different Kind of Indians," 284.
11 Robbins, *Colony and Empire*, xi, 61–82; see also Emmons, "Constructed Province," 437–59; Jenson et al., "A Roundtable," 461–86.
12 *The North-West*, Oct. 25, 1860; *Weekly Message*, Feb. 25, 1870; *Argus*, Oct. 9, 1875; Stevens, *Report of Explorations for a Route for the Pacific Railroad*, 469.
13 Wrobel, *Promised Lands*, 2–3.
14 Schwantes, *The Pacific Northwest*, 227; Pomeroy, *The American Far West*, 16–17. The Immigration Aid Society would appear to be the first formally organized county development effort. However, it derived from the exertions of individuals rather than county or city government – all of which was quite minimalist until the 1890s in Washington (Ficken, *Washington State*, 126–33). A simple trustee form of city government was initiated in 1860. A city council and mayor replaced the trustees in 1878 (Daly and Gregory, "Port Townsend" in *With Pride in Heritage*,

64; Gregory, "Profiles of Pioneers" in *With Pride in Heritage,*
366). A chamber of commerce was established in 1890, and it did
work with the city council on development projects in succeeding
years; especially important was the input of the chamber in the
location of the Crown Zellerbach pulp and paper mill in Port
Townsend in 1928 (Thiele, "Chamber of Commerce" in *With
Pride in Heritage,* 81; Simpson et al., *City of Dreams,* 167–8).
However, until the 1890s, development projects were organized
by individuals working together; the Immigration Aid Society is
an example. Another example is the Port Townsend Southern
Railroad, incorporated by Port Townsend businessmen in 1887.
County residents provided the required $100,000 bonus paid to
the Oregon Improvement Company when that organization took
over the Port Townsend Southern Railroad, intending to complete
the line between Port Townsend and Olympia.

15 For further discussion of the booster press, see Boorstin, *The
Americans,* 124–34; Doyle, *The Social Order of a Frontier Community,* 62–4; Hamer, *New Towns in the New World,* 52, 60;
Moehring, *Urbanism and Empire,* 197–210; Wrobel, *Promised
Lands,* 6, 48–9, 203–4n22; Dykstra, *The Cattle Towns,* 149–50,
163–6. See Schwantes, *The Pacific Northwest,* 278–9, for a discussion of the Pacific Northwest frontier press. For further discussion of Jefferson County's early newspapers see McCurdy, *By
Juan de Fuca's Strait,* 142–6.

16 *Register,* July 26, 1860.

17 Ibid., Nov. 14, 1860.

18 *The North-West,* July 8, 1860.

19 *Argus,* May 4, 1877.

20 *Democratic Press,* Aug. 31, 1877.

21 The *Democratic Press* consolidated with the *Argus* on Jan. 21,
1881, turning over to the *Argus* its "business, good will and patronage" (*Argus,* Jan. 21, 1881).

22 *Port of Entry Times,* Jan. 12, 1884.

23 The *Port Townsend Leader* was renamed the *Jefferson County
Leader* several years ago.

24 McCurdy, *By Juan de Fuca's Strait,* 143.

25 *The North-West*, Jan. 18, 1862.

26 Prosch, *Reminiscences of Washington Territory*, 7, 11. See also Satterlee, *Dub of South Burlap*, 7–10).

·27 Hamer, *New Towns in the New World*, 60.

28 *The North-West*, July 8, 1860.

29 *Register*, July 26, 1860; *Argus*, July 26, 1877; *Weekly Message*, Aug. 20, 1868; *Leader*, Jan. 12, 1892; *The Quilcene Queen*, Oct. 22, 1891.

30 Prosch, *Reminiscences of Washington Territory*, 11, 36.

31 Ibid., 15.

32 *Argus*, July 3, 1879.

33 *Register*, May 2, 1860.

34 *Weekly Message*, Sept. 3, 1868; Apr. 8, 1870; Apr. 4, 1871.

35 *The North-West*, Oct. 25, 1860.

36 Sources for the customs house controversy are: local and territorial newspapers – especially *The North-West*, Sept. 1861 to Oct. 1862, and Marian Parks's biography of Smith, "A Man for His Season"; McCurdy, *By Juan de Fuca's Strait*, 54–9, and Ficken, *Washington Territory*, 70–5. Campbell, "The Victor Smith Saga" in With *Pride in Heritage*, 114–19, and Morgan, *Last Wilderness*, 45–54, have also written about the controversy.

37 Ficken, *Washington Territory*, 72.

38 Quoted in ibid., from *The North-West*, Mar. 15, 1862.

39 Parks, "A Man for His Season," 15–35.

40 Smith reported that he had decreased the cost per patient in the hospital from $2 per day to $1.50; dismissed unnecessary inspectors from the Customs service; decreased remaining employees' salaries; and proposed changing purchasing procedures, which would also lower expenditures. Smith even found a cheaper office for Customs, reducing the monthly rent from $600 to $180 ("with better accommodations"); total savings were $12,000 in the first six months (*The North-West*, June 14, 1862; July 12, 1862).

41 *The North-West*, Sept. 26, 1861; Oct. 3, 1861; Feb. 1, 1862.

42 *The North-West*, Mar. 8, 1862.

43 Parks, "A Man for His Season," 60.

44 *The North-West*, Nov. 2, 1861.

45 Letter from *Overland Press* (Olympia, Washington), quoted in *The North-West*, Jan. 25, 1862.

46 *Overland Press* quoted in *The North-West* Jan. 25, 1862; *The North-West* Nov. 16, 1861.

47 *The North-West*, Nov. 16, 1861.

48 Ibid., Mar. 22, 1862.

49 *Washington Standard*, Jan. 25, 1862; Feb. 8, 1862.

50 To list a few of Damon's accusations: Damon said that Smith had received financial gain from the sale of the U.S. Revenue Cutter *Jefferson Davis* (*The North-West*, Jan. 11, 1862); that Smith used appointments in the Customs Service to influence legislators to withdraw support of Joint Resolution No. 3 (Jan. 18, 1862); that he used Revenue Service Cutter crewmen to work on his property in Port Angeles (Feb. 8, 1862); that he found employment for family members in government service when they were not competent to do the work; that Smith received kickbacks from Dr Allyn, the newly appointed head of the Marine Hospital; as well, making improper use of government services and supplies for his family needs (June 14, 1862).

51 *The North-West*, Dec. 28, 1861; Jan. 18, 1862; Feb. 1, 1862; Feb. 8, 1862; *Washington Standard*, Jan. 25, 1862.

52 *The North-West*, Jan. 11, 1862.

53 Letter from Victor Smith to Secretary of the Treasury Salmon P. Chase, quoted in Parks, "A Man for His Season," 41. Smith had moved the Marine Hospital three miles from town in the fall of 1861.

54 *The North-West*, Mar. 22, 1862. The grand jury's complaint was dated Feb. 17, 1862.

55 *Washington Standard*, July 19, 1862.

56 Quoted in Parks, "A Man for His Season," 80.

57 *The North-West* May 24, 1862.

58 Ibid., July 5, 1862; Parks, "A Man for His Season," 77–8.

59 Parks, "A Man for His Season," 78.

60 *The North-West*, Aug. 21, 1862, quotations from the petition, "To the President, Abraham Lincoln, and to the Senate and House of Representative of the United States, in Congress assembled," "numerously signed."

61 *The North-West*, Aug. 9, 1862.

62 Parks, "A Man for His Season," vii, 43; Eutalain, "Abraham Lincoln," 3–22. See also Johannsen, "The Secession Crisis and the Frontier," 415–40; Lang, *Confederacy of Ambition*, 148, 177, 111– 83; Ficken, *Washington Territory*, 71–3.

63 *Washington Standard*, Aug. 16, 1862; *The North-West*, Aug. 31, 1862.

64 *The North-West*, Oct. 2, 1862; Parks, "A Man for His Season," 83.

65 Parks, "A Man for His Season," 83–9.

66 Ibid., 89–102.

67 McCurdy, *By Juan de Fuca's Strait*, 54–9, quotation, 58–9.

68 Immigration Aid Society, *North-Western Washington*, 24.

69 Parks, "A Man for His Season," 38.

70 Ibid., 44, 58–9; *Washington Standard*, Nov. 8, 1862.

71 *San Francisco Bulletin* (San Francisco, California), quoted in *The North-West*, Aug. 21, 1862.

72 Edwards, "'Terminus Disease'," 163–77; *Argus*, June 27, 1871; May 2, 1872.

73 Governor Marshall Moore, quoted in the *Weekly Message*, Mar. 11, 1870.

74 Schwantes, *The Pacific Northwest*, 171, 173; Richards, *Isaac I. Stevens*, 47.

75 See Johansen and Gates, *Empire of the Columbia*, 305–15; Meinig, *The Shaping of America*, 82, 83; Schwantes, *Railroad Signatures*, 14–18, 50–80, for discussions of Pacific Northwest railroad building. For a discussion of the intense interest displayed by Puget Sound communities in capturing the Northern Pacific terminus, see Edwards, "'Terminus Disease'," 163–77.

76 Quoted by Edwards, "'Terminus Disease'," 164; Ficken, *Washington Territory*, 2.

77 *Washington Standard*, June 11, 1870, quoted by Edwards, "'Terminus Disease'," 164.

78 *Weekly Message*, Feb. 25, 1870.

79 Turner, "Inventory of James G. Swan Papers," 6; Lucile McDonald, *Swan among the Indians*, 139–52; Doig, *Winter Brothers*, 135–9.

80 Stevens, Isaac I. *Report of Explorations for a Route for the Pacific Railroad*, 469; James G. Swan to Thomas H. Canfield, Esq., Gen Agent Northern Pacific RR, Burlington, Vermont, Dec. 3, 1868, Swan Papers.

81 James G. Swan to Thomas H. Canfield, Esq, General Agent Northern Pacific Rail Road Co, No 54 Broadway, NY, Feb. 27, 1869, Swan Papers.

82 James G. Swan to Thomas H. Canfield Esq, General Agent Northern Pacific Rail Road Co, May 12, 1869, Swan Papers.

83 Richards, *Isaac I. Stevens*, 326; *Register*, Apr. 18, 1860. Swan later published the report he made to Canfield in a pamphlet (C.H. Hanford to Hon. J.G. Swan, Port Townsend, Aug. 19, 1885, Swan Papers).

84 *Weekly Message*, Mar. 18, 1871.

85 Swan, "Washington Sketches," 8; Johansen and Gates, *Empire of the Columbia*, 308.

86 *Weekly Message*, Feb. 25, 1870.

87 *Argus*, June 27, 1871.

88 *Weekly Message*, Feb. 25, 1870.

89 *Argus*, Oct. 9, 1875.

90 *The North-West*, Oct. 25, 1860. See also, Ficken, *Washington Territory*, 6, 32–5.

91 *Democratic Press*, Apr. 26, 1878.

92 James G. Swan to Thomas H. Canfield, Esq, General Agent Northern Pacific Rail Road Co, No 54 Broadway, NY, Feb. 27, 1869, Swan Papers.

93 *Weekly Message*, Aug. 20, 1868; Sept. 3, 1868. Such a road would have been built along Hood Canal.

94 *Weekly Message*, Aug. 20, 1868.

95 *North-Western Washington*, 40, 42.

96 *North-Western Washington*, 16–17.

97 *Democratic Press*, Apr. 6, 1880.

98 *Argus*, May 15, 1879.

99 Ibid., June 26, 1879.

100 Ibid., July 3, 1879.

101 *Democratic Press*, Nov. 6, 1879.

102 Ibid., Apr. 6, 1880.

103 Ibid.

104 *Argus*, July 17, 1879. The *Argus*, Apr. 15, 1880, listed the society's charter members, men who were directly engaged in promotional activities. Thomas T. Minor was an important public figure in Port Townsend. He was president of the Immigration Aid Society and also politically active in the Republican Party, serving as a delegate to the 1876 and 1880 national conventions. He was twice mayor of Port Townsend; he moved to Seattle in 1882, where he was mayor (Gregory, "Profiles of Pioneers" in *With Pride in Heritage*, 396–7).

H.H. Learned settled in Port Townsend in 1865, was postmaster for many years, and business partner of his uncle, Enoch Fowler. Fowler was a prominent political figure and merchant who built and operated one of the first wharves and a hotel as well as owning other properties (Gregory, 388, 390, 367–8).

Allen Weir was the son of a pioneering family in nearby Clallam County. He bought the *Puget Sound Argus* in 1877, selling his interest in 1889 when he moved to Olympia (Gregory, 418–19).

D.C.H. Rothschild, who came to Port Townsend in 1858, was a merchant, shipping agent, and ship chandler. His two sons became active partners in his various enterprises in 1877 (Gregory, 403).

Samuel Hadlock was a capitalist, lumberman, land speculator, and landlord. He established a town site, named Port Hadlock, in 1870 and was one of the original incorporators of the Puget Sound Iron Company and its first superintendent. He and H.C. Willison were partners in real estate development in Irondale. In 1884 he and other investors built a lumber mill at Hadlock, which they sold to the burned-out Washington Mill Company in 1885 (Gregory, 371).

William Dodd was a lumberman associated with the Port Discovery mill and later manager of the Port Townsend Mill Company (McCurdy, *From Juan de Fuca's Strait*, 78).

Frank Bartlett was the son of Charles Bartlett, who settled in Port Townsend in 1864, operating a hotel and various successful stores. In 1880 the family built the Bartlett business block at a cost of $50,000. Frank Bartlett invested in several Port Townsend industrial ventures and served as a director of the Port Townsend Mill Company, treasurer of the Puget Sound Telegraph Company, and President of the Port Townsend Steel, Wire and Nail Company (Gregory 352, 354).

Granville O. Haller, a retired army officer, "engaged in farming and a number of business ventures at Port Townsend" (Gregory, 372).

Nathaniel D. Hill was another Port Townsendite deeply involved in local commercial ventures. He was a pharmacist and merchant and helped organize the First National Bank, the Port Townsend Southern Railroad, and the Puget Sound Telegraph company. He also invested in the Port Townsend Mill Company, a foundry, a water company, a wharf, and the Port Townsend Steel, Wire and Nail Company; he was active in county politics as well (Gregory, 376).

Joseph A. Kuhn, a commercial photographer and lawyer, was active in county and territorial politics and prominent in commercial enterprise. He was associated with three Port Townsend banks and helped organize the Port Townsend Southern Railroad and several other enterprises (Gregory, 384–5).

Last but not least, James Swan was also a member of the Immigration Aid Society. (There was insufficient information to profile W.H. Roberts, D.W. Smith – an attorney – Thomas Phillips, O.H. Holcomb, William Anderson, and L. Smith.)

105 *Democratic Press*, Apr. 15, 1880.

106 *Argus*, Apr. 15, 1880. Whether or not such immigrants and their cash ever materialized in the county is unknown.

107 *Democratic Press*, Apr. 21, 1880.

108 Ficken and LeWarne, *Washington*, 33–4.

109 *Democratic Press*, Apr. 6, 1880.

110 *Argus*, Jan. 28, 1881.

111 Myers became editor in August 1879 (*Democratic Press*, Aug. 21, 1879).

112 Blanchard; James Jones, a Port Townsend merchant and insurance agent; E.L. Canby; and Samuel Hadlock arranged incorporation of the company – see discussion below. Cyrus Walker of the Puget Sound Mill Company – located in Port Gamble, Kitsap

County, but owned by the San Francisco Pope and Talbot Company – was one of the directors. The other trustees were San Francisco men (Britton, *The Iron and Steel Industry in the Far West*, 151).

113 Ibid., 9–22. The mill reopened for a time in 1901 under different ownership (17, 22).

114 He was also appointed to offices by three territorial governors and was an elected delegate to the state constitutional convention (McCurdy, *By Juan de Fuca's Strait*, 145; Britton, *The Iron and Steel Industry in the Far West*, 15; Gregory, "Profiles of Pioneers" in *With Pride in Heritage*, 419–20).

115 Cox, *Mills and Markets*, 116, 240, n40; "Hadlock" in *With Pride in Heritage*, 210;

116 See Schwantes, *Radical Heritage*, 6–11, for a discussion of the effect travel literature and promotional efforts by local boosters – such as the Immigration Aid Society – as well as the railroads, had upon immigrants' expectations of the Northwest. Overall, the Northwest was portrayed as having endless resources and "get-rich-quick opportunities." It was also said to be "a veritable farmers' paradise" (8).

117 Schwantes, *The Pacific Northwest*, 205–6.

118 The prairies were the remnants of more extensive prairies of 3,000 to 4,000 years ago. When climatic cooling fostered heavy forests – which covered much of Western Washington by the time Euro-American settlement began – Native Americans maintained some of the prairies by systematic burning (Gorsline, "The Cultural Transformation of Sequim Prairie" in *Shadows of Our Ancestors*, 218); Simpson et al., *City of Dreams*, 10–11, 48–9, 163.

119 *North-Western Washington*, 9,11.

120 See White, *Land Use, Environment, and Social Change*, 55–61, 113–16, quotation, 56, for a discussion of the fertility of forested and logged-off land.

121 *North-Western Washington*, 10–11, 18. For further discussion of this type of family farming, see Watkins, *Rural Democracy*, 22–7. Richard White also discusses farming in nearby Island County. See especially the sections about farming on marginal lands (White, *Land Use, Environment, and Social Change*, 35–70, 113–

41). Archie Binns's memories of his boyhood on a Puget Sound "stump farm" are both perceptive and amusing; see "Stump Farm" in *The Roaring Land*, 2–27.

122 *Argus*, Apr. 3, 1875; Dec. 15, 1876.

123 Ibid., July 16, 1880; July 23, 1880.

124 *Democratic Press*, Apr. 26, 1878; *North-Western Washington*, 13.

125 White, *Land Use, Environment and Social Change*, 115–16.

126 Harmon, "A Different Kind of Indians," 284, 286; Tenth and Eleventh United States Censuses, 1880, 1890.

CHAPTER FOUR

1 *Washington Standard*, Nov. 22, 1862.

2 Leighton, *Life at Puget Sound*, 17, 81; Swan, *San Francisco Evening Bulletin*, May 9, 1859.

3 *Weekly Message*, Feb. 11, 1870; Swan, *San Francisco Evening Bulletin*, May 10, 1859.

4 *Washington Standard*, Nov. 22, 1862.

5 Photograph, E.M. Starrett Collection.

6 "Earliest Settlers of Port Townsend," Washington Pioneer Project, 2; *Washington Standard*, Nov. 22, 1862.

7 *Weekly Message*, Mar. 18, 1870; Jan. 3, 1871; Swan, Diaries, Jan. 7, 1874; *Democratic Press*, Aug. 7, 1879; *Argus*, Mar. 29, 1883.

8 *Port Townsend Daily Call* (hereinafter cited as the *Call*), May 14, 1895.

9 Swan, *San Francisco Evening Bulletin*, May 10, 1859; "Loren Bingham Hastings," Washington Pioneer Project, 3.

10 Hamer, *New Towns in the New World*, 45–6, quotation 40, 45–7, 58–9.

11 Swan, *San Francisco Evening Bulletin*, May 19, 1859.

12 *The North-West*, Nov. 16, 1861.

13 *Register*, Mar. 28, 1860.

14 For mention of rough areas in other frontier towns and residents' attempts to come to terms with the attendant vice and potential for violence in such areas, see Norman H. Clark, *Mill Town*, 101–2, and also his chapter, "The 'Hell-Soaked Institution,'" in

The Dry Years, 54–63; Dykstra, *The Cattle Towns*, 239–92; Malone, *The Battle for Butte*, 57–79; Morgan, *Skid Road*, 6–7; Morrissey, *Mental Territories*, 52–5, 182n80; Rettmann, "Business, Government, and Prostitution," 77–83; Sale, *Seattle*, 56–8.

15 Murphy, *Mining Cultures*, xvi; also see Wood, *The Freedom of the Streets*.

16 Dykstra, *The Cattle Towns*, 263–85.

17 Malone, *The Battle for Butte*, 71; Barber, *Reno's Big Gamble*, 9.

18 Morrissey, *Mental Territories*, 52, 54, 182n80. See also Rettmann, "Business, Government, and Prostitution."

19 While these issues may have been played out politically, evidence for this is lacking. According to Robert Ficken, local governments were "traditionally informal" during the territorial period (*Washington State*, 126–33). It may be that petitions to the city council were the extent of such informal efforts at moral reform.

20 Weir, "Roughing It on Puget Sound," 74.

21 Swan, *San Francisco Evening Bulletin*, May 10, 1859.

22 McCurdy, *By Juan de Fuca's Strait*, 81–8; Dunbar, "In the Days of McGuffey's Reader" in *With Pride in Heritage*, 30–5.

23 Schaub et al., "Churches" in *With Pride in Heritage*, 84–90; Letter to Chamber of Commerce from Mrs Percy E. Davidson, LS, Oct. 5, 1959, MSS 3D, Archival Collections, McCurdy Historical Research Library.

24 "Lodges and Clubs in Port Townsend," TMS, MSS 100, Archival Collections, McCurdy Historical Research Library. Formation of other fraternal orders was more gradual: International Order of Good Templars, 1867 (*Argus*, July 5, 1883); the Improved Order of Red Men, 1872; Independent Order of Odd Fellows, 1877; Brotherhood of the Protective Order of Elks, 1895; Fraternal Order of Eagles, 1901. The program for Port Townsend's Memorial Day parade on May 30, 1891, lists several social organizations: Grand Army of the Republic, Women's Relief Corps, Knights of Pythias, Odd Fellows, Independent Order of Good Templars, Red Men, Ancient Order of United Workmen, and Sons of St George ("Lodges and Clubs in Port Townsend;" "Memorial Day, Port Townsend, Washington, 1891, May Thirti-

eth," Program, MSS 1, Archival Collections, McCurdy Historical
Research Library.)

25 McCurdy, *By Juan de Fuca's Strait*, 229; Daly and Gregory, "Port
Townsend" in *With Pride in Heritage*, 64; Gregory, "Profiles of
Pioneers" in *With Pride in Heritage*, 366.

26 Ficken, *Washington State*, 126.

27 McCurdy, *By Juan de Fuca's Strait*, 67. See chapter 3.

28 *Register*, Jan. 18, 1860, also reprinted in *Weekly Message*, Mar.
4, 1870. For a similar description of a frontier courtroom scene,
see Swan, *The Northwest Coast*, 292–303; also, a collection of
anecdotes by Swan, "James Swan," TMS, MSS 15a, Archival
Collections, McCurdy Historical Reference Library.

29 Leighton, *Life at Puget Sound*, 84; *Register*, Mar. 28, 1860.

30 Ficken, *Washington State*, 140–3.

31 Quotations from a female correspondent to the *Argus*, Jan. 1,
1876, and Clark Crandall, a Portland newsman who visited the
Sound region in 1871 (Edwards, "'Terminus Disease'," 173).

32 *The Northwest*, Nov. 29, 1860; May 9, 1861.

33 *Weekly Message*, May 21, 1868; July 23, 1868; and Sept. 1,
1869. *Argus*, June 27, 1871; May 2, 1872; June 2, 1875; Oct. 6,
1876; Apr. 4, 1877; May 18, 1877. County population in 1860
was 531; in 1870, 1,268; in 1880, 1,712; in 1890, 8,368 (Federal
Population Census).

34 "R.L. Polk & Co's Puget Sound Directory," 1887; ibid., 1890;
Samuelson, "List compiled from incomplete collection of liquor
license applications; Satterlee, *Dub of South Burlap*, 243.

35 "Hill, Howard ... Port Townsend," Washington Pioneer Project, 2.

36 "Port Townsend, Washington," Sanborn fire insurance map,
1888; "Robert Gow: Last of the Native Born Chinese," 88–90;
"Richard Francis McCurdy: The Early Years," 43–4; "Hill Family, 6; Swan, Diaries, Feb. 28, Mar. 1, 1877.

37 "Old Pilot Notes"; Perry, *Seabeck*, 104, 108.

38 Samuelson, "List Compiled from Incomplete Collection of City
Arrest Records, November 1879–June 1913."

39 "Petition to Honorable Mayor and Common Council of the City
of Port Townsend," D, Jan. 3, 1879, MSS 3A; "Petition to the

Hon. Mayor and Common Council of Port Townsend, Wash.
Terr.," D, undated, MSS 3A; "Petition to the Honorable Mayor
and Common Council of the City of Port Townsend," D, August
1892, MSS 3A; "Petition To the Honorable the Mayor and City
Council of Port Townsend, Wash.," D, undtd., MSS 3A (all petitions are Archival Collections, McCurdy Historical Research Library). I would date the second petition between 1885 and 1889,
since at least one of the signators (George Starrett) did not move
to Port Townsend until 1885, and Washington ceased to be a
territory in 1889. The fourth petition is addressed to Port
Townsend, Washington, rather than Washington Territory, and
it is signed by James Swan, who died in 1900; a probable range
of dates is therefore between 1889 and 1900 (Gregory, "Profiles
of the Pioneers" in *With Pride in Heritage*, 409).

40 *Argus*, Mar. 22, 1886; Apr. 1, 1886. Also see *Leader*, May 11,
1890; May 13, 1890; May 14, 1890; May 17, 1890.

41 Brad Asher, "Their Own Domestic Difficulties," n82, 208.

42 *Democratic Press*, Sept. 28, 1877.

43 County newspaper coverage was limited until 1868, when the
Weekly Message began publication, after which events in Jefferson County were routinely covered by at least one and often two
newspapers.

44 There is an extensive literature on frontier violence focused on
"whether the incidence of interpersonal killing ... was – or was
not – as commonplace and large in volume as widely thought"
(Dykstra, "Quantifying the Wild West," 321). For the purposes
of this discussion for Jefferson County, violence is broadly
defined.

45 *The North-West*, May 23, 1861.

46 *Weekly Message*, July 16, 1868.

47 Ibid., Dec. 3, 1868.

48 Ibid., Aug. 11 and Sept. 15, 1869.

49 Ibid., Oct. 6, 1869.

50 Ibid., Apr. 4, 1871.

51 Ibid., May 23, 1871.

52 *Democratic Press*, Sept. 7, 1877.

53 Ibid., Apr. 5, 1878.

54 Ibid., Sept. 23, 1878. Also see *Weekly Message*, July 9, 1868;
    Sept. 15, 1869; May 9, 1871; *Democratic Press*, Sept. 21, 1877;
    Sept. 23, 1878; Dec. 19, 1879; Aug. 26, 1880, for other incidents
    involving violence. Swan also noted many incidents of violence.
    See Swan, Diaries, Nov. 6, 1872; Aug. 30, 1873; Feb. 21, 1874;
    Mar. 4, 1874; Jan. 15, 1875; Mar. 11, 1877; Apr. 26, 1886.

55 Weir, "Roughing It on Puget Sound in the Early Sixties," 74.

56 "Oral History of Mrs. Florence Pittman," 5.

57 Swan, *San Francisco Evening Bulletin*, May 10, 1859.

58 Pilcher, "The Port Townsend of 1868," Washington Pioneer
    Project, 2–3.

59 "Oral History of Mrs. Florence Pitman,"4–5. Mrs Pitman came
    to Port Townsend from England in 1882. Probably an adolescent
    when she arrived, her aunt and uncle immediately put her to
    work as a domestic laborer in their boarding house. She lived the
    rest of her life in Jefferson County.

60 Satterlee, *Dub of South Burlap*, 19.

61 *Argus*, Apr. 20, 1879.

62 Dorothy McLarney to author, LS, Oct. 23, 1995, in possession of
    author. Mrs McLarney, who was born in Port Townsend in 1906,
    was a student of Port Townsend's history throughout her life. I
    am indebted to her for the time and trouble she took to corre-
    spond with me about many aspects of Port Townsend's history,
    but especially about the divisions between downtown and up-
    town. Mrs McLarney died, May 19, 2001 (Redmen Cemetary
    Records). See also: "Richard Frances McCurdy: The Early
    Years," 15, 44, 83–4; "Horace Winslow McCurdy," 93.

63 *Argus*, Dec. 30, 1885.

64 "Port Townsend, Washington," Sanborn fire insurance map,
    1888; "R.L. Polk & Co's Puget Sound Directory," 1887; Wash-
    ington Territorial Census, 1889. County population in 1887 was
    3,393 and Washington Territory's population was 140,014 (cited
    in Wynne, "Reaction to the Chinese," Appendix II, 493).

65 Wynne, "Reaction to the Chinese," 493.

66 I have assumed that the nine single women with no listed occupa-
    tion whose address was the beach or Water Street were prosti-
    tutes. The actual figure would have been higher, I surmise.

67 "Louis Herman Hansen," 118.

68 *The North-west*, July 26, 1860.

69 Ibid., July 26, 1860.

70 Ibid., Nov. 1, 1860.

71 *Weekly Message*, Nov. 21, 1867. See also ibid., Oct. 3, 1868; Feb. 24, 1869 and Apr. 21, 1869, for similar entries.

72 Ibid., Dec. 18, 1868.

73 *Democratic Press*, Oct. 5, 1877.

74 *Weekly Message*, Oct. 27, 1869.

75 Ibid., May 18, 1871.

76 Ibid., Mar. 23, 1871.

77 *Argus*, Sept. 21, 1876.

78 *Weekly Message*, July 9, 1868.

79 Ibid., Mar. 25, 1870.

80 *Democratic Press*, Feb. 15, 1878.

81 Norman H. Clark, *The Dry Years*, 26. Washington residents – following trends established throughout the United States – made several attempts to control or eliminate the use of alcohol, which culminated in the 1914 law prohibiting the sale and manufacture of liquor in Washington, a measure which was rejected in Jefferson County by 56% of voters (116; see also 32–5, 81–94).

82 Of the first thirty-three cases heard by the First Judicial Circuit Court held in Port Townsend in 1854 and 1855, twenty-one were brought against either people accused of selling liquor to Native Americans, or Native Americans involved in incidents of violence (Harmon, "Different Kind of Indians," 256 n12). According to Harmon, the new territorial government (established in 1854) was determined to establish the supremacy of American law not only over Native Americans, but also over settlers who had been accustomed to managing without the law, especially where relations between Native Americans and themselves were concerned, meting out punishment for supposed wrongs and selling them liquor (199–205). The prohibition law may have been connected to this effort. Supporting this reasoning, Norman H. Clark found that those counties with significant numbers of Native Americans living in close proximity with settlers – as in Jefferson County –

voted "yes," to this first legislative effort for prohibition (*The Dry Years*, 21–7).

83 Lucile McDonald, *Swan among the Indians*, 77. Swan was known to be a heavy drinker who periodically swore off.

84 *Register*, Mar. 28, 1860. The Moral Reform Club of Port Townsend (which may have been the same organization) held a meeting in April (*Register*, Apr. 11, 1860). The longevity of these clubs is unknown, but it is worth noting that they were more likely similar to the Dashaway Club.

85 Norman H. Clark, *The Dry Years*, 28.

86 *Argus*, July 5, 1883; Mar. 13, 1879; May 31, 1883; *Democratic Press*, Jan. 4, 1878; Satterlee, *Dub of South Burlap*, 243; *Argus*, Feb. 4, 1886; Norman H. Clark, *The Dry Years*, 28; Satterlee, *Dub of South Burlap*, 243.

87 *Weekly Message*, Dec. 10, 1869; *Argus*, June 2, 1875; Mar. 13, 1879; June 26, 1879; July 3, 1879; May 31, 1883; July 5, 1883; Feb. 4, 1886.

88 *Argus*, July 5, 1883, qtn.; Norman H. Clark, *The Dry Years*, 34. See also *Argus*, Feb. 4, 1886.

89 *Leader*, Jan. 24, 1892; Jan. 30, 1892; Feb. 2, 1892; Feb. 5, 1892; Feb. 17, 1892; quotations Jan. 30 and Feb. 2, 1892; Satterlee, *Dub of South Burlap*, 243.

90 Letter from "W.L." LS, June 18, 1877, MSS 38, Archival Collections, McCurdy Historical Research Library. "W.L." was probably William Learned, writing to his son William Henry Harrison Learned. Alphonso was William's elder son and a partner with Enoch Fowler in a merchandising and shipping business that sold liquor in Port Townsend (Gregory, "Profiles of Pioneers" in *With Pride in Heritage*, 387–8).

91 *Democratic Press*, Feb. 23, 1879; June 19, 1879; June 26, 1879; July 3, 1879 (quotation).

92 *Argus*, Dec. 18, 1879.

93 The law was declared unconstitutional by the territorial supreme court in 1888. See Norman H. Clark, *The Dry Years*, 28–30, 35–6, 38–40, 81–107, for a discussion of the various attempts in Washington to inaugurate the local option. The failure of the

local option eventually prompted prohibitionists to work for a
state law prohibiting the sale and manufacture of liquor.

94 *Argus*, Jan. 28, 1886.

95 Ibid., Feb. 4, 1886.

96 Ibid., Apr. 29, 1886; see also Mar. 18, 1886.

97 "Proceedings of the County Commissioners of Jefferson County,
W.T., Regular Meeting Monday, May 7, 1877," reported in
Argus, May 18, 1877.

98 *Leader*, May 4, 1892.

99 *Argus*, May 18, 1877.

100 *Weekly Message*, Oct. 27, 1869.

101 *Democratic Press*, June 7, 1878; Dec. 12, 1878; *Argus* Aug. 30,
1883; Sept. 6,1883.

102 *Argus*, Aug. 29, 1883.

103 *Weekly Message*, May 18, 1871.

104 *Argus*, July 16, 1880.

105 *Weekly Message*, July 23, 1868.

106 Ibid., Oct. 27, 1869.

107 *Democratic Press*, Dec. 12, 1878.

108 *Argus*, Aug. 2, 1883.

109 *Democratic Press*, Dec. 11, 1879.

110 *Leader*, May 13, 1890.

111 "Petition to the Hon. Mayor and Common Council of Port
Townsend, Wash. Terr."; "Petition To the Honorable the Mayor
and City Council of Port Townsend, Wash."

112 McCurdy, *By Juan de Fuca's Strait*, 203–4; Swan, Diaries, Mar. 3,
1874; Mar. 4, 1874.

113 *Register*, Mar. 28, 1860; *Leader*, May 7, 1890.

114 *Leader*, Jan. 10, 1892, Feb. 10, 1892.

CHAPTER FIVE

1 Officially, Chinese immigration to the area began in the 1860s;
the 1860 census records only one Chinese resident in Washington
Territory (U.S. Census, Federal Population Schedules, 1860).
Other sources than the census, however, suggest larger numbers.
See Buchanan, "Lumbering and Logging"; *Register*, Mar. 7,

1860; *The North-West*, Mar. 8 and Oct. 30, 1862; Affidavit, Sing Lee, June 3, 1886, in "Report of the Governor of Washington Territory to Secretary of the Interior, Oct. 8, 1866" (hereinafter cited as Squire's Report to Interior).

2 In response to anti-Chinese pressure, the 1868 Burlingame Treaty between China and the United States – which allowed free immigration between China and the United States – was renegotiated, and a new treaty ratified in 1881 required that China accept limitations, regulation, and/or suspension of immigration by Chinese laborers. The 1882 Exclusion Act and its amendments and successors of 1884, 1888, 1892, 1893, 1894, and 1902 limited and denied entry into the United States to Chinese laborers who could not prove previous American residence. Between 1888 and 1894 the Scott Act denied re-entry even to previously resident laborers. Only merchants, their dependent families, American-born Chinese and their children, various professionals, students, and government officials and their dependents were allowed to enter and establish residence in the United States. The Immigration Act of 1924 prohibited the immigration of any persons ineligible for citizenship, which included Chinese who had been forbidden naturalization through various acts of Congress. After 1930 the wives of resident Chinese were allowed to immigrate. Chinese exclusion was repealed in 1943 and replaced with a quota system; in addition, persons of Chinese descent or origin were to be eligible for naturalization. Further legislation in 1945 and 1946 granted entry to "alien spouses and alien minor children" and fiancées. The quota system was removed in 1965. See Daniels, *Guarding the Golden Door*, 3–26, 91–5, quotation 94. Also see Erika Lee, *At America's Gates*, 19–26; Takaki, *Strangers from a Different Shore* , 235; Tsai, *The Chinese Experience*, 62–7, 72–6; Yung, *Unbound Voices*, 9–16.

3 Schwantes, "From Anti-Chinese Agitation," 176; see also Schwantes, "Protest in a Promised Land."

4 Schwantes, "From Anti-Chinese Agitation," 175.

5 Ibid., 176.

6 Posters, "Great Anti-Chinese Mass Meeting! [Tacoma, Washington]," June 3, 1885, EPH-A 979.778031, An87G, 1885 and

EPH-A 979.778031, W434, 1885, Fuller Collection; Karlin, "The Anti-Chinese Outbreaks in Seattle," 103–5, and "The Anti-Chinese Outbreak in Tacoma," 271–3; Schwantes, "From Anti-Chinese Agitation," 176–7.

7 *Seattle Post-Intelligencer*, (hereinafter cited as *Post Intelligencer*), Sept. 10, 1885; Letter to L.Q.C. Lamar, Secretary of the Interior, from Watson C. Squire, Governor of Washington Territory, Oct. 12, 1885, Squire's Report to Interior; McGraw, "The Anti-Chinese Riots of 1885," 388–9.

8 By spontaneous I mean those expulsions which occurred with little apparent advance planning. At Squak Valley and the coal mines, groups of non-Chinese workers had tried to force employers to let Chinese employees go; when these efforts failed, violent expulsions followed. Later expulsions such as those from Tacoma and Seattle were planned by movement organizers over a period of time.

9 Territorial census figures for 1885 list ninety-five Chinese residents for Jefferson County (figures quoted in Wynne, "Reaction to the Chinese," Appendix II, 493–4). However, according to the *Argus*, the population, at the end of December 1885, was about 300, which may be more accurate. Port Townsend's Chinese population may have been larger than the official figures because of refugees fleeing the violence and expulsions in Tacoma, Seattle, and other territorial towns. Also, illegal immigrants would have avoided an official census taker, but their numbers may have been apparent to residents; see discussion below (*Argus*, Dec. 24, 1885). Further, following the reasoning of Cole Harris and Robert Galois as stated in their analysis of the 1881 British Columbia census, census takers may have had a tendency to underestimate Chinese and Native American numbers, their focus being more nearly directed to Euro-Americans (See their chapter, "A Population Geography of British Columbia in 1881," in Harris, ed., *The Resettlement of British Columbia*, 137–60, esp. 137–8).

10 For early treatments of the expulsions, see Adams, *To and Fro*, 431–2; Evans, *History of the Pacific North West*, 51; Bancroft, *History of Washington*, 294; Grant, *History of Seattle*, 187; Hawthorne, *History of Washington*, 310; Kinnear, *Anti-Chinese*

Riots, 3; McGraw, "The Anti-Chinese Riots," 389–90. For works that focus on working-class participation in the movement, see Karlin, "The Anti-Chinese Outbreaks in Seattle," 103–29, and "The Anti-Chinese Outbreak in Tacoma," 271–83; Morgan, *Puget's Sound*, 212–52; Schwantes, *Radical Heritage*; Schwantes, "Protest in a Promised Land," 373–90; and Schwantes, "From Anti-Chinese Agitation," 174–84. For works that focus on middle-class participation, see Halseth and Glasrud, "Anti-Chinese Movements in Washington," 117–18; Wynne, "Reaction to the Chinese," 275, 283; Shuman, "The Role of Seattle's Newspapers," 51; Cloud, "Laura Hall Peters," 28–36. Also see Dettman, "Anti-Chinese Violence in the American Northwest"; Todd Stevens, "Brokers between Worlds"; and Pfaelzer, *Driven Out*.

11 Willson and MacDonald, "Port Townsend's Pioneer Chinese Merchants," 20 and Willson and MacDonald, "Racial Tension at Port Townsend," 1, 6–11.

12 Liestman, "'The Various Celestials among Our Town'," 93–104.

13 A conservative estimate of the 1885 Lower Sound Chinese community – Clallam, Island, Jefferson, Kitsap, San Juan, Skagit, Snohomish, and Whatcom counties – based upon official figures is 373 (in Wynne, "Reaction to the Chinese," Appendix II, 493–4), although, for reasons as cited in n9, official figures may fall short of the real number.

14 Port Townsend's Chinese community has long been a subject of interest. See Forwood, "Port Townsend ... Parts I-V"; "Robert Gow: Last of the Native Born Chinese"; Liestman, "'The Various Celestials among Our Town'"; McCurdy, *By Juan de Fuca's Strait*, 207–15; Simpson et al., *City of Dreams*, 51–3; Willson and MacDonald, "Port Townsend's Pioneer Chinese Merchants" and "Racial Tension at Port Townsend."

15 U.S. Census, Federal Population Schedules, 1890; *Leader*, Feb. 9, 1890.

16 There was one in 1860, 234 in 1870, 3,186 in 1880, 3,260 in 1890, 3,629 in 1900, and 2,790 in 1910 (U.S. Census, Federal Population Schedules, 1860, 1870, 1880, 1890, 1900, 1910).

17 *Register*, Mar. 7, 1860; Buchanan, "Lumbering and Logging"; *The North-West*, Mar. 8, 1862. Another early reference: a

Chinese man was fined $40 for attacking a fellow employee in a
Port Townsend home in 1868 (*Weekly Message*, May 6, 1868).
In addition, a dozen or more Chinese are also known to have
worked in a coal mine near Bellingham in 1862 (*The North-West*,
Oct. 30, 1862). Chin Chun Hock, Seattle's first Chinese immigrant, arrived in 1860, founding that city's first Chinese mercantile establishment in 1868 – a business that remained active until
the 1950s (Lucile McDonald, "Seattle's First Chinese Resident."
For further discussion of Chinese employment on Puget Sound,
see Art Chin, *Golden Tassels*, 35–41, 44–6; and Wynne, "Reaction to the Chinese," 79–84.

18 U.S. Census, Federal Population Census Schedules, 1870. Nine-
    teen Chinese residents are listed in the 1870 federal census for
    Jefferson County; 96 for 1880; 209 for 1887; and 331 for 1889
    (1887 and 1889 figures in Wynne, "Reaction to the Chinese,"
    Appendix II, 493).

19 Sam Sing is listed in the 1870 census as a laundryman, and he ap-
    parently came to Port Townsend even earlier, since he was known
    to have been a "house servant" first. He remained in business
    until 1890 (U.S. Census, 1870; Swan, Diaries, Jan. 30, 1883;
    Mar. 7, 1884; *Leader*, Feb. 15, 1890; *Democratic Press*, Oct. 9,
    1879).

20 Chinese names are spelled as they appear the various sources used
    for this study.

21 The Zee Tai Company continued under ownership of the Ng fam-
    ily until 1930, when the property was sold (Willison and Mac-
    Donald, "Port Townsend's Pioneer Chinese Merchants," 20).

22 In 1880 there were twenty-one woodchoppers at work near Chi-
    macum employed by Sheriff Ben Miller, perhaps clearing land for
    the Puget Sound Ironmaking Co. (U.S. Census, Federal Popula-
    tion Schedules, 1880; *Democratic Press*, Oct. 26, 1880; Nov. 4
    1880).

23 See Cassel, "Introduction," in *The Chinese in America*, 1–18;
    Daniels, "Majority Issues" in *Nativism, Discrimination, and Im-
    ages of Immigrants*, 74–9; Lyman, *Chinatown and Little Tokyo*,
    37–68; Mei, "Socioeconomic Origins of Emigration: Guangdong
    to California" in *Labor Immigration under Capitalism*, 219–45;

Takaki, *Strangers from a Different Shore*, 21–42; Tsai, *The Chinese Experience in America*, 12, 1–10.

24 See Chen, "The Internal Origins of Chinese Emigration," 544; Liu, "The Social Origins of Early Chinese Immigrants," 21–36; and Valentine, "Chinese Placer Mining in the United States" in *The Chinese in America*, 37–53, for a reappraisal of the reasons for nineteenth-century Chinese emigration to the United States.

25 Mei, "Socioeconomic Origins of Emigration," 232–3, 235–8; Takaki, *Strangers from a Different Shore*, 119; Tsai, *The Chinese Experience in America*, 8.

26 Takaki, *Strangers from a Different Shore*, 10–11; Cheng Hirata, "Free, Indentured, Enslaved," 5.

27 "Emigrant" means "sojourner" in Chinese (Daniels, "Majority Issues," 78). Estimates vary, but it is likely that more than 50% of nineteenth-century Chinese emigrants to the United States never returned permanently to China (Lyman, *Chinatown and Little Tokyo*, 42; Mei, "Socioeconomic Origins of Emigration", 238–9; Takaki, *Strangers from a Different Shore*, 116). Whatever the return figure – large or small – it does not diminish the sojourner ideal. For many there was movement back and forth between China and the United States, although accurate numbers are difficult to estimate especially for the period following the 1882 Exclusion Act. For discussion of Chinese American transnationalism, see Sucheng Chan, "Introduction" in *Chinese Americans*; Chen, *Chinese San Francisco*; Hsu, *Dreaming of Gold*; Liu, "Transnational Historiography," 135–53; Scott K. Wong, " Review Essay."

28 *Leader*, Nov. 27, 1890; Zee Tai to Washington Mill Company, LS Dec., 17, 1887, MSS 43, Washington Mill Company Papers (hereinafter cited as WMC Papers). I have identified the following Jefferson County labor contractors: Zee Tai Company, established in 1878; Yee Sing Wo Kee Company, established by at least 1887 and probably earlier; Hong Kee Company, in operation from at least 1890 through 1903; Zee Sing and Company in operation in at least 1884. The Hong Yung Company combined a restaurant with labor contracting at least throughout 1887–90. There may have been others, and the dates are not conclusive. Many con-

cerns may have been in operation earlier than available sources indicate ("R.L. Polk & Co's Puget Sound Directory," 1887; "R.L. Polk & Co's Port Townsend City Directory," 1890; "Port Townsend, Washington," Sanborn fire insurance map, 1888; McCurdy Historical Research Library; Fong Chong of Hong Kee to Washington Mill Company, LS, Nov. 9, 1900; Feb. 20, 1902; Apr. 25, 1902; June 9, 1902; Aug. 2, 1902; Sept. 9, 1903, WMC Papers; *Argus*, Mar. 20, 1884; Willison and MacDonald, "Port Townsend's Pioneer Chinese Merchants," 21.)

29 Daniels, "Majority Issues," in *Nativism, Discrimination, and Images of Immigrants*, 79–86; Mei, "Socioeconomic Developments," 381–2, 392–7; Takaki, *Strangers from a Different Shore*, 82–92; Tsai, *The Chinese Experience in America*, 10–15; Wynne, "Reaction to the Chinese," 12–105.

30 Mei, "Socioeconomic Origins of Emigration," 239–41; Gedosch, "Seabeck," 121; *Leader*, Nov. 27, 1890; Liestman, "'The Various Celestials among Our Town,'" 98.

31 The mills were the Port Townsend Mill, the Washington Mill Company at Seabeck and Port Hadlock, the Port Discovery Mill, and the Puget Mill Company at Port Ludlow.

32 Sources used to construct this profile of Jefferson County Chinese labor: *Washington Standard*, Sept. 25, 1885; W.J. Adams, to Washington Mill Co., LS, Nov. 7, 1888, WMC Papers; Wa Chong to WMC, LS, Sept. 6, 1894; Mar. 28, 1895; Dec. 30, 1896; Apr. 25, 1897, WMC Papers; Fong Chong of Hong Kee to WMC, LS, Nov. 9, 1900; Feb. 20, 1902; Apr. 25, 1902; June 9, 1902; Aug. 2, 1902; Sept. 9, 1903, WMC Papers; Washington Territorial Census, 1880, 1889; U.S. Census, Federal Population Census Schedules, 1870, 1880, 1900, 1910, 1920; Chin, *Golden Tassels*, 39; Gedosch, "Seabeck," 121–2; "Robert Gow: Last of the Native Born Chinese," 9, 12, 56, 88; Liestman, "'The Various Celestials among Our Town,'" 96; McCurdy, *From Juan de Fuca's Strait*, 212; Simpson et al., *City of Dreams*, 131. The Port Townsend Mill Company replaced its Chinese millworkers with Euro-Americans at the height of the 1885–86 anti-Chinese agitation. The Washington Mill Company first contracted for Chinese laborers in 1883 and continued to do so into the first decade of the new

century. Approximately sixty men worked for the mill in 1889, although by 1900 there were only eight. The Port Discovery Mill also employed Chinese, approximately twenty-one laborers in 1889 and several cooks. Chinese do not appear to have worked in the logging camps except as cooks. The Puget Sound Iron Company appears to have employed Chinese workers as well – thirteen laborers listed in 1889 for Irondale, where the foundry was the only large-scale employer (W. J. Adams to Washington Mill Company, LS, Nov. 17, 1888, WMC Papers; "Robert Gow: Last of the Native Born Chinese," 9, 12).

33 During the twentieth century, Chinese were also employed by the military at Fort Worden, 1902–53, and by several Port Townsend fish canneries: the Puget Sound Sardine Co, 1902–3, and the Hillside Packing Company and Key City Packing Company, which were salmon canneries, 1906–16. The Zee Tai Company also contracted Chinese labor to salmon canneries in Washington and Alaska, and after the Port Townsend canneries closed, some Chinese residents continued such work far afield, returning to Port Townsend in the off-season (*Leader*, Sept. 9, 1903; June 9 and Aug. 11, 1906; Mar. 28 and Aug. 13, 1908; "Robert Gow: Last of the Native Born Chinese," 9, 102–3).

34 One garden of approximately eight acres was located near Port Townsend on North Beach; the other of sixty acres was at Station Prairie, near Fort Townsend. This farm employed approximately twenty Chinese in the 1890s, although the 1900 census lists only nine Chinese farmers in that area. From 1905 to 1920 one Charlie Tuey farmed at Station Prairie. The North Beach "Chinese Gardens" were well established by at latest 1892 and probably much earlier. According to Robert Gow's recollections, between 1910 and 1917 approximately twenty Chinese were employed in the operation. This farm dominated the fresh vegetable market until at least the Second World War and continued to be worked into the 1960s. (U.S. Census, Federal Population Census Schedules, 1900; H.C. Willison, Health Officer, to Mayor and Council, Port Townsend, Washington, LS, Apr. 3, 1892, MSS 3a, Archival Collections, McCurdy Historical Research Library; "Robert Gow: Last of the Native Born Chinese," 12; McCurdy, *By Juan*

de Fuca's Strait, 205; *Leader*, Sept. 29, 1914; Forwood, "Port Townsend ... Part II and IV"; Simpson et al., *City of Dreams*, 10–11; Liestman, "'The Various Celestials among Our Town,'" 96). For discussion of Chinese truck gardens in Portland, Oregon, see Marie Rose Wong, *Sweet Cakes, Long Journey*, 211–20.

35 Laundries might employ as many as ten laborers at a time. U.S. Census, Federal Population Census Schedules, 1870, 1880, 1890, 1900, 1910, 1920; Washington Territorial Census, 1880, 1889; *Register*, Mar. 7, 1860; T.R. Delaney, Chief of Police and D.H. Hill, Chief of Fire Department to Mayor and City Council, Port Townsend Washington, LS, Feb. 16, 1892, MSS-3a, Archival Collections, McCurdy Historical Research Library; "R.L. Polk & Co's Puget Sound Directory," 1887; "R.L. Polk & Co's Port Townsend City Directory," 1890, 1897, and 1907; Swan, Diaries, Jan. 30, 1883; Mar. 7, 1884; July 5, 1884; Forwood, "Port Townsend ... Part I and III"; Liestman, "'The Various Celestials among Our Town,'" 96. In 1892, eight Chinese laundries were listed in a city council fire safety and sewage drainage report (Delaney and Hill to Mayor and City Council). The city directories variously mention from two to five laundries between 1887 and 1907, although neither the city directories nor the census necessarily provide exhaustive information about the county's Chinese residents.

36 For further discussion, see Liestman, "'The Various Celestials among Our Town,'" 98–9.

37 For further discussion of Chinatowns, see Daniels, "Majority Issues," 85–6; Takaki, *Strangers from a Different Shore*, 117–31; Tsai, *The Chinese Experience in America*, 33–42.

38 Art Chin, *Golden Tassels*, 41.

39 "R.L. Polk & Co's Port Townsend Directory," 1887, 1890, 1897, 1907, 1912; *Leader*, Sept. 9, 1903; Forwood, "Port Townsend ... Part I"; *Leader*, Jan. 21, 1890; Jan. 25, 1895; Jan. 28, 1911.

40 Numerous beer, wine, and ale bottles were found during an excavation of what had been Chinese businesses and living quarters during the nineteenth and early-twentieth centuries (Kannenberg, "Chinese in Port Townsend," 9–10).

41 "Robert Gow: Last of the Native Born Chinese," 9–11; Forwood,

"Port Townsend ... Parts II, III." Opium was legal until the pas-
sage of the 1914 Harrison Narcotic Act. Subject to expensive du-
ties and taxes, it was smuggled into the United States, often from
Victoria, B.C. to Jefferson County, by both Euro-Americans and
Chinese Americans. Customs officials were responsible for polic-
ing this illegal trade, which they did with little success (Liestman,
"'The Various Celestials among Our Town,'" 99–101; DeLorme,
"The United States Bureau of Customs," 77–88, 81).

42 Forwood, "Port Townsend ... Part II"; *Peninsula Daily News*,
Sept. 12, 1993; "Robert Gow: Last of the Native Born Chinese,"
16–17.

43 *Leader*, Jan. 30 and Feb. 3, 1895; "Robert Gow: Last of the Native Born Chinese," 9–11, 63–5; Forwood, "Port Townsend ...
Parts II and III"; Liestman, "'The Various Celestials among Our
Town,'" 101, *Leader*, Nov. 5, 1909; Nov. 11, 1909; Nov. 12,
1909.

44 Forwood, "Port Townsend ... Part V"; "Robert Gow: Last of the
Native Born Chinese," 18; McCurdy, *By Juan de Fuca's Strait*,
210; Friday, *Organizing Asian American Labor*, 55.

45 See Cheng Hirata, "Free, Indentured, Enslaved" and Pascoe,
"Gender Systems in Conflict" for discussions of Chinese prostitution. See Friday, *Organizing Asian American Labor*, 54–5, for
discussion of homosexual relationships among Chinese men
working in the salmon canning industry.

46 U.S. Census, Federal Population Census Schedules, 1880; also see
Forwood, "Port Townsend ... Part IV"; Liestman, "'The Various
Celestials among Our Town,'" 94.

47 Wing Sing Company, Wing Lee Company, and Hong Chung
Company, all merchant stores – first mentioned in city directories
in 1890, 1897, and 1907, respectively – were also located on the
site, as well as an unnamed laundry (Kannenberg, "Chinese in
Port Townsend," 5, 9–10). In Sept. 1886, Swan recorded that a
fire in a Chinese laundry burned a dance house (Swan, Diaries,
Sept. 24, 1886.).

48 *Leader*, Nov. 23, 1889.

49 Cheng Hirta, "Free, Indentured, Enslaved," 5; Pascoe, "Gender
Systems in Conflict," 142, 144–6; *The Weekly Message*, Aug. 15,

1867; Wynne, "Reaction to the Chinese," 79; Friday, *Organizing Asian American Labor*, 51; *Leader*, Feb. 5, 1892; Liestman, "'The Various Celestials among Our Town,'" 94.

50 Takaki, *Strangers from a Different Shore*, 123–6.

51 *Leader*, Apr. 16, 1895. See McCunn, *Thousand Pieces of Gold*.

52 Lyman, *Chinatown and Little Tokyo*, 142–7. The Zhigongtang really had nothing to do with the Masons. The perceived link arose through one of the Masons' countermoves against anti-Masonic feeling in the early nineteenth century. Trying to establish an ancient lineage, the Masons speculated that in the distant past an "ancient order" of religious and philosophical learning had split into eastern and western societies. The Masonic Order was the western society. Seeing similarities between Masonic and Triad Society symbols, some Masons argued that the Chinese Triad Society – of which the Zhigongtang was a connection – was the eastern result of the "mythic division." The Zhigongtang was not loath to use this connection to legitimate itself with Euro-Americans, and the society became known to Euro-Americans as the Chinese Freemasons. Any formal connection was denied by the Masons, although informal contact did occasionally occur (Lyman, "Chinese Secret Societies," 82–9).

53 Swan, Diaries, Apr. 21, 1883. A second chapter was organized in 1902 (Liestman, "'The Various Celestials among Our Town,'" 94).

54 Liestman, "'The Various Celestials among Our Town,'" 94.

55 Lyman, *Chinatown and Little Tokyo*, 146. Lyman suggests that the Zhigongtang functioned as the central authority within the small, early Chinese communities of British Columbia. The first was formed in 1862, thus operating for many years before Victoria's CCBS was established in 1884 (Lyman, "Chinese Secret Societies," 95; Lyman, *Chinatown and Little Tokyo*, 126; see also Chung, "Between Two Worlds."

56 For a discussion of the Zhigongtang's involvement in Chinese political and dynastic affairs, see Lyman, "Chinese Secret Societies," 92–7. Some North American members of the organization gave important support to Sun Yat-sen's revolutionary movement, 1894 to 1912 (93). Port Townsend's second Zhigongtang may

have had an express interest in Sun Yat-sen's revolutionary movement. This group was sometimes also involved in vice operations
(Lyman, *Chinatown and Little Tokyo*, 145).

57 For further information on social organizations, see Doug and
Art Chin, *Up Hill*, 23–4, 28–31; Chung, "Between Two Worlds";
Daniels, "Majority Issues," 86–9; Douglas W. Lee, "Sacred Cows
and Paper Tigers," 86–103; Lyman, *Chinatown* and Little Tokyo,
111–224; Lyman, "Chinese Secret Societies," 95–102; Takaki,
Strangers from a Different Shore, 118–19; Tsai, *The Chinese Experience in America*, 45–55.

58 Daniels, "Majority Issues," 87–9.

59 "Robert Gow: Last of the Native Born Chinese," 25; Forwood,
"Port Townsend ... Part II" and Part IV. Euro-Americans usually
used the name of the Zee Tai Company as if it were the name of
the owner; this was a common Euro-American misunderstanding,
and the Euro-American residents interviewed by Forwood made
this mistake. The fact that some Chinese merchants signed their
correspondence with the name of the company rather than a personal signature may be, in part, the source for this confusion.
(Swan, Diaries, Feb. 13, 1885; *Leader*, Mar. 1, 1890; July 4,
1903; Zee Tai and Co. to Mr. Kendrick, Washington Mill Company, LS, Dec. 17, 1887, WMC Papers; Wa Chong Co. to Washington Mill Company, LS, Sept. 6, 1894; Mar. 28, 1895; Dec. 30,
1896; Apr. 25, 1897, WMC Papers).

60 According to the *Leader*, in 1890 the Zee Tai Company paid duties "equal to that of every other business house in the city" and
had approximately $100,000 worth of Chinese and Japanese
goods in stock (Oct. 12, 1890; Oct. 15, 1890).

61 "Robert Gow: Last of the Native Born Chinese," 25; Forwood,
"Port Townsend ... Part IV."

62 Art and Doug Chin, *Up Hill*, 23–4. The clan name of a merchant
indicates the presence of that clan, as well as its organization centered in the store. See also Mei, "Socioeconomic Origins of Emigration," 237–8, for a discussion of pre-existing ties between
immigrants and their clans or district associations in the United
States.

63 Washington Territorial Census 1889; Willson and MacDonald,

"Port Townsend's Pioneer Chinese Merchants," 20–1; Art and
Doug Chin, *Up Hill*, 24–5.

64 There were smaller merchant stores as well, some formed primarily so that the owners would be able to define themselves as merchants in order to get around the 1882 Exclusion Act and its
subsequent refinements and extensions, which excluded "laborers," but allowed the entry of merchants, their wives, and dependent children. Thus, some Chinese pooled enough resources
to give themselves at least the appearance of merchant status in
order to enter or return to the United States. The Yet Wo Company and the Get Kee Company may have been this type of store,
and as such would not have had the same place in the power
structure of the community as did the Zee Tai, Wing Sing ,or Yee
Sing Wo Kee companies (Tsai, *The Chinese Experience in America*, 66; McCurdy, *By Juan de Fuca's Strait*, 209).

65 Jimmy Mar, son of one of the original Mars, said that his father's
store shared premises with a gambling establishment, but was itself an export-import store (*Peninsula Daily News*, Sept. 12, 1992).

66 "R.L. Polk & Co's Port Townsend Directory," 1887, 1990, 1897,
1907; *Leader*, May 12, 1914; Mar. 3, 1892; Fung Chong to
Washington Mill Company, LS, Nov. 9, 1900; Feb. 20, 1902; Apr.
25, 1902; June 9, 1901; Aug. 2, 1902; Sept. 30, 1903, WMC Papers; Liestman, "'The Various Celestials among Our Town,'" 94;
Willson and MacDonald, "Port Townsend's Pioneer Chinese Merchants," 21–2. The Eng and Mar Clans were well established in
Seattle also (Art and Doug Chin, *Up Hill*, 20).

67 *Argus*, Aug. 23, 1883.

68 During the 1880s, Puget Sound Customs issued the second largest
number of Chinese labor certificates. Mei, "Socioeconomic Developments," 370; Coolidge, *Chinese Immigration*, 498; Wynne,
"Reaction to the Chinese," 68; Doug and Art Chin, *Up Hill*, 8;
DeLorme, "The United States Bureau of Customs," 81.

69 U.S. Bureau of Census, *Historical Statistics*, in Tsai, *The Chinese
Experience in America*, 194.

70 DeLorme, "The United States Bureau of Customs," 80; Kim and
Markov, "The Chinese Exclusion Laws," 19; Memorial of
Tacoma Chamber of Commerce; Letter to Watson C. Squire,

Governor of Washington Territory, from D. Manning, Secretary
of Treasury, Dec. 9, 1885, Squire's Report to Interior. Over time a
federal bureaucracy was developed, which became more efficient
at "gatekeeping," although Chinese immigrants became at the
same time increasingly adept at getting around bureaucratic
means for prohibiting Chinese immigration. See Erika Lee, *At
America's Gates*, 12; and Wong, *Sweet Cakes, Long Journey*.

71 De Lorme, "The United States Bureau of Customs," 77.

72 *Argus*, Aug. 2, 1883. See also *Leader*, May 14, 1890; June 13,
1890; May 7, 1892; July 16, 1914; Forwood, "Port Townsend ...
Parts II and IV"; McCurdy, *By Juan de Fuca's Strait*, 209–10; De-
Lorme, "The United States Bureau of Customs," 77–88. The waters between Victoria, B.C. and Jefferson County are often
dangerous. In the space of just three months in 1892, the *Leader*
reported the deaths of fourteen Chinese – twelve men and two
women – who drowned during stormy crossings. Such danger
may have increased the popularity over time of crossing the border by land – from Vancouver, B.C. (*Leader*, Mar. 8, 1892; Kim
and Markov, "The Chinese Exclusion Laws," 20–1). See Liestman, "'The Various Celestials among Our Town,'" 102, for a discussion of legendary stories about smugglers who supposedly
would push their Chinese customers – who were said to be
chained together – overboard if approached by the authorities.
There is no substantive evidence that such events occurred, although one smuggler claimed to have witnessed such an event
(*Argus*, Dec. 30, 1885).

73 Forward, "Port Townsend ... Part II"; McCurdy, *From Juan de
Fuca's Strait*, 209–10; DeLorme, "The United States Bureau of
Customs," 77, 79, 83–4; *Argus*, Aug. 2, 1883; *Leader*, May 2,
1890; May 14, 1890; June 13, 1890; Mar. 8, 1892; Mar. 17,
1903; Apr. 17, 1903. See also Kim and Markov, "The Chinese
Exclusion Laws," 16–30; Erika Lee, *At America's Gates*, 151–61.
A federal Special Agent reported in May 1893 that there were up-
wards of 1,000 Chinese en route at that time between China and
the United States, some making their second attempt at entry
(Kim and Markov, 25). An 1891 Customs estimate was that at
Coupeville (on Whidby Island in the Lower Sound) alone thirty

or more Chinese were landed per week, and that ten were landed
at Dungeness nightly – for how long is not stated (DeLorme, 79).
While none of these figures is conclusive as to numbers, they do
indicate numerous illegal entries. Until the Exclusion Act of 1923,
restriction of Chinese immigration to Canada consisted primarily
of "head taxes" of increasing amounts: 1886 – $50; 1901 – $100;
1903 – $500. See Roy, *White Man's Province*, 61–2, 66–7, 100–
2, 107, 118, 155–7, 232, 234–5, 266. After the institution of the
$500 head tax, illegal entries to Washington were greatly dimin-
ished and gradually became a thing of the past (Liestman, "'The
Various Celestials among Our Town,'" 103).

74 According to Robert Gow and Mattie Gow Chong, those who
entered illegally used the papers of someone who had died, or
borrowed papers from someone of similar age and description
(Forwood, "Port Townsend ... Part II"; Todd Stevens, "Brokers
Between Worlds," 228–9).

75 Liestman, "'The Various Celestials among Our Town,'" 101.

76 *Leader*, May 6, 12, 14, June 7, 30, July 1, 17, 22, 1891; De-
Lorme, "The United States Bureau of Customs," 84, 86–7.

77 Swan, Diaries, July 5, 24, 1884; Mar. 23, 1885; Jan. 23, 24, 26,
28, 30, Feb. 17, Mar. 23, Apr. 29, May 5, 6, 1886; Aug. 19, 20,
1887; *Leader*, Mar. 8, 1892; Nov. 6, 1898.

78 *Leader*, Nov. 30, 1889; July 13, 1897; Nov. 12, 1909; Lucile
McDonald, "Revenue Cutter," 131. There were other ways of
effecting illegal entry. The destruction of San Francisco municipal
records during the 1906 earthquake allowed certain resident
Chinese to claim – without proof – that they had been born in
San Francisco. As citizens they could bring their wives from
China. Before the earthquake created this loophole, only small
numbers of Chinese women came to the United States, but some
10,000 wives emigrated between 1907 and 1924, when the Immigration Act of 1924 essentially prohibited the immigration of any
Chinese. Anyone born in the United States is an American citizen,
and the children of American citizens are American citizens wherever they are born. Thus, Chinese-born children of Chinese Americans were eligible to immigrate to the United States. Many real
sons did immigrate, but there were also "paper sons" who pur-

chased or used the birth certificates of real sons in order to immigrate. Apparently few daughters immigrated (Takaki, *Strangers from a Distant Shore*, 234–9).

79 *Argus*, Dec. 17, 1880.

80 Ibid., Aug. 2, 1883.

81 Ibid. See also ibid., Aug. 16, 23, 30, 1883. Included are reprints from the Seattle *Chronicle* and the Tacoma *Ledger* praising Weir's efforts.

82 *Argus*, Mar. 11, 1886.

83 Immigration Aid Society, *North-Western Washington*.

84 Ibid., 40.

85 A sampling of such thinking from local newspapers: The Chinese were "a vastly inferior race," recognized as such by even "the untutored savage" Indians (*Democratic Press*, Sept. 25, Oct. 9, 1879); Chinese were "alien" to American culture and society, and they and their offspring "to the remotest generation would be aliens" (*Democratic Press*, Sept. 19, 1878); Chinese religious ceremonies might be "interesting ... to civilized spectators, but their communities were "sickening scenes of filth, disease and misery" (*The North-West*, Nov. 15, 1860; *Argus*, Sept. 29, 1876); laborers were castigated for "virtually starv[ing] out all other classes of laborers [by] liv[ing] on 7 cents a day" (*Democratic Press*, Oct. 9, 1879). When James Swan wanted to express his liking for a Chinese man, he could only say that, "Charlie Hing was the nearest to a white man of any Chinaman I have seen" (Swan, Diaries, Apr. 27, 1886). The editor of the *Democratic Press* argued that unless something was done quickly "to prevent the flood of Chinese emigration into this Territory ... the mills of Puget Sound will be run by Chinese labor. Our coal mines and ... every branch of labor by which white men barely can earn a livelihood will be filled by Chinamen, and white men will be compelled to starve or work for a Chinaman's wage and live on Chinaman's fare – one rat and a pound of rice per week." Without immediate action "the more difficult it will be to overcome the evil" (*Democratic Press*, May 20, 1879). In another instance, the *Democratic Press* expressed fear of competition between American steamships and the China Merchants' Steamship Company, "a corporation pos-

sessing great wealth and chiefly composed of Mandarins and Chinese merchants," which planned to establish a run between China and the United States. "If the line can be successfully operated then there is no branch of commerce and no manufacturing field that will not be blighted by competition capitalized in China" (*Democratic Press*, Nov. 6, 1879). The murder of a Chinese resident in Portland, reputedly an assassin for one of "these Chinese Companies," also roused the anger of the *Press* editor. Fulminating about this "class of people we permit to come to our shores and enter into competition with our white citizens," he argued that "the time is not far distant when [they] may deem it to their advantage to have some of our leading white citizens put out of the way ... They are a dangerous element ... and the sooner we get rid of them the better." (*Democratic Press*, Apr. 21, 1880).

86 *Democratic Press*, Oct. 26, 1880; July 17, 1879; Dec. 28, 1877; June 19, 1879; July 17, 1879; July 31, 1879. Meyers reprinted material from other newspapers similar to his own anti-Chinese ravings. See *Democratic Press*, Oct. 9, 1879; Mar. 11, 1880.

87 Ibid., Oct. 3, 1878.

88 Ibid., Oct. 2, 1879; Aug. 28, 1879; Sept. 18, 1879. See also *Democratic Press*, Oct. 9, 1879; Oct. 16, 1879, for related letters to the editor. Although it is not stated in any of the articles, I would assume that because the laundrymen owned neither real property nor taxable personal property, they paid no property taxes.

89 *Argus*, Aug. 7, 1879.

90 Ibid., Feb. 19, 1880.

91 Ibid., July 5, 1883.

92 Ibid., Aug. 2, 1883.

93 Ibid., Aug. 30, 1883.

94 *Democratic Press*, Nov. 9, 1877.

95 *Argus*, Feb. 9, 1877.

96 Ibid., Mar. 4, 1886.

97 *Port of Entry Times*, Feb. 23, 1884.

98 *Argus*, Feb. 20, 1879. Weir's statistics were taken from a congressional joint committee report.

99 Ibid., Aug. 30, 1883.

100 Ibid., Aug. 16, 1883.

101 Ibid., Aug. 30, 1883.

102 Ibid., Feb. 11, 1886.

103 Ibid., Mar. 20, 1884; *Washington Standard*, Sept. 25, 1885.

104 *Argus*, Feb. 11, 1886.

105 Ibid., Dec. 24, 1885.

106 Ibid., Feb. 11, 1886.

107 Ibid., Feb. 18, 1886.

108 Ibid., Feb. 11, 1886. Also see ibid., Feb. 18, 1886; Mar. 4, 1886; Mar. 11, 1886; Mar. 25, 1886; Apr. 1, 1886; May 6, 1886, for articles deploring violence against the region's Chinese. When trouble visited perpetrators of anti-Chinese violence, Weir was delighted, as when the *News* of Tacoma, "the leading organ of the anti-Chinese agitators," went bankrupt. He moralized that "the class of people who take part mostly in [mob violence] are not in the habit of contributing largely to the support of newspapers. Had the *News* 'made a gallant fight' against violence, it might have been a more profitable concern." Again, when Mayor Weisbach – one of the leaders of Puget Sound's expulsion forces – was troubled with labor agitations in Tacoma, the paper crowed: "Mayor Weisbach is probably realizing by this time what it [is] to have chickens come home to roost. The dragon's teeth he sowed at the head of a mob ... are springing up now" (*Argus*, Feb. 18, 1886; Apr. 1, 1886).

109 *Argus*, Mar. 11, 1886.

110 Ibid., Feb. 11, 1886.

111 Karlin, "Anti-Chinese Outbreaks in Seattle," 122–3.

112 *Argus*, Feb. 18, 1886.

113 Swan, Diaries, Feb. 12, 1886; Feb. 14, 1886.

114 James Swan to Mrs. Willoughby, LS, Feb. 13, 1886, MSS 8, Archival Collecitons, McCurdy Historical Research Library. See Karlin, "Anti-Chinese Outbreaks in Seattle."

115 *Argus*, Feb. 18, 1886.

116 Ibid., Mar. 4, 1886, Mar. 25, 1886.

117 Ibid., Mar. 11, 1886.

118 Ibid., Mar. 18, 1886.

119 Ibid., Mar. 25, 1886.

120 *Blaine Journal*, quoted in *Argus*, Mar. 25, 1886.

121 Reported in the *Argus*, Mar. 11, 1886; Mar. 25, 1886.

122 *Argus*, Mar. 11, 1886; Feb. 25, 1886; Apr. 29, 1886.

123 See Liestman, "'The Various Celestials among Our Town,'" for further discussion of the failed boycott, 99.

124 *Argus*, Mar. 11, 1886.

125 Cox, *Mills and Markets*, 199–226. The Port Townsend Mill relied primarily on the local market, but it would have benefitted from the building boom caused by increasing immigration to the area during the 1880s.

126 Liestman, "'The Various Celestials among Our Town,'" 98.

127 Schwantes, "Protest in a Promised Land," 373, 380. See also Schwantes, "The Concept of the Wageworkers' Frontier."

128 *Post-Intelligencer*, Sept. 21, 24, and 29, 1885.

129 Ibid., Oct. 8 and 9, 1885; Todd Stevens, "Brokers between Worlds," 241.

130 See, Karlin, "Anti-Chinese Outbreaks in Seattle"; Todd Stevens, "Brokers between Worlds," 240–53.

131 Naylor, "Expulsion." Business and legal ties between Chinese merchants and certain members of the Opera-House gang would continue into the twentieth century (Ficken, *Washington State*, 137; Todd Stevens, "Brokers Between Worlds," 253–6.

132 *Leader*, Apr. 10, 1892.

133 H.C. Willison, Health Officer, to Hon. Mayor and Council of the City of Port Townsend, LS, Apr. 3, 1892, MSS 3a, Archival Collections, McCurdy Historical Library; *Leader*, Mar. 29, 1892; Apr. 10, 1892.

134 For other examples, see *Weekly Messenger*, May 6, 1868; *Leader*, Oct. 4, 1889; Mar. 18, 1892.

135 James Swan noted in his journals that he had received gifts from "Zee Tai" and his laundryman, Sam Sing: a white silk handkerchief and china bowl in 1883; a China teapot from "Zee Tai" in 1886. Sometimes laundrymen gave blossoming lilies to their female Euro-American customers at the New Year, or just before Christmas, they would give narcissus bulbs planted in gravel-filled shallow pottery bowls. Customers were told that if they put the bowls away in the dark, by Chinese New Year they would bloom and bring good luck to the recipient. Swan, Diaries, Jan.

30, 1883; Feb. 7, 1883; Feb. 13, 1886; *Leader*, Jan. 19, 1890; Forwood, "Port Townsend ... Part I."

136 For some of the more recent literature which addresses resistance, see, e.g., Chen, *Chinese San Francisco*; Erika Lee, *At America's Gates*; Ma, "Chinatown Organizations"; McKeown, "Transnational Chinese Families"; Peffer, *If They Don't Bring Their Women Here*; Salyer, *Laws Harsh as Tigers*; Tong, *Unsubmissive Women*; Marie Rose Wong, *Sweet Cakes, Long Journey*; Yung, *Unbound Voices*; Scott K. Wong, "Cultural Defenders and Brokers"; Zhu, *A Chinaman's Chance*, especially 1–6.

137 Chinese population was 233 in 1900 and 102 in 1910 (U.S. Census, Federal Population Census Schedules, 1890, 1900, 1910).

CONCLUSION

1 McCurdy, *By Juan de Fuca's Strait*, 300.

2 Johansen and Gates, *Empire of the Columbia*, 311, 313; Schwantes, *The Pacific Northwest*, 169, 188–9; Schwantes, *Railroad Signatures*, 50–80; Ficken, *Washington Territory*, 146–65; Ficken, *Washington State*, 22.

3 Schwantes, *The Pacific Northwest*, 177.

4 Johansen and Gates, *Empire of the Columbia*, 316.

5 Ficken, *Washington State*, vi-vii, quotation vi.

6 *Argus*, Nov. 24, 1887.

7 For instance, Seattle's population grew from 3,533 in 1880 to 42,837 in 1890 (Johansen and Gates, *Empire of the Columbia*, 329).

8 Ficken, *Washington State*, vi.

9 The population was 2,641 in 1885; 3,393 in 1887; and 5,740 in 1889 (Wynne, "Reaction to the Chinese," Appendix II, 493).

10 *Argus*, Dec. 30, 1885.

11 "Loren Bingham Hastings," Washington Pioneer Project, 3–4.

12 Wright, *Lewis and Dryden's Marine History*, 381, 77–8.

13 Cox, *Mills and Markets*, 199–226.

14 Coman and Gibbs, *Time, Tide and Timber*, 110–11, 152.

15 *Argus*, Dec. 31, 1885.

16 *Register*, Feb. 15, 1860; *Argus*, Dec. 31, 1885.

17 Swan, Diaries, July 31, 1885; Nov. 22, 1885; Feb. 7, 1886; May
    10, 1886; June 25, 1886; June 26, 1886; July 15, 1886; July 23,
    1886; quotation, July 15, 1886.

18 Perry, Seabeck, 58–9; McCurdy, By Juan de Fuca's Strait, 80;
    Simpson et al., City of Dreams, 160.

19 Argus, June 19, 1875; Apr. 27, 1877; July 13, 1877.

20 McCurdy, By Juan de Fuca's Strait, 80; "Port Townsend, Wash-
    ington," Sanborn Fire Insurance Map, 1888.

21 Until 1889, when the mill closed due to assorted problems, the
    Puget Sound Iron mill operated the largest furnace on the west
    coast (Ficken, Washington State, 62).

22 Argus, Dec. 30, 1885; Call, July 27, 1889; McCurdy, By Juan de
    Fuca's Strait, 299.

23 Argus, Dec. 30, 1885.

24 McCurdy, By Juan de Fuca's Strait, 292.

25 Squires is referring to a triangular system of fortifications which
    had been recently recommended by the military for the protection
    of Puget Sound. Congress did not authorize funding until 1896
    and the forts – Fort Casey on Whidbey Island across Admiralty
    Inlet from Port Townsend, Fort Flagler at the north end of Mar-
    rowstone Island across the bay from Port Townsend, and Fort
    Worden at Point Wilson in Port Townsend – were not built until
    after the turn of the century (see below). See Gregory, Keepers at
    the Gate; McCurdy, By Juan de Fuca's Strait, 306–8; Simpson et
    al., City of Dreams, 90–6.

26 Argus, Dec. 30, 1885.

27 Post-Intelligencer, reported in Argus, Dec. 8, 1887.

28 The trustees were A.D. Moore, Robert C. Hill, L.B. Hastings,
    Charles Eisenbeis, Henry Landes, S.W. Levy, and J.A. Kuhn as
    president (McCurdy, By Juan de Fuca's Strait, 289).

29 Sources for the history of the Port Townsend Southern Railroad
    are: James G. Swan Papers (hereinafter cited as Swan papers); Jef-
    ferson County newspapers; McCurdy, By Juan de Fuca's Strait,
    286–302; Gray, "Historic Railroads of Washington," 3–5, 12–18;
    Schrenk, "The Port Townsend Southern Railroad."

30 Jefferson County residents were inspired by Seattle investors who,
    frustrated by Tacoma's monopoly of the Northern Pacific, tried

unsuccessfully to establish a Seattle-based, trans-Cascade connection to the Northern Pacific (McCurdy, *By Juan de Fuca's Strait*, 288–9; Meinig, *The Shaping of America*, 83; Johansen and Gates, *Empire of the Columbia*, 312–13; Schwantes, *The Pacific Northwest*, 238.

31 *Argus*, Nov. 24, 1887.

32 James Swan to Hon. J.A. Kuhn, President Port Townsend Southern RR, LS, July 25, 1888, Swan papers. Swan had earlier correspondence with Adams on the same subject, but had received a polite brush-off (Charles F. Adams, President, The Union Pacific Railway Company, to James G. Swan, Esq., LS, July 9, 1885, Aug. 15, 1885, Oct. 9, 1885, Swan papers).

33 D.W. Smith to Hon James G. Swan, LS, July 19, 1888, Swan papers; J.A. Kuhn to Hon. J.G. Swan, LS, June 30, 1888, Swan papers.

34 McCurdy, *By Juan de Fuca's Strait*, 189–90.

35 Ibid., 291.

36 Ibid., 294.

37 Ibid., 299.

38 Ibid., 297.

39 In the subsequent reorganization of Union Pacific's interests – which included the troubled Oregon Improvement Company – the Port Townsend Southern Railroad was sold. The Northern Division from Port Townsend to Quilcene continued in operation under several owners until 1925, when the line from Port Discovery to Quilcene was shut down. The line from Port Townsend to Port Discovery was connected to a track from Port Angeles and has been used sporadically to connect Port Townsend and Port Angeles (Gray, 15–18). See Schwantes, *Railroad Signatures*, 70–80, for a larger discussion of the close of what Schwantes calls the "first [Pacific Northwest] railway age."

40 McCurdy, *By Juan de Fuca's Strait*, 299.

41 *The Quilcene Queen*, June 11, 1891.

42 *Leader*, Aug. 27, 1891.

43 A Port Townsend chamber of commerce was organized in 1890. Chambers of commerce and boards of trade began to appear in the United States in significant numbers by the mid-nineteenth

century, but "in the older rather than the newer states." However, if post-frontier boosterism became increasingly institutionalized, frontier boosterism was the purview of individuals and informally organized local groups (Pomeroy, *The American Far West*, 16–17). Local government in frontier Washington was much less formal, as well, and played a lesser role in boosterism than would be true in the post-frontier period (Ficken, *Washington State*, 126).

44 Swan, "A Description of the City of Port Townsend," reported in the *Leader*, June 25, 1891. See also "Port Townsend: Its Advantages."

45 James G. Swan to President Winters and the Directors of the Northern Pacific Rail Road, LS, Aug. 1896, Swan papers; James G. Swan to Hon. Charles Francis Adams, LS, June 6, 1899, Swan papers; James G. Swan to President James J. Hill, Great Northern Railway Company, LS, June 22, 1899, Swan papers; James J. Hill to James G. Swan, Esq., LS, July 6, 1899, Swan papers.

46 Lucile McDonald, *Swan among The Indians*, 209.

47 McCurdy, *By Juan de Fuca's Strait*, 199.

48 Lucile McDonald, *Swan among the Indians*, 204, 213, 221. During summer 1889, the *Leader* estimated the dollar value of that year's building boom as over $400,000. Eleven two- or three-storey business buildings or blocks were under construction – some of which were never completed – one college building, three shops in the uptown area, three churches, twenty rental cottages and tenements, and thirty private homes (*Leader*, Oct. 2, 1889). See also Simpson et al., *City of Dreams*, 17–21.

49 *Leader*, Oct. 2, 1889.

50 McCurdy, *By Juan de Fuca's Strait*, 299, 304, qtn.

51 Britton, *The Iron and Steel Industry*, 20–2; according to Ficken, "poor design, bad management and distance from markets," led to the shut down of the mill (*Washington State*, 62).

52 *Leader*, July 30, 1891. Although they suffered through the 1890s, the county's other two cargo mills – the Washington Mill Company at Hadlock and the Puget Mill Company at Port Ludlow – did survive. The Port Townsend Mill – never a cargo mill – also continued to operate in a much-reduced capacity, supplying the small lumber needs of Port Townsend (McCurdy, *By Juan de Fuca's Strait*, 80).

53 Cox, *Mills and Markets*, 199–226, 226.

54 Griffiths, *Shipping Reminiscences*, 40.

55 See Cox, *Mills and Markets*, 284–96; Ficken, *The Forested Land*, 78–117.

56 Ficken and LeWarne, *Washington*, 46.

57 Cox, *Mills and Markets*, 284.

58 Ibid., 285–7.

59 Ibid., 287–91.

60 Ibid., 291–5; *Leader*, July 30, 1891.

61 Cox, *Mills and Markets*, 296.

62 The Washington Mill Company's inability to weather economic troubles in the lumber industry during 1907 was exacerbated by the death of the owner, W.H. Adams, that same year.

63 Cox, *Mills and Markets*, 292–3.

64 James G. Swan to Thomas H. Canfield, Esq., Gen Agent Northern Pacific RR, Burlington, Vermont, LS, Dec. 3, 1868, Swan papers.

65 Edwin Ames to Mr. W.H. Talbot, San Francisco, LS, July 1899–October 1899, Edwin Ames Papers (hereinafter cited as Ames papers).

66 Edwin Ames to Messrs. Pope & Talbot, San Francisco, California, LS, Ames papers.

67 Figures in Wynne, "Reaction to the Chinese," Appendix II, 493; Appendix III, 495.

68 Seattle grew from 3,533 in 1880 to 42,837 in 1890; Tacoma from 1,098 to 36,006. Seattle had a dozen sawmills and nearly as many sash and door and furniture plants in 1890, as well as slaughterhouses, foundries, canneries, and flour mills. Tacoma had more lumber-working plants than any city on the West Coast, and more wholesale dry goods, hardware, and grocery sales than Seattle or Spokane. Also, the Northern Pacific Railroad shops, a smelter, grain elevators, a network of Sound and San Francisco steamship lines, towing companies, etc. were located there (Johansen and Gates, *Empire of the Columbia*, 329–31).

69 Britton, *The Iron and Steel Industry*, 151–9; Simpson et al., *City of Dreams*, 131.

70 McCurdy, *By Juan de Fuca's Strait*, 307.

71 *Leader*, Sept. 9, 1903; June 9 and Aug. 11, 1906; Mar. 28 and

Aug. 13, 1908; "Robert Gow: Last of the Native Born Chinese,"
9, 102–3; McCurdy, *By Juan de Fuca's Strait*, 308. There were
three fish canneries: the Puget Sound Sardine Co, 1902–3, the
Hillside Packing Company, and Key City Packing Company,
1906–1914.

72 McCurdy, *By Juan de Fuca's Strait*, 308.

73 Ibid., 308–10; Simpson et al., *City of Dreams*, 167–71.

74 Ibid., 167–71, quotation 167; McCurdy, *By Juan de Fuca's Strait*,
308–10.

75 Ibid., 300.

76 Swan, "Washington Sketches," 5.

77 Pomeroy, *The American Far West*, 19.

78 Harmon, "A Different Kind of Indians," 437n58. See 390–5 for a
discussion of the role relations between Indians and settlers
played in this literature; McCurdy, *By Juan de Fuca's Strait*, 310,
62, 216; "Bars and Bordellos – 'Satisfaction Guaranteed.'"

79 For a similar focus, see Camfield, *Port Townsend: An Illustrated
History*, and Camfield, *Port Townsend: The City That Whiskey
Built*. G. Thomas Edwards discusses Port Townsend's failed
hopes in "Dreams and Developments."

BIBLIOGRAPHY

ARCHIVAL COLLECTIONS AND UNPUBLISHED MANUSCRIPTS

Alexander Sampson Papers. Manuscripts and University Archives Division. Suzzallo & Allen Library. University of Washington. Seattle, Washington.

Ancient Order of United Woodman Papers. Manuscripts and Archives Division. Suzzallo & Allen Library. University of Washington. Seattle, Washington.

Archival Collections. McCurdy Historical Research Library. Jefferson County Historical Society. Port Townsend, Washington.

"Bars and Bordellos – 'Satisfaction Guaranteed' – February 1, 1997 to August 24, 1997," Exhibit brochure. Jefferson County Historical Society, Port Townsend, Washington. In possession of author.

Dorothy McLarney to Elaine Naylor. October 23, 1995. Letter in possession of author.

Edmond Meany Papers. Manuscripts and University Archives Division. Suzzallo & Allen Library. University of Washington. Seattle, Washington.

Edwin Ames Papers. Manuscripts and University Archives Division. Suzzallo & Allen Library. University of Washington. Seattle, Washington.

E.M. Starrett Collection, Jefferson County Historical Society, Port Townsend, Washington.

Fuller Collection, Washington State Historical Society, Tacoma, Washington.

Gray, Henry L., "Historic Railroads of Washington." MSS 29, McCurdy Historical Research Library. Jefferson County Historical Society. Port Townsend, Washington.

Greene, Gary. "Early Shipbuilding on the Kitsap Peninsula and Bainbridge Island," TMS, 1994. In possession of author.

"Hill Family," TMS, MSS 3888, 2/25, Manuscripts and University Archives Division, Suzzallo & Allen Library, University of Washington, Seattle, Washington.

"History of Quilcene." McCurdy Historical Research Library, Jefferson County Historical Society, Port Townsend, Washington.

"Horace Winslow McCurdy: Boyhood in Port Townsend," interviewed by Sue Sidle, Witness to the First Century, no. 3, TMS, 1989, McCurdy Historical Research Library, Jefferson County Historical Society. Port Townsend, Washington.

James G. Swan Papers. Special Collections. University of British Columbia. Vancouver, British Columbia.

Kannenberg, Bud. "Chinese in Port Townsend," TMS, February 17, 1990, McCurdy Historical Research Library, Port Townsend, Washington.

"Louis Herman Hansen: Port Townsend Man on the Street," interviewed by James Hermanson, Witness to the First Century (oral history series), no. 4, TMS, 1989, McCurdy Historical Research Library, Jefferson County Historical Society. Port Townsend, Washington.

Memorial of Tacoma Chamber of Commerce to President of the United States, November 3, 1885.

"Old Pilot Notes." TMS, MSS 54. McCurdy Historical Research Library. Jefferson County Historical Society. Port Townsend, Washington.

"Oral History of Mrs. Florence Pitman." TMS, MSS 121. McCurdy Historical Research Library. Jefferson County Historical Society. Port Townsend, Washington.

"Petition to Honorable Mayor and Common Council of the City of Port Townsend," January 3, 1879, MSS 3A, McCurdy Historical Research Library, Jefferson County Historical Society, Port Townsend, Washington.

Plum, Ida. "Diary of Ida Plum Wife of Captain John Plum, From the Log, Nov. 3, 1886–Sept. 6, 1888." TMS, MSS 54, McCurdy Historical Research Library. Jefferson County Historical Society, Port Townsend, Washington.

Pope and Talbot Papers. Manuscripts and University Archives Division. Suzzallo & Allen Library. University of Washington. Seattle, Washington.

Redmen Cemetary Records. http.wajcgs.org/wp-content/uploads/2011/02.

"Richard Francis McCurdy: The Early Years: 1910–1930," interviewed by Sue Sidle, Witness to the First Century (oral history series), no. 9, TMS, 1989, McCurdy Historical Research Library, Jefferson County Historical Society, Port Townsend, Washington.

"Robert Gow: Last of the Native Born Chinese," interviewed by Robert Boardman, Witness to the First Century (oral history series), no. 5, TMS, 1989, McCurdy Historical Research Library, Jefferson County Historical Society, Port Townsend, Washington.

Samuelson, Marge. "List Compiled from Incomplete Collection of City Arrest Records, November 1879–June 1913, for Bars and Bordellos Exhibit, February 1, 1997–August 24, 1997." McCurdy Historical Research Library. Jefferson County Historical Society. Port Townsend, Washington.

– "List Compiled from Incomplete Collection of Liquor License Applications, issued between the years 1860 and 1903, for ninety different saloons for Bars and Bordellos Exhibit – February 1, 1997 to August 24, 1997." McCurdy Historical Research Library. Jefferson County Historical Society. Port Townsend, Washington.

Sayward, William T. "Additional Statement of Capt. Wm. T. Sayward." Bancroft Library. University of California at Berkeley. Berkeley, California.

Schrenk, L.P. "The Port Townsend Southern Railroad." MSS 29. McCurdy Historical Research Library. Jefferson County Historical Society. Port Townsend, Washington.

Swan, James G., Diaries, 1868–1897. Manuscripts and University Archives Division, Suzzallo & Allen Library. University of Washington. Seattle, Washington.

– "Washington Sketches." (Port Townsend, 1878). HM, BANL MSS P-B

20. The Bancroft Library, University of California, Berkeley, California.

Turner, Jane, "Inventory of James G. Swan Papers, 1852–1907." Special Collections, University of British Columbia, Vancouver, British Columbia, May 1990.

Washington Mill Company Papers. McCurdy Historical Research Library. Jefferson County Historical Society. Port Townsend, Washington.

Washington Mill Company Papers. Manuscripts and University Archives Division. Suzzalo & Allen Library. University of Washington. Seattle, Washington.

Washington Pioneer Project, Jefferson County. Washington State Library, Washington Room, Olympia, Washington.

"An Outline of the History of Jefferson County, Washington," TMS, 1936.

Bishop, Jonathan J. "Why the 'Duke of York' Was Friendly to the Whites," TMS, 1936.

"Earliest Settlers of Port Townsend: As Told to Gilbert Pilcher by James G. McCurdy, A Son of A Pioneer of 1857," TMS, 1936.

"Early Days in Quilcene: As Told to Gilbert Pilcher by Samuel H. Cottle," TMS, 1936.

"Hill, Howard ... Port Townsend," TMS, 1936.

"Loren Bingham Hastings: Son of the First White Woman to Settle at Port Townsend," TMS, 1936.

Pilcher, Gilbert. "The Port Townsend of 1868: (Being an Excerpt from Harper's Magazine Published in 1869)," TMS, 1936.

"Randall Dalgardno, Port Townsend," TMS, MSS 8, 1936.

"The Prince of Wales: Present Chief of the Clallams," TMS, 1936.

"Washington State, Believe It or Not, Has Its Own 'Royal Family' of the Olympics," TMS, 1936.

Witness to the First Century. Oral History Series. McCurdy Historical Research Library. Jefferson County Historical Society. Port Townsend, Washington.

NEWSPAPERS

Alta California, San Francisco, California, March 26, 1858.
Democratic Press, Port Townsend, Washington, 1877–81.
Pacific Tribune, Olympia, Washington, August 26, 1874.
Peninsula Daily News, Bremerton, Washington, September 12, 1992.
Pioneer & Democrat, Olympia, Washington, 1855; 1858.
Port of Entry Times, Port Townsend, Washington, 1884.
Port Townsend Call, Port Townsend, Washington, 1885–1910.
Port Townsend Leader, Port Townsend, Washington, 1889–1969.
Port Townsend Register, Port Townsend, Washington, 1859–61.
Puget Sound Argus, Port Townsend, Washington, 1870–90.
Puget Sound Herald, Steilacoom, Washington, 1858.
San Francisco Evening Bulletin, San Francisco, California, May 9, 10, 19, 1859.
Seattle Post-Intelligencer, Seattle, Washington, December 8, 1887.
Seattle Times, Seattle, Washington, September 11, 1955, March 9, 1958–March 30, 1958.
The North-West, Port Townsend, Washington, 1860–62.
Washington Standard. Olympia, Washington, 1861–70; 1885.
Weekly Message, Port Townsend, Washington, 1869–71.

PRINTED WORKS

"A Portfolio of Klallam Photos." *Shadows of Our Ancestors: Readings in the History of Klallam-White Relations*, ed. Jerry Gorlsine. Port Townsend, Washington: Empty Bowl, 1992, 101–20.
Abbott, Carl. *Boosters and Businessmen: Popular Economic Thought and Urban Growth in the Antebellum Middle West*. Westport, Connecticut: Greenwood Press, 1981.
– *How Cities Won The West: Four Centuries of Urban Change in Western North America*. Albuquerque: University of New Mexico Press, 2008.
Adams, Emma H. *To and Fro, Up and Down in Southern California, Oregon and Washington Territory with Sketches in Arizona, New Mexico, and British Columbia*. Chicago: Cranston & Stowe, 1888.

American National Biography. Vol. 3, eds., John A. Garraty and Mark C. Carnes. Oxford and New York: Oxford University Press, 1991, 758–60.

Armitage, Sue. "Are We There Yet? Some Thoughts on the Current State of Western Women's History." *Montana: The Magazine of Western History* 29, no. 3 (Autumn 2009): 70–3.

Asher, Brad. "'Their Own Domestic Difficulties': Intra-Indian Crime and White Law in Western Washington Territory, 1873–1889." *Western Historical Quarterly* 27 (Summer 1996): 189–209.

Bancroft, Hubert Howe, *History of Washington, Idaho and Montana*. San Francisco: History Co., 1890.

Barber, Alicia. *Reno's Big Gamble: Image and Reputation in the Biggest Little City*. Lawrence: University Press of Kansas, 2008.

Barsh, Russell Lawrence. "Ethnogenesis and Ethnonationalism from Competing Treaty Claims." *The Power of Promises: Rethinking Indian Treaties in the Pacific Northwest*, ed. Alexandra Harmon. Seattle: University of Washington Press, 2008: 215–44.

Barth, Gunther. *Bitter Strength: A History of the Chinese in the United States, 1850–1870*. Cambridge, Massachusetts: Harvard University Press, 1964, 3rd Printing, 1974.

Bartlett, Richard A. *The New Country: A Social History of the American Frontier, 1776–1890*. New York: Oxford University Press, 1974.

Benson, Todd. "The Consequences of Reservation Life: Native Californians on the Round Valley Reservation, 1871–1884." *Pacific Historical Review* 60 (1991): 221–44.

Berner, Richard C. "The Port Blakely Mill Company, 1876–89." *Pacific Northwest Quarterly* 57 (1966): 158–71.

Binns, Archie. *The Roaring Land*. New York: R.M. McBride and Company, 1942.

Birder, Bradley J. "Expanding Creative Destruction: Entrepreneurship in the American Wests." *Western Historical Quarterly* 30 (Spring 1999): 45–63.

Blodgett, Jan. *Land of Bright Promise: Advertising the Texas Panhandle and South Plains, 1870–1917*. Austin, Texas: University of Texas Press, 1988.

Boag, Peter G. *Environment and Experience: Settlement Culture in Nineteenth-Century Oregon*. Berkeley: University of California Press, 1992.

Bonacich, Edna and Lucie Cheng, "Introduction: A Theoretical Orientation to International Labor Migration." *Labor Immigration under Capitalism*, eds. Lucie Cheng and Edna Bonacich. Berkeley and Los Angeles: University of California Press, 1984, 1–59.

Boorstin, Daniel. *The Americans: The National Experience*. New York: Random House, 1965.

Boxberger, Daniel L. *To Fish in Common: The Ethnohistory of Lummi Indian Salmon Fishing*. Seattle: University of Washington Press, 1989, 2000.

Boyd, Robert. *The Coming of the Spirit of Pestilence: Introduced Infectious Diseases and Population Decline among Northwest Coast Indians, 1774–1874*. Vancouver: University of British Columbia Press, 1999.

Britton, Diane F. *The Iron and Steel Industry in the Far West: Irondale, Washington*. Boulder: University of Colorado Press, 1991.

Brosnan, Kathleen. *Uniting Mountain and Plain: Cities, Law, and Environmental Change Along the Front Range*. Albuquerque: University of New Mexico Press, 2002.

Brown, Margaret L. "Asa Whitney and His Pacific Railroad Publicity Campaign." *The Mississippi Valley Historical Review* 20, no. 3 (1933): 209–24.

Browne, J. Ross. *Crusoe's Island: A Ramble in the Footsteps of Alexander Selkirk With Sketches of Adventure in California and Washoe*. New York: Harper & Brothers, 1864.

– *J. Ross Browne: His Letters, Journals and Writings*, ed. Lina Fergusson Browne. Albuquerque: University of New Mexico Press, 1969.

– "The Coast Rangers." *Harper's New Monthly Magazine* (February 1862): 289–301.

Buchanan, Iva L. "Lumbering and Logging in the Puget Sound Region in Territorial Days." *Pacific Northwest Quarterly* 2 (1936): 34–53.

Bunting, Robert. *The Pacific Raincoast: Environment and Culture in an American Eden, 1778–1900*. Lawrence: University Press of Kansas, 1997.

Camfield, Thomas W. *Port Townsend: An Illustrated History of Shanghaiing, Shipwrecks, Soiled Doves and Sundry Souls*. Port Townsend, Washington: Ah Tom Publishing, 2000.

– *Port Townsend: The City That Whiskey Built*. Port Townsend, Washington: Ah Tom Publishing, 2002.

Cassel, Susie Lan. "Introduction: One Hundred and Fifty Years of Chinese in America: The Politics of Polarity." *The Chinese in America: A History from Gold Mountain to the New Millennium*, ed. Suzie Lan Cassel. Walnut Creek, California: Altamira Press, 2002, 1–18.

Chambers, William N. *Old Bullion Benton, Senator From the New West*. Boston: Little Brown, 1956.

Chan, Anthony B. *Gold Mountain: The Chinese in the New World*. Vancouver: New Star Books, 1983.

Chan, Sucheng. "Introduction: Chinese American Historiography: What Difference Has The Asian American Movement Made." *Chinese Americans and the Politics of Race and Culture*, eds. Sucheng Chan and Madeline Y. Hsu. Philadelphia: Temple University Press, 2008, 1–61.

Chen, Yong. *Chinese San Francisco: A Trans-Pacific Community, 1850–1943*. Stanford: Stanford University Press, 2000.

– "The Internal Origins of Chinese Emigration to California Reconsidered." *Western Historical Quarterly* 28 (Winter 1997): 521–46.

Cheng Hirata, Lucie. "Free, Indentured, Enslaved: Chinese Prostitutes in Nineteenth-Century America." *Signs: Journal of Women in Culture and Society* 5 (1979): 3–29.

Chin, Art. *Golden Tassels: A History of the Chinese in Washington. 1957–1977*. Privately printed, in possession of Portland State University Library, 1977.

Chin, Doug and Art. *Up Hill: The Settlement and Diffusion of the Chinese in Seattle, Washington*. Seattle: Shorey Book Store, 1973.

Chung, Sue Fawn. "Between Two Worlds: The Zhigongtang and Chinese American Funerary Rituals." *The Chinese in America: A History from Gold Mountain to the New Millennium*, ed. Susie Lan Cassel. Walnut Creek, California: Altamira Press, 2002, 217–23.

Clark, Donald Hathaway. "An Analysis of Forest Utilization as a Factor in Colonizing the Pacific Northwest and in Subsequent Population Transitions." PHD dissertation. University of Washington, 1952.

Clark, Norman H. *Mill Town: A Social History of Everett, Washington, From Its Earliest Beginnings on the Shores of Puget Sound to the Tragic and Infamous Event Known As the Everett Massacre*. Seattle: University of Washington Press, 1970.

– *The Dry Years: Prohibition and Social Change in Washington*. Seattle: University of Washington Press, 1965; reprint, 1988.

Cloud, Barbara. "Laura Hall Peters: Pursuing the Myth of Equality."
  Pacific Northwest Quarterly 74 (January 1983): 28–36.
Cole, Douglas. *Captured Heritage: The Scramble for Northwest Coast
  Artifacts.* Vancouver: Douglas & McIntyre, 1985.
Collins, Cary C. "Subsistence and Survival: The Makah Indian Reser-
  vation, 1855–1933." *Pacific Northwest Quarterly* 87 (Fall 1996):
  180–93.
Collins, June M. "Distribution of the Chemakum Language," *Indians
  of the Urban Northwest.* ed. Marian W. Smith. New York: AMS
  Press, 1949; reprint 1969, 147–160.
Coman, Edwin T., Jr. and Helen M. Gibbs. *Time, Tide and Timber: A
  Century of Pope and Talbot.* Stanford: Stanford University Press, 1949.
Coolidge, Mary Roberts. *Chinese Immigration.* New York: H. Holt
  and Company, 1909; Authorized facsimile by University Micro-films,
  Ann Arbor, Michigan, 1967.
Cox, Thomas R. *Mills and Markets: A History of the Pacific Coast
  Lumber Industry to 1900.* Seattle: University of Washington Press,
  1974.
Cronon, William. *Nature's Metropolis: Chicago and the Great West.*
  New York: W.W. Norton, 1991.
Daniels, Roger. *Guarding the Golden Door: American Immigration
  Policy and Immigrants since 1882.* New York: Hill and Wang, 2004.
– "Majority Issues – Minority Realities: A Perspective on Anti-Orien-
  talism in the United States." *Nativism, Discrimination, and Images
  of Immigrants*, ed. George E. Pozzetta. New York: Garland, 1991,
  73–126.
Delanty, H.M. *Along The Waterfront: Covering a Period of Fifty Years
  on Grays Harbor and the Pacific Northwest.* [Aberdeen, Washington:
  Quick Print Co.] Private Distribution, 1943.
DeLorme, Roland L. "The United States Bureau of Customs and
  Smuggling on Puget Sound, 1851 to 1913." *Prologue: The Journal of
  the National Archives* 5 (Summer 1973): 77–88.
Dettman, Jeffrey Allen. "Anti-Chinese Violence in the American
  Northwest: From Community Politics to International Diplomacy,
  1885–1888." PHD dissertation, University of Texas at Austin, 2002.
Deverell, William. "Fighting Words: The Significance of the American
  West in the History of the United States." *Western Historical Quar-
  terly* (Summer 1994): 185–205.

Dillon, Richard H. "J. Ross Browne." *American National Biography*,
Vol. 3. eds. John A. Garranty and Mark C. Carnes, Oxford and New
York: Oxford University Press, 1991, 758–60.

– *J. Ross Browne: Confidential Agent in Old California*. Norman: University of Oklahoma Press, 1965.

Doig, Ivan. *Winter Brothers: A Season at the Edge of America*. New
York: Harcourt Brace Jovanovich, 1980.

Doyle, Don Harrison. *The Social Order of a Frontier Community:
Jacksonville, Illinois, 1825–1870*. Urbana: University of Illinois
Press, 1978.

Dykstra, Robert R. "Quantifying the Wild West: The Problematic Statistics of Frontier Violence." *Western Historical Quarterly* (Autumn
2009): 321–47.

– *The Cattle Towns*. New York: Knopf, 1968.

Edwards, G. Thomas."Dreams and Developments: A Comparison of
Two of Washington's Most Historic Towns, Port Townsend and
Walla Walla, 1850–1900." *Columbia* 16, no.3 (2002): 30–42.

– "'Terminus Disease': The Clark P. Crandall Description of Puget
Sound in 1871. *Pacific Northwest Quarterly* 70 (1979): 163–77.

Eells, Myron, "Ten Years of Missionary Work Among the Indians at
Skokomish, Washington Territory, 1874–1884." *Shadows of Our An-
cestors: Readings in the History of Klallam-White Relations*, ed. Jerry
Gorsline. Port Townsend, Washington: Empty Bowl, 1992: 74–97.

– *The Twana, Chemakum, and Klallam Indians of Washington Territory*. Washington, D.C.: The Smithsonian Institution, 1889; reprint,
Fairfield, Washington: Ye Galleon Press, 1996.

Eifler, Mark. *Gold Rush Capitalists: Greed and Growth in Sacra-
mento*. Albuquerque: University of New Mexico Press, 2002.

Elkins, Stanley and Eric McKitrick. "A Meaning for Turner's Frontier." *Political Science Quarterly* LXIX (1954): 321–53, 565–602.

Emmons, David M. "Constructed Province: History and the Making
of the Last American West." *Western Historical Quarterly* 25
(1994): 437–59.

– *Garden in the Grasslands: Boomer Literature of the Central Great
Plains*. Lincoln: University of Nebraska Press, 1971.

– *The Butte Irish: Class and Ethnicity in an American Mining Town:
1875–1925*. Champaign: University of Illinois Press, 1989.

Engle, Nancy Arlene Driscol. "Benefitting a City: Women, Respectability and Reform in Spokane, Washington, 1886–1910." PHD dissertation, University of Florida, 2003.

Etulain, Richard W. "Abraham Lincoln: Political Founding Father of the American West." *Montana: The Magazine of Western History* 59, no. 2 (Summer 2009): 3–22.

– *Beyond the Missouri: The Story of the American West.* Albuquerque: University of New Mexico Press, 2006.

Evans, Elwood. *History of the Pacific North West,* Vol. II. Portland, Oregon: North Pacific History Company, 1889.

Fenn, Elizabeth A. *Pox Americana: The Great Smallpox Epidemic of 1775–82.* New York: Hill and Wang, 2001.

Ficken, Robert E. *The Forested Land: A History of Lumbering in Western Washington.* Seattle : University of Washington Press, 1988.

– *Washington State: The Inaugural Decade, 1889–1899.* Pullman: Washington State University Press, 2007.

– *Washington Territory.* Pullman: Washington State University Press, 2002.

Ficken, Robert E. and Charles P. LeWarne. *Washington: A Centennial History.* Seattle: University of Washington Press, 1988.

Findlay, John M. "Closing the Frontier in Washington: Edmond S. Meany and Frederick Jackson Turner." *Pacific Northwest Quarterly* 82 (1991): 59–69.

– "An Elusive Institution: the Birth of Indian Reservations in Gold Rush California." *State and Reservation: New Perspectives on Federal Indian Policy,* eds. George Pierre Castile and Robert L. Bee. Tucson: University of Arizona Press, 1992. 13–37.

Forwood, Margaret. "Port Townsend and the Mysterious East, Parts I–V." *Port Townsend Leader,* February 13, 20, 27 and March 6, 13, 1969.

Friday, Chris. *Organizing Asian American Labor: The Pacific Coast Canned-Salmon Industry, 1870–1942.* Philadelphia: Temple University Press, 1994.

Gates, Charles M. "The Indian Treaty of Point No Point." *Pacific Northwest Quarterly* 46 (1955): 52–8.

Gedosch, Thomas Frederick. "Seabeck 1857–1886: The History of A Company Town." MA thesis, University of Washington, 1966.

Gibbs, George. "Tribes of Western Washington and Northwestern Oregon." *Contributions to North American Ethnology I* (1877): 157–242.

Gitlin, Jay, Barbara Berglund, And Adam Arenson. "Introduction: Local Crossroads, Global Networks, and Frontier Cities." *Frontier Cities: Encounters at the Crossroads of Empire*, eds. Jay Gitlin, Barbara Berglund, and Adam Arenson. Philadelphia: University of Pennsylvania Press, 2013, 1–8.

Glaab, Charles N. "Jesup W. Scott and a West of Cities." *Ohio History 73* (1964).

– *Kansas City and the Railroads: Community Policy in the Growth.* Lawrence: University Press of Kansas, 1962, reprint, 1993.

Glaab, Charles N. and Theodore Brown. *A History of Urban America.* New York: Macmillan, 1967.

Gleason, Madeleine Rowse. *The Voyages of the Ship Revere: 1849–1883.* Palo Alto, California: Glencannon, 1994.

Goetzmann, William H. *New Lands, New Men: America and the Second Great Age of Discovery.* New York: Viking, 1986.

Goldfield, David R. *Cotton Fields and Skyscrapers: Southern City and Region, 1607–1980.* Baton Rouge: Louisiana State University Press, 1982.

Goodman, David Michael. *A Western Panorama, 1849–1875: The Travels, Writings and Influence of J. Ross Browne on the Pacific Coast, and in Texas, Nevada, Arizona and Baja California, as the First Mining Commissioner, and Minister to China.* Glendale, California: A.H. Clark Co., 1966.

Gorsline, Jerry, ed. *Shadows of Our Ancestors: Readings in the History of Klallam-White Relations.* Port Townsend, Washington: Empty Bowl, 1992.

Graebner, Norman A. *Empire on the Pacific: A Study in American Continental Expansion.* New York: Ronald Press Co., 1955.

Grant, Frederick James. *History of Seattle.* New York: American Publishing and Engraving Co., 1891.

Gregory, V. J. *Keepers at the Gate.* Port Townsend, Washington: Port Townsend Publishing Company, 1976.

Griffiths, James. *Shipping Reminiscences of 62 Years, 1874–1936.* Privately printed. Reprint, Seattle, 1965.

Halseth, James A. and Bruce A. Glasrud. "Anti-Chinese Movements in Washington, 1885–86: A Reconsideration." *The Northwest Mosaic: Minority Conflicts in Pacific Northwest History*, eds. James A. Halseth and Bruce A. Glasrud. Boulder, Colorado: Pruett Publishing Co., 1977: 116–39.

Hamer, David. *New Towns in the New World: Images and Perceptions of the Nineteenth-Century Urban Frontier*. New York: Columbia University Press, 1990.

Harmon, Alexandra. "A Different Kind of Indians: Negotiating the Meanings of 'Indian' and 'Tribe' in the Puget Sound Region, 1820s–1970s." PhD dissertation, University of Washington, 1995.

– *Indians in the Making: Ethnic Relations and Indian Identities around Puget Sound*. Berkeley: University of California Press, 1999.

– "Introduction: Pacific Northwest Indian Treaties in National and International Historical Perspective." *The Power of Promises: Rethinking Indian Treaties in the Pacific Northwest*. Seattle: University of Washington Press, 2008: 3–31.

– "Lines in Sand: Shifting Boundaries Between Indians and Non-Indians in the Puget Sound Region." *Western Historical Quarterly* 26 (Winter 1995): 429–53.

– ed. *The Power of Promises: Rethinking Indian Treaties in the Pacific Northwest*. Seattle: University of Washington Press, 2008.

Harris, Cole, ed. *The Resettlement of British Columbia: Essays on Colonialism and Geographical Change*. Vancouver: University of British Columbia Press, 1997.

Hawthorne, Julian. *History of Washington: The Evergreen State From Early Dawn to Daylight*. New York: American Historical Publishing, 1893.

Hine, Robert V. and John Mack Faragher. *Frontiers: A Short History of the American West*. New Haven and London: Yale University Press, 2007.

Holbrook, Steward H. *Holy Old Mackinaw: A Natural History of the American Lumberjack*. New York: Macmillan, 1938.

Hsu, Madeline Yuan-yin. *Dreaming of Gold, Dreaming of Home: Transnationalism and Migration Between the United States and South China, 1882–1943*. Stanford: Stanford University Press, 2000.

Immigration Aid Society of North-Western Washington. *North-Western*

Washington: It's [sic] Soil, Climate, Productions and General Resources, with Detailed Description of the Counties of Jefferson, Clalam [sic], Island, San Juan and Whatcom. Port Townsend, Washington: Immigration Aid Society of North-Western Washington, 1880.

Jameson, Elizabeth. *All That Glitters: Class, Conflict, and Community in Cripple Creek.* Champaign: University of Illinois Press, 1998.

Jefferson County Quick Facts from the US Census Bureau. http://quickfacts.census.gov/qfd/states/53/53031.

Jenson, Joan M., A. Yvette Huginnie, Albert L. Hurtado, Charles Reagan Wilson, Edward L. Ayers, William Cronon, and David A. Emmons, "A Roundtable: Six Responses to 'Constructed Province' and a Final Statement by the Author." *Western Historical Quarterly* 25 (1994): 461–86.

Johannsen, Robert W. "The Seccession Crisis and the Frontier: Washington Territory, 1860–1861. *The Mississippi Valley Historical Review* 39, no. 3 (1952): 415–40.

Johansen, Dorothy O., and Charles M. Gates. *Empire of the Columbia: A History of the Pacific Northwest,* 2nd ed. New York: Harper & Row, 1967

Johnston, Robert D. *The Radical Middle Class: Populist Democracy and the Question of Capitalism in Progressive Era Portland, Oregon.* Princeton: Princeton University Press, 2003.

Judson, Phoebe Goodell. *A Pioneer's Search For An Ideal Home.* Bellingham, Washington, 1925; reprint, Lincoln: University of Nebraska Press, 1984.

Karlin, Jules Alexander. "The Anti-Chinese Outbreaks in Seattle, 1885–1886." *Pacific Northwest Quarterly* 39 (1948): 103–30.

– "The Anti-Chinese Outbreak in Tacoma, 1885." *Pacific Historical Review* 23 (1954): 271–83.

Kim, Hyung-chan and Richard W. Markov. "The Chinese Exclusion Laws and Smuggling Chinese into Whatcom County, Washington, 1890–1900." *Annals of the Chinese Historical Society of The Pacific Northwest* (1983): 16–30.

Kinnear, George. *Anti-Chinese Riots at Seattle, Wn., February 8, 1886.* Seattle: Privately published, 1911.

Klingle, Matthew. *Emerald City: An Environmental History of Seattle.* New Haven: Yale University Press, 2007.

Lang, Robert E., Deborah Epstein Popper, and Frank J. Popper. "'Progress of the Nation': The Settlement History of the Enduring American Frontier." *Western Historical Quarterly* 26, (Autumn, 1995): 289–307.

Lang, William L. *Confederacy of Ambition: William Winlock Miller and the Making of Washington Territory*. Seattle: University of Washington Press, 1996.

Langness, L.L. "A Case of Post Contact Reform Among the Klallam." *Shadows of Our Ancestors: Readings in the History of Klallam-White Relations*. ed. Jerry Gorsline. Port Townsend, Washington: Empty Bowl, 1992, 167–71.

Lee, Douglas W. "Sacred Cows and Paper Tigers: Politics in Chinese America, 1880–1900." *Annals of the Chinese Historical Society of the Pacific Northwest* (1983): 86–103.

Lee, Erika. *At America's Gates: Chinese Immigration During the Exclusion Era, 1882–1943*. Chapel Hill: University of North Carolina Press, 2003.

Lee, W. Storrs, ed. *Washington State: A Literary Chronicle*. New York: Funk & Wagnalls, 1967, 276–7.

Leighton, Caroline C. *Life at Puget Sound with Sketches of Travel in Washington Territory, British Columbia, Oregon and California*. Boston: Lee and Shepard, and New York: C.T. Dillingham, 1884; reprint, 1980.

"Letter from J. Ross Browne, special agent of the Treasury Department to the Commissioner of Indian Affairs, Reviewing the Origin of the Indian War of 1855–56, in the Territories of Oregon and Washington," dtd., December 4, 1857, 35th Cong., 1st., 1858, H.E.D. 38, (Serial 955).

Liestman, Daniel. "'The Various Celestials Among Our Town': Euro-American Response to Port Townsend's Chinese Colony." *Pacific Northwest Quarterly* 85 (Summer 1994): 93–104.

Limerick, Patricia Nelson. "Haunted by Rhyolite: Learning from the Landscape of Failure." *American Art* 6, no. 4 (Autumn, 1992): 18–39.

Limerick, Patricia Nelson, Clyde A. Milner, and Charles E. Rankin, eds. *Trails: toward a New Western History*. Lawrence: University of Kansas Press, 1991.

Liu, Haiming. "The Social Origins of Early Chinese Immigrants: A Revisionist Perspective." *The Chinese in America: A History from*

Gold Mountain to the New Millennium, ed. Susie Lan Cassel. Walnut Creek, California: Altamira Press, 2002, 21–36.

– "Transnational Historiography: Chinese American Studies Reconsidered." *Journal of the History of Ideas, Inc.* 65, no. 1 (2004): 135–53.

Lutz, John. "After the Fur Trade: The Aboriginal Laboring Class of British Columbia 1849–1890." *Journal of the Canadian Historical Association* 3 (1992): 69–94.

Lyman, Stanford Morris. *Chinatown and Little Tokyo: Power, Conflict, and Community Among Chinese and Japanese Immigrants in America*. Millwood, New York: Associated Faculty Press, Inc., 1986.

– "Chinese Secret Societies in the Occident: Notes and Suggestions for Research in the Sociology of Secrecy." *The Canadian Review of Sociology and Anthropology* 1 (February 1964): 79–103.

Ma, L. Eve Armentrout. "Chinatown Organizations and the Anti-Chinese Movement, 1882–1914." *Entry Denied: Exclusion and the Chinese Community in America: 1882–1943*. ed. Sucheng Chan. Philadelphia: Temple University Press, 1991: 147–69.

MacGregor, Carol Lynn. *Boise, Idaho, 1882–1910: Prosperity in Isolation*. Missoula, Montana: Mountain Press Publishing Company, 2006.

Mahoney, Timothy R. *River Towns in the Great West: The Structure of Provincial Urbanization in the American Midwest, 1820–1870*. Cambridge: Cambridge University Press, 1990.

Malone, Michael P. *The Battle for Butte: Mining and Politics on the Northern Frontier, 1864–1906*. Seattle: University of Washington Press, 1981.

"Map of the Quimper Peninsula, Jefferson County, Washington, 1997." Office of the Assessor, Jefferson County Courthouse, Port Townsend, Washington.

May, Dean L. *Three Frontiers: Family, Land, and Society in the American West, 1850–1900*. Cambridge: Cambridge University Press, 1994.

McCunn, Ruthanne Lum. *Thousand Pieces of Gold*. Boston: Beacon Press, 1981.

McCurdy, James G. *By Juan de Fuca's Strait: Pioneering Along the Northwestern Edge of the Continent*. Portland, Oregon: Metropolitan Press, 1937.

McDonald, Lucile. "A Seafaring Visit to Puget Sound in 1853." *The Seattle Times Magazine*. March 23, 1958.

– "A Woman's Views of Puget Sound in 1850s." *The Seattle Times Magazine*. March 9, 1958.

– "Events of 1853 at Port Discovery." *The Seattle Times Magazine*. April 6, 1958.

– "Life in Puget Sound Ports 105 Years Ago." *The Seattle Times Magazine*. March 30, 1958.

– "Revenue Cutter 'Oliver Wolcott." *The Sea Chest: Journal of the Puget Sound Maritime Historical Society* 9, no. 4 (June 1976): 128–32.

– "Seattle's First Chinese Resident." *The Seattle Times Magazine*. September 11, 1955.

– *Swan among the Indians: Life of James G. Swan, 1818–1900*. Portland, Oregon: Binfords & Mort, 1972.

McDonald, Norbert. *Distant Neighbors: A Comparative History of Seattle and Vancouver*. Lincoln: University of Nebraska Press, 1987.

McGraw, John H. "The Anti-Chinese Riots of 1885 by Gov. John H. McGraw." *Washington State Historical Society Publications II* (1915): 388–9.

McKeown, Adam. "Transnational Chinese Families and Chinese Exclusion, 1875–1943." *Journal of American Ethnic History* (Winter 1999): 73–110.

Meany, Edmond S. *History of the State of Washington*. New York: Macmillan, 1909.

Mei, June. "Socioeconomic Developments among the Chinese in San Francisco, 1848–1906." *Labor Immigration under Capitalism*. eds. Lucie Cheng and Edna Bonacich. Berkeley: University of California Press, 1984, 370–401.

– "Socioeconomic Origins of Emigration: Guangdong to California, 1850–1882." *Labor Immigration Under Capitalism*. eds. Lucie Cheng and Edna Bonacich. Berkeley: University of California Press, 1984, 219–45.

Meinig, D.W. *The Shaping of America: A Geographical Perspective on 500 Years of History, Vol. 3, Transcontinental America, 1850–1915*. New Haven: Yale University Press, 1998.

Menzies, Archibald. *Rainshadow: Archibald Menzies and the Botanical Exploration of the Olympic Peninsula*, ed. Jerry Gorsline. Port Townsend, Washington: Jefferson County Historical Society, 1992.

Mickelson, Sig. *The Northern Pacific Railroad and the Selling of the West: A Nineteenth-Century Public Relations Venture*. Sioux Falls, South Dakota: Center for Western Studies, 1993.

Moehring, Eugene P. *Urbanism and Empire in the Far West, 1840–1890*. Reno: University of Nevada Press, 2004.

Morgan, Murray. *Skid Road: An Informal Portrait of Seattle*. Sausalito, California: Comstock Editions, revised ed., 1978.

– *The Last Wilderness*. New York: Viking Press, 1955.

– *Puget's Sound: A Narrative of Early Tacoma and the Southern Sound*. Seattle: University of Washington Press, 1979.

Morrissey, Katherine G. *Mental Territories: Mapping the Inland Empire*. Ithaca: Cornell University Press, 1997.

Murphy, Mary. *Mining Cultures: Men, Women and Leisure in Butte, 1914–41*. Champaign: University of Illinois Press, 1997.

Naylor, Elaine. "Chet-ze-moka, J. Ross Browne, and 'the Great Port Townsend Controversy,'" *Pacific Northwest Quarterly* 93 (Spring 2002): 59–68.

– "Expulsion: Puget Sound, Washington, 1885–88," conference paper delivered at WHA Conference, Fort Worth, Texas, October 8–11, 2003.

Newell, Gordon, ed. *The H.W. McCurdy Marine History of the Pacific Northwest*. Seattle: Superior Publishing Company, 1966.

– *Ships of the Inland Sea: The Story of the Puget Sound Steamboats*. Portland, Oregon: Binfords & Mort, 1951.

Nobles, Gregory H. *American Frontiers: Cultural Encounters and Continental Conquest*. New York: Hill & Wang, 1997.

Nordhoff, Charles. *Nordhoff's West Coast: California, Oregon and Hawaii*. 1874, part I, 1875, part II; London: KPI, reprint (distributed by Methuen, Routledge & Keegan Paul), 1987.

Owram, Doug. *Promise of Eden: The Canadian Expansionist Movement and the Idea of the West, 1856–1900*. Toronto: University of Toronto Press, 1980, reprint, 1992.

Oxford Encyclopedic English Dictionary. eds R.E. Allen and Joyce Hawkins. New York: Oxford University Press, 1991.

Parks, Marian. "A Man For His Season: Victor Smith, 1826–1865." MA thesis, Claremont Graduate School, 1981.

Pascoe, Peggy. "Gender Systems in Conflict: The Marriages of Mission-Educated Chinese American Women, 1874–1939." *Unequal Sisters: A Multi-cultural Reader in U. S. Women's History*, 2nd ed., eds. Vicki L. Ruiz and Ellen Carol Dubois. New York: Routledge, 1994, 139–156.

Peffer, George Anthony. *If They Don't Bring Their Women Here: Chinese Female Immigration before Exclusion*. Urbana and Chicago: University of Illinois Press, 1999.

Perry, Fredi. *Seabeck: Tide's Out, Table's Set*. Bremerton, Washington: Perry Publishing, 1993.

Pfaelzer, Jean. *Driven Out: The Forgotten War against Chinese Americans*. New York: Random House, 2007.

Pomeroy, Earl. *The American Far West in the Twentieth Century*. New Haven: Yale University Press, 2008.

"Port Gamble sawmill, oldest continuously operating sawmill in the U.S., closes on November 30, 1995," accessed January 20, 2013; http://www.historylink.org/index.cfm?DisplayPage=output.cfm& file_id=5487.

"Port Townsend: Its Advantages, Resources, and Prospects." Port Townsend, Washington: Leader Publishing Company, 1890, reprint Port Townsend Publishing Co., 1997.

"Port Townsend, Washington, 1888." Sanborn Fire Insurance Map. McCurdy Historical Library, Jefferson County Historical Society, Port Townsend, Washington.

Prosch, Charles. *Reminiscences of Washington Territory*. Fairfield, Washington: Ye Galleon Press, 1969.

Prucha, Francis Paul. *American Indian Treaties: The History of a Political Anomaly*. Berkeley: University of California Press, 1994.

– *The Great Father: The United States Government and the American Indians*. Vol. 1 Lincoln: Nebraska University Press, 1984.

Rajala, Richard A. "The Forest as Factory: Technological Change and Worker Control in the West Coast Logging Industry, 1880–1930." *Labour/LeTravail* 32 (1993): 73–104.

"Report of the Governor of Washington Territory to Secretary of the Interior, October 8, 1886" (cited as Squire's Report to Interior), Serial Set 2468, 40th Cong. 2nd Sess. H. Ex. Docs. V. 9, n.1 pt 5, University of Washington.

"Report on the Conditions of the Indian Reservations in the Territories of Oregon and Washington, from J. Ross Browne, special agent of the Treasury Department to the Commissioner of Indian Affairs, dtd. November 17, 1857," 35th Cong., 1st Sess., 1858, H.E.D. 39, (Serial 955).

Reps, John W. *The Making of Urban America: A History of City Planning in the United States.* Princeton: Princeton University Press, 1965.

Rettmann, Jef. "Business, Government, and Prostitution in Spokane, Washington, 1889–1910." *Pacific Northwest Quarterly* 89 (Spring 1998): 77–83.

Richards, Kent D. *Isaac I. Stevens: Young Man in a Hurry.* Provo, Utah: Brigham Young University Press, 1979.

Rivera, Trinita. "Diet of a Food-Gathering People, With Chemical Analysis of Salmon and Saskatoons." *Indians of the Urban Northwest.* New York, 1949; reprint, 1969, 19–36.

"R.L. Polk & Co's Puget Sound Directory, 1887." Typewritten copy. McCurdy Historical Research Library. Jefferson County Historical Society. Port Townsend, Washington.

"R.L. Polk & Co's Port Townsend City Directory, 1890." McCurdy Historical Research Library. Jefferson County Historical Society. Port Townsend, Washington.

"R.L. Polk & Co's Port Townsend City Directory, 1897." McCurdy Historical Research Library. Jefferson County Historical Society. Port Townsend, Washington.

"R.L. Polk & Co's Port Townsend City Directory, 1907." McCurdy Historical Research Library. Jefferson County Historical Society. Port Townsend, Washington.

"R.L. Polk & Co's Port Townsend City Directory, 1912." McCurdy Historical Research Library. Jefferson County Historical Society. Port Townsend, Washington.

Robbins, William G. *Colony and Empire: The Capitalist Transformation of the American West.* Lawrence: University Press of Kansas, 1994.

– "In Pursuit of Historical Explanation: Capitalism as a Conceptual Tool for Knowing the American West." *Western Historical Quarterly* 30 (Autumn 1999): 277–93.

– *Landscapes of Promise: The Oregon Story: 1800–1940.* Seattle: University of Washington Press, 1997.

Roy, Patricia E. *White Man's Province: British Columbia Politicians and Chinese and Japanese Immigrants, 1858–1914*. Vancouver: University of British Columbia Press, 1989.

Ruby, Robert H. and John A. Brown. *Indians of the Pacific Northwest: A History*. Norman, Oklahoma: University of Oklahoma Press, 1981

Sale, Roger. *Seattle: Past to Present*. Seattle: University of Washington Press, 1976.

Salyer, Lucy. *Laws Harsh as Tigers: Chinese Immigrants and the Shaping of Modern Immigration Law*. Chapel Hill: University of North Carolina Press, 1995.

Sandos, James A. "Between Crucifix and Lance: Indian-White Relations in California, 1769–1848." *California History* 76 (1997): 196–229.

Satterlee, Brandon. *Dub of South Burlap: The Story of a Newspaperman Who Made a Holler in the Wilderness of Washington State ... Jefferson County ... Quilcene*. Port Townsend, Washington: Exposition Press, 1952, reprint, 1992.

Saxton, Alexander. *The Indispensable Enemy: Labor and the Anti-Chinese Movement in California*. Berkeley: University of California Press, 1971.

Schwantes, Carlos A. "From Anti-Chinese Agitation to Reform Politics: The Legacy of the Knights of Labor in Washington and the Pacific Northwest." *Pacific Northwest Quarterly* 88 (1997): 174–84.

– *Long Day's Journey: The Steamboat and Stagecoach Era in the Northern West*. Seattle: University of Washington Press, 1999.

– "Protest in a Promised Land: Unemployment, Disinheritance, and the Origin of Labor Militancy in the Pacific Northwest, 1885–1886," *Western Historical Quarterly* 13 (1982): 373–90.

– *Radical Heritage: Labor, Socialism and Reform in Washington and British Columbia, 1885–1917*. Seattle: University of Washington Press, 1979.

– *Railroad Signatures across The Pacific Northwest*. Seattle: University of Washington Press, 1992.

– "The Concept of the Wageworkers' Frontier: A Framework for Future Research." *Western Historical Quarterly* 18, no. 1 (1987): 39–55.

– *The Pacific Northwest: An Interpretive History*, rev. and enl. ed. Lincoln: University of Nebraska Press, 1996.

– "Unemployment, Disinheritance, and Labor Militancy." *Experiences in a Promised Land: Essays in Pacific Northwest History*, eds. G. Thomas Edwards and Carlos A. Schwantes. Seattle: University of Washington Press, 1986, 170–94.

Schwantes, Carlos Arnaldo and James Ronda. *The West the Railroads Made*. Seattle: University of Washington Press, 2008.

Scott, Jesup W. "Our Cities – Atlantic and Interior." *Hunt's Merchants' Magazine XIX* (1848).

Shuman, Howard Henry. "The Role of Seattle's Newspapers in the Anti-Chinese Agitation of 1885–1886." MA thesis, University of Washington, 1968.

Simpson, Peter. "We Give Our Hearts To You." *Shadows of Our Ancestors: Readings in the History of Klallam-White Relations*, ed. Jerry Gorsline. Port Townsend, Washington: Empty Bowl, 1992, 133–4.

Simpson, Peter, Robin Biffle, Jim Heymen, Nora Porter, and Mark Welch. *City of Dreams: A Guide to Port Townsend*, ed. Peter Simpson. Port Townsend, Washington: Bay Press, 1986.

Smith, Henry Nash. *Virgin Land: The American West as Symbol and Myth*. Cambridge, Massachusetts: Harvard University Press, 1950; reprint: New York, 1957.

Smith, Marian W. "The Indians and Modern Society." *Indians of the Urban Northwest*. New York: Columbia University Press, 1949; reprint: AMS Press, 1969: 3–18.

Snyder, Eugene E. *Early Portland: Stump Town Triumphant: Rival Townsites on the Willamette, 1831–1854*. Portland, Oregon: Binfords & Mort, 1970.

Steinberg, Ted. *Down to Earth: Nature's Role in American History*. New York and Oxford: Oxford University Press, 2002, 2009.

Steiner, Michael. "From Frontier to Region: Frederick Jackson Turner and the New Western History." *Pacific Historical Review* (1995): 470–501.

Stelter, Gilbert A. and Alan F.J. Artibise, eds. *Shaping the Urban Landscape: Aspects of the Canadian City-Building Process*. Ottawa: Carleton University Press, 1982.

Stevens, Isaac I. *Report of Explorations for a Route for the Pacific Railroad, near the Forty-Seventh and Forty-Ninth Parallels of North*

Latitude, from St. Paul to Puget Sound, 1853. The Michigan Historical Reprint Series. Ann Arbor, Michigan: University of Michigan
Library, 2011.

– "Reports of the Explorations and Surveys to Ascertain the Most
Practicable and Economical Route for a Railroad from the Mississippi to the Pacific Ocean." Washington, D.C., 1885, 33rd Congress,
2nd Sess., Senate Ex. Doc. No. 78.

Stevens, Todd. "Brokers between Worlds: Chinese Merchants and
Legal Culture in the Pacific Northwest, 1852–1925." PHD dissertation. Princeton University, 2003.

Stock, Catherine. *Main Street in Crisis: The Great Depression and the
Old Middle Class on the Northern Plains.* Chapel Hill, North Carolina: University of North Carolina Press, 1992.

Suttles, Wayne, ed. Vol. 7 of *Handbook of North American Indians,*
gen. ed. William C. Sturtevant. Washington, D.C.: Smithsonian Institution, 1990.

Swadish, Morris. "The Linguistic Approach to Salish Prehistory."
Indians of the Urban Northwest. New York, 1949; reprint 1969,
161–73

Swan, James G. "A Description of the City of Port Townsend, Jefferson County, State of Washington, U.S.A." Port Townsend, Washington, 1891. Reprint, *Port Townsend Leader,* June 25, 1891.

– *Almost Out of The World: Scenes From Washington Territory, The
Strait of Juan de Fuca, 1859–1861.* Reprint, Tacoma, Washington:
Washington State Historical Society, 1971.

– *The Northwest Coast: Or, Three Years' Residence in Washington
Territory.* New York: Harper, 1857; reprint, Seattle, Washington:
University of Washington Press, 1972.

Takaki, Ronald T. *Iron Cages: Race and Culture in Nineteenth-
Century America.* New York: Knopf , 1979.

– *Strangers from a Different Shore: A History of Asian Americans.*
Boston: Little Brown, 1998.

Tattersall, James N. "The Economic Development of the Pacific
Northwest to 1920." PHD dissertation. University of Washington,
1960.

Taylor, Alan. *Williams Cooper's Town: Power and Persuasion on the
Frontier of the Early American Republic.* New York: Knopf, 1995.

Throckmorton, Arthur L. *Oregon Argonauts: Merchant Adventurers on the Western Frontier*. Portland, Oregon: Oregon Historical Society, 1961.

Thrush, Coll. *Native Seattle: Histories from the Crossing-Over Place*. Seattle, Washington: University of Washington Press, 2007.

Thrush, Coll-Peter and Robert H. Keller, Jr. "'I See What I Have Done': The Life and Murder Trial of Xwelas, a S'Klallam Woman." *Western Historical Quarterly* 26 (Summer 1995): 168–83.

Tong, Benson. *Unsubmissive Women: Chinese Prostitutes in Nineteenth-Century San Francisco*. Norman: University of Oklahoma Press, 1994.

"Treaty with the S'Klallam, 1855." *Indian Affairs: Laws and Treaties*, Vol. 2, ed. Charles J. Kappler, 1904; reprint Washington D.C.: Government Printing Office, 1971, 674.

Tsai, Henry Shih-Shan. *The Chinese Experience in America*. Bloomington, Indiana: Indiana University Press, 1986.

Tulloch, James Francis. *The James Francis Tulloch Diary: 1875–1910*, ed. Gordon Keith. Portland, Oregon: Binfords & Mort, 1978.

Turner, Frederick Jackson. *The Frontier in American History*. New York, 1920, 1947; reprint, New York: Holt, Rinehart and Winston, 1962.

United States Censuses. Federal Population Census Schedules. Jefferson County, Washington. 1860–1920. National Archives, Washington, D.C.

United States Census, 1860: *Manufactures*. Washington, D.C.: Government Printing Office, 1865.

United States Census, 1870: *Manufactures*. Washington, D.C.: Government Printing Office, 1872.

Valadez, Jamie, Trina Bridges, Kathy Duncan, Gina Beckwith, Marie Hebert, and Tallis Woodward. "The S'Klallam: Elwha, Jamestown and Port Gamble." *Native Peoples of the Olympic Peninsula: Who We Are / by the Olympic Peninsula Intertribal Cultural Advisory Committee*, ed. Jacilee Wray. Norman: University of Oklahoma Press, 2002

Valentine, David. "Chinese Placer Mining in the United States: An Example from American Canyon, Nevada." *The Chinese in America: A History from Gold Mountain to the New Millenium*, ed. Susie Lan Cassel. Walnut Creek, California: Altamira Press, 2002, 37–53.

Van West, Carroll. *Capitalism on the Frontier: Billings and the Yellowstone Valley in the Nineteenth Century*. Lincoln: University of Nebraska Press, 1993.

Vincent, Mary Ann Lambert. *Dungeness Massacre and Other Regional Tales*. Privately printed, 1961; reprint, Sequim, Washington, 1991.

Wade, Richard D. *The Urban Frontier: Pioneer Life in Early Pittsburgh, Cincinnati, Lexington, Louisville and St. Louis*. Chicago: University of Illinois Press, 1964.

Washington Territorial Census, 1880. McCurdy Historical Research Library. Jefferson County Historical Society. Port Townsend, Washington.

Washington Territorial Census, 1889. McCurdy Historical Research Library. Jefferson County Historical Society. Port Townsend, Washington.

Watkins, Marilyn P. *Rural Democracy: Family Farmers and Politics in Western Washington, 1890–1925*. Ithaca: Cornell University Press, 1995.

Weaver, John C. *The Great Land Rush and the Making of the Modern World, 1650–1900*. Montreal and Kingston: McGill-Queens University Press, 2003, 2006.

Weir, Allen. "Roughing It on Puget Sound in the Early Sixties: A Paper Read Before The Washington Pioneer Association in 1891." *The Washington Historian*. 2, no. 2 (January 1900): 70–5.

White, Richard. *"It's Your Misfortune and None of My Own": A History of the American West*. Norman: University of Oklahoma Press, 1991.

– *Land Use, Environment, and Social Change: The Shaping of Island County, Washington*. Seattle, Washington, 1980, reprint, Seattle, Washington: University of Washington Press, 1992.

– "Treaty at Medicine Creek: Indian-White Relations on Upper Puget Sound, 1830–1880." MA thesis, University of Washington, 1972.

Wilkins, David E. and K. Tsianina Lomawaima. *Uneven Ground: American Indian Sovereignty and Federal Law*. Norman, Oklahoma: University of Oklahoma Press, 2001.

Willingham, William F. *Starting Over: Community Building on the Eastern Oregon Frontier*. Portland, Oregon: Oregon Historical Society Press, 2005.

Wills, Jocelyn. *Boosters, Hustlers, and Speculators: Entrepreneurial Culture and the Rise of Minneapolis and St. Paul, 1840–1883*. St. Paul, Minnesota: Minnesota Historical Society, 2005.

Willson, Margaret and Jeffery L. MacDonald. "Port Townsend's Pioneer Chinese Merchants." *Landmarks* 2 (Winter 1983): 20–4.

– "Racial Tension at Port Townsend and Bellingham Bay: 1870–1886." *Annals of the Chinese Historical Society of the Pacific Northwest* (1983):1–15.

Winthrop, Theodore. *Canoe and Saddle*. 1862; reprint, Portland, Oregon: Binfords & Mort, Nisqually Edition, n.d.

With Pride in Heritage: History of Jefferson County. Jefferson County Historical Society, ed. Port Townsend, Washington: Professional Publishing Printing, Inc., 1966:

Campbell, Patricia, "The Victor Smith Saga," 114–19.

Daly, William J. "The Legal Creation," 4–10.

Daly, William J. and V.J. Gregory. "Port Townsend," 64.

Dunbar, Ednis. "In the Days of McGuffey's Reader,"30–5.

Fletcher, Lena. "Valley of the Hoh," 216–38.

Gregory, V.J., "The Duke of York," 131.

–"Profiles of Pioneers, 1850-1892," 125–6.

"Hadlock," 210.

Schaub, Rev. Gary B., et al., "Churches," 84–90.

Swanson, Arthur. "High Tide at Ludlow," 180.

Taylor, Eva Cook. "Quilcene," 162–9.

Thiele, Paul W. "Chamber of Commerce," 81.

Witgen, Michael J. "An Infinity of Nations: How Indians, Empires and Western Migration Shaped National Identity in North America." PHD dissertation. University of Washington, 2004.

Wong, Rose Marie. *Sweet Cakes, Long Journey: The Chinatowns of Portland, Oregon*. Seattle, Washington: University of Washington Press, 2004.

Wong, Scott K. "Cultural Defenders and Brokers: Chinese Responses to the Anti-Chinese Movement." *Claiming America: Constructing Chinese American Identities During the Exclusion Era*. eds., K. Scott Wong and Sucheng Chan. Philadelphia, Pennsylvania: Temple University Press, 1998, 3–40.

– "Review Essay: Still Climbing, Still Digging." *Journal of Asian American Studies* (October 2003): 313–20.

Wood, Sharon. *The Freedom of the Streets: Work, Citizenship, and Sexuality in a Gilded Age City.* Chapel Hill, North Carolina: University of North Carolina Press, 2005.

Worster, Donald. *Dust Bowl: The Southern Plains in the 1930s.* New York: Oxford University Press, 2004.

Wright, E.W., ed. *Lewis and Dryden's Marine History of the Pacific Northwest.* New York: Lewis & Dryden Printing Co., 1895; reprint, New York: Antiquarian Press, 1961.

Wrobel, David M. "Global West, American Frontier." *Pacific Historical Review* 78, no. 1 (February 2009): 1–26.

– *Promised Lands: Promotion, Memory, and the Creation of the American West.* Lawrence: University of Kansas Press, 2002.

Wunder, John R. "What's Old About the New Western History: Race and Gender, Part 1." *Pacific Northwest Quarterly* (1994): 50–9.

– "What's Old About the New Western History: Environment and Economy, Part 2." *Pacific Northwest Quarterly* (1998): 84–94.

Wynne, Robert Edward. "Reaction to the Chinese in the Pacific Northwest and British Columbia, 1850 to 1910." PHD dissertation, University of Washington, 1964.

Yonce, Frederick Jay. "Public Land Disposal in Washington." PHD dissertation. University of Washington, 1969.

Yung, Judy. *Unbound Voices: A Documentary History of Chinese Women in San Francisco.* Berkeley: University of California Press, 1999.

Zhu, Liping. *A Chinaman's Chance: The Chinese on the Rocky Mountain Mining Frontier.* Bolder: University Press of Colorado, 1997.